52 WEEKEND
GARDEN
PROJECTS

Other Books by the Same Author:

The Adventurous Gardener
The Country Journal Book of Vegetable Gardening
The New Seed Starter's Handbook
Root Cellaring (written with Michael Bubel)
Vegetables Money Can't Buy
Working Wood (written with Michael Bubel)

52 WEEKEND
GARDEN
PROJECTS

◆ Grow a Fast Food Garden ◆ Choose Herbs for a Shady Corner ◆ Create a Butterfly Garden ◆ Get a Head Start on Tomatoes ◆ Save Your Own Seed ◆ Learn to Root Cuttings ◆ Harvest Flowers for Drying ◆ And Much More!

By Nancy Bubel

Illustrations by Carol Inouye

Rodale Press, Emmaus, Pennsylvania

Portions of this book previously appeared in *Country Journal, Horticulture, The Mother Earth News,* and *New Shelter* magazines.

Senior Managing Editor: Margaret Lydic Balitas
Senior Editor: Barbara W. Ellis
Editor: Sally Roth
Associate Editor/Research Associate: Heidi A. Stonehill
Copy Editor: Nancy N. Bailey
Indexer: Sandi Schroeder

Cover and book design by Lynn N. Gano
Cover and interior illustrations by Carol Inouye

If you have any questions or comments concerning this book, please write:
Rodale Press
Book Reader Service
33 East Minor Street
Emmaus, PA 18098

Library of Congress Cataloging-in-Publication Data

Bubel, Nancy.
  52 weekend garden projects / by Nancy Bubel.
      p.   cm.
  Includes bibliographical references and index.
  ISBN 0–87857–963–X hardcover
  ISBN 0–87857–964–8 paperback
  1. Gardening. I. Title. II. Title: Fifty-two weekend garden projects.
  III. Title: Garden projects.
  SB453.B827   1991
  635—dc20   91–27282
                                                                              CIP

Distributed in the book trade by St. Martin's Press

2 4 6 8 10 9 7 5 3 1 hardcover
2 4 6 8 10 9 7 5 3 1 paperback

To all my friends whose gardens have
enriched my own, especially Rebecca
Francis, Harriet Heaney, Dot Brown, and
Kate and Nevin Reinard

C O N T E N T S

ACKNOWLEDGMENTS

I gratefully acknowledge the kindness of Dr. Kim Hummer, Research Leader/Curator, National Clonal Germplasm Laboratory, Corvallis, Oregon, in granting permission to print parts of her study of *Ribes* restrictions in the list of gooseberry restrictions in chapter 17.

I appreciate the generosity of the people who answered my questions about wisteria, including: the late Hal Bruce, horticulturist at Winterthur Museum and Gardens, Winterthur, Delaware; William Frederick, landscape architect, Wilmington, Delaware; Clarence Hubbuch, horticulturist at the Bernheim Arboretum, Clermont, Kentucky; Ed Moulin, horticulturist at the Brooklyn Botanic Garden, Brooklyn, New York; and Judy Zuk, who was director of the Scott Foundation Plant Collection at Swarthmore College, Swarthmore, Pennsylvania, at the time of our conversation.

Fairman and Kate Jayne of Sandy Mush Herb Nursery in Leicester, North Carolina, have been unfailingly gracious in allowing us to visit their herb garden and in answering questions on the phone. Cyrus Hyde of Well-Sweep Herb Farm in Port Murray, New Jersey, took time to give us a tour of his wonderful demonstration herb garden. Thanks also to the staff of the National Wildflower Research Center in Austin, Texas, the staff of Bowman's Hill Wildflower Preserve in Washington Crossing, Pennsylvania, and Claire Herzog of the Marie Selby Botanical Gardens in Sarasota, Florida, for answering my questions. Jane Elshami and Rose Ann Soloway at the National Capitol Poison Center at Georgetown University Hospital cheerfully helped me double-check flower edibility. Janice Lymburner and Priscilla Wilson of Gourdcraft Originals in Cleveland, Georgia, generously shared their gourd-growing and crafting expertise.

Sally Roth has been a wonderfully astute, helpful, and accessible editor, and I'd like to thank her for all the good energy she has put into this book. Thanks, too, to editor Ellen Phillips, who guided the book through its initial planning stages with such heartening enthusiasm, and to Barbara Ellis and Heidi Stonehill, for their helpful suggestions. Carol Inouye's illustrations and Lynn Gano's design have helped to turn a rough manuscript into a readable book.

Loving thanks to my husband, Mike, who helped me with the chapters on grapes and grafting.

None of these good people is responsible for errors or misinterpretation that may appear in text. That responsibility is mine alone.

INTRODUCTION

Does anyone read book introductions before delving into those chapters that look most interesting? I hope so, because I'd like to take a moment to explain my intentions in writing these chapters, and my hopes for you, my reader.

This book is a collection of gardening adventures—a path of exploration leading into a lifetime of learning, appreciation, and experimenting. So much to try . . . seed saving, food drying, herb growing, plant propagating. I'm a quilter as well as a gardener, and among quilters it is common to admit to a "life list" of often dozens of quilt patterns one wants to create while there is still time. In my gardening, I feel the same way—full of awe and fascination for the variety, dependability and surprises in the world of growing things, and ever eyeing the next plant I want to learn to grow, the next technique to try.

The projects I describe in this book are those that have caught my interest over 34 years of gardening. Some I've only begun to explore; others I've pursued in some depth. I don't work at all of them in any one year, and I can't imagine that you would either, but I hope you'll find here both the encouragement and the information you need to start on whichever of these gardening adventures appeals to you most. Each chapter stands on its own as a guide to a specific project or area of gardening exploration, including principles and how-to. Every chapter gives you the information you need to successfully complete a project, or to begin to learn about an area of interest. Many of the projects can be pursued and developed in greater depth over a period of years—sometimes many years.

Even a small backyard can hold a world of discovery for the gardener who is willing to try new methods and taste new foods. If you take pleasure in providing the freshest and best food for your table, in quality and variety not to be found in any store, I hope you'll find this book a helpful guide to branching out in areas you've not yet explored. If it has always seemed to you unfortunate to arbitrarily divide the vegetable from the flower garden, you'll find here that flowers have not been forgotten. And if you sometimes like to experiment just for the stimulation of trying something new, why, then, I hope you'll find encouragement in these pages when the doldrums hit or when you're looking for new gardening experiences.

Many of the projects in this book, and many of the individual steps involved in pursuing a particular area of interest, can be completed in a weekend. Mostly, though, I've had in mind "weekend" in the larger sense—the time you devote to true relaxation, creative endeavors, satisfying physical work, planning and dreaming. Every weekend should allow for some space and time not taken up by catching up with the laundry or sorting trash for recycling—some time for renewal, recharging. Weekend projects are those that nourish the inner person . . . projects you can start some Saturday and pick up again whenever you have a chance. The satisfaction to be gained from completing a new kind of growing cycle, developing a new gardening skill, or mastering the care of a new plant can do wonders for both physical and mental health.

Travel is exhilarating, study is challenging, work is absorbing. But at last we all come home, and it is at home, on our own ground, where we can most freely and fully follow our whims, grow what we want, nurture a passion for daylilies or heirloom tomatoes or cottage gardens, plant and tend and harvest. I hope this book will encourage you to delve more deeply into familiar territory and to try something new. Find out for yourself, "I can do it!"

Happy gardening, friends!

PART ONE

S weet spring, full of sweet days and roses.

—George Herbert (1593–1633)

SPRING

Grow a
Fast Food Garden

In the days when most people depended on stored root-cellar crops to see them through until the next harvest, the weeks in March when the larder got low were called the hungry gap. You could see the bottom of the food barrel, but spring crops weren't ready yet. Today we have canned and frozen foods, and markets are full of shipped-in produce. Still, in late winter, we gardeners begin to crave some fresh green food of our own growing. Despite full potato bins and still-glowing shelves of canned tomatoes, we long for something crisp, leafy, or pungent picked from our own garden. Sure, we know that gardening teaches patience, but it also confers a keen appreciation for what tastes good. Plant some of these earliest garden foods, and you'll have something fresh and tasty—and fast.

COUNTING THE DAYS

If you've grown vegetables before, you know that their maturity dates seldom correspond exactly to catalog descriptions. When you compare catalogs, you'll notice that there can be a disparity of as much as 7 to 10 days between dates listed by different companies for the same cultivar. Variables of rainfall, temperature, soil type, and exposure can shift things around even more. So if your 40-day lettuce takes 43 days, or even 45, don't despair, but do check to see whether it needs a windbreak or more watering, or perhaps a different spot where it would get some reflected warmth from a nearby wall. And keep watching those radishes. They'll be ready before you know it.

Lively Flavor

Wake up your taste buds with the sharp tang of peppergrass, radishes, and spring onions. Peppergrass grows fast enough for even the most impatient gardener, and the others will be ready for eating in only a few short weeks.

Peppergrass

Peppergrass (*Lepidium sativum*), sometimes called curly grass or garden cress, can be ready for harvest in ten days. Yes, ten days. Seed starts to germinate in a day—and within two weeks you'll have snippings to garnish sandwiches and soups. Real, fresh greens, with a mustardlike pungency.

You can even grow this eager green on your kitchen windowsill, without soil. Just scatter the seeds on damp paper towels pressed into a shallow pan. Once they sprout, keep them moist in a well-lit spot. Start a new pan each week until the ground outside is diggable. Outdoors, plant small patches of peppergrass in earliest spring. Cover with cut-down plastic gallon jugs to ward off late freezes (use a sharp knife to saw the jugs in half). Peppergrass seedlings tolerate crowding and don't need to be thinned. Use a pair of scissors to snip the green sprouts as you need them.

Radishes

Many cultivars of radishes are ready for picking in three weeks from planting. Radishes grow best in cool weather and abundant moisture. Plant them directly in the ground as soon as the soil is dry enough to work. Earliest plantings germinate more slowly in cold ground, so start the seeds indoors for a head start. Scatter them on damp paper towels pressed into a shallow pan. Plant the sprouted seeds in soil well supplied with organic matter to retain moisture. Make sure the sprouted seeds don't dry out until their leaves show aboveground. I've liked 'Champion', 'Cherry Belle', 'French Breakfast', and 'White Icicle', all widely available. 'Cherry Beauty', an extra-early radish (17 days till maturity), may be a little harder to find but is worth the search.

Onions

Onion sets, the miniature bulbs that appear in grocery and hardware stores even before the seed-packet racks are set up in spring, can give you a bonus of piquant green top leaves. In our house, onion tops snipped over baked potatoes or soups are a delicious and reassuring sign of spring. Plant onion sets as early in spring as you can get the ground dug and raked. The tops will be ready to pluck within five weeks. Just poke the little bulbs 2 to 3 inches into the ground, root side down, about 4 inches apart. I plant wide rows of four to five bulbs across. When picking, take only one or two of the tubular leaves from each onion.

3

Tender Roots

The satisfying crunch of kohlrabi makes it a good choice for nibbling raw or adding to salads. Early beets and turnips give you tender roots in about six weeks. Soup greens from thinnings are a bonus.

Turnips

Some turnips store well, others grow fast—so you can have good roots and nutritious greens both early and late. The early turnips are quick and good—and usually escape the maggot damage that often defaces later crops. Try 'Tokyo Cross' or 'Presto', which produce small tender roots in 30 to 35 days. 'Shogoin' will give you good cuttings of turnip tops for greens in 30 days, and roots by the end of the second month.

A month before your last spring frost date, sow the seeds where plants are to grow, in well-composted soil. Keep the plants well watered for rapid, tender growth. Thin plants to stand 3 inches apart. You can even transplant young turnips, if you can't bear to toss thinnings on the compost heap. Uproot them carefully before they develop their second true leaves, and water them in well.

Beets

Small, tender, Ping-Pong–sized beet roots make a delightful early crop. Beet leaves are delicious and full of vitamins, too. Try 'Little Egypt', 'Early Red Ball', or 'Early Wonder', all about 48 days from seed. Plant outdoors where the plants are to grow, about six weeks before your last frost date. Or sow indoors or in cold frames in early March, and set outside in mid-April for mid-May harvest. The most tender beets are grown quickly in loose, fine soil with a steady supply of moisture. The seed is actually a compound seedball containing several seeds. That's why, no matter how carefully you space the seeds, your beet planting will usually need thinning.

Kohlrabi

Never tried kohlrabi? Its solid, round, aboveground bulbs sprout leafy stalks and contain crisp, sweet flesh. Most kohlrabi cultivars mature in 45 to 50 days, but 'Kolpak', a new, extra-early cultivar, is ready to pick in only 38 days.

Plant kohlrabi in the garden about a month before your last spring frost and thin seedlings to 6 inches apart. Pick nonhybrid kohlrabis at about 2 inches in diameter, before they grow large and woody. Hybrid kolhrabis like 'Kolpak' retain their good texture longer than some of the older cultivars.

Leafy Greens

If you're tired of pale iceberg-lettuce salads, try the tender flavors of fast-growing spinach and lettuce. Or experiment with the new taste of exotic mizuna and tyfon.

Spinach

Short-lived as it is, spinach is a wonderful early spring crop with tender, crisp leaves. Plant the seeds where they are to grow as early in spring as the soil can be worked, in your richest ground. The seeds germinate in soil as cool as 40°F. Spinach is a heavy feeder and well-composted soil makes a noticeable difference in its vigor. You can crowd spinach a bit if your soil is rich, but for picture-perfect plants, thin to 6 inches apart.

Plan on a harvest in about 39 days if you plant 'Indian Summer'. 'Tyee' is ready approximately a week later, but is also slower to bolt to seed when weather warms up. I often plant a double row, with 'Indian Summer' on one side and 'Tyee' on the other.

Lettuce

What would spring be without leaf lettuce? That brave little patch of light green looks so encouraging in the still-frosty garden, and the melting, tender leaves bring spring to the table. 'Black-seeded Simpson', at 42 days, is about as early a lettuce as you can get, and fortunately it's a good one and widely available.

Sow lettuce seeds right in the garden soon after you plant spinach. Plant the fine seeds thinly and shallowly. They will germinate while soil temperature is still in the forties. Thin leaf lettuce to 8-inch spacing. For "forcing" lettuce—starting it even earlier, in a cold frame, plastic tunnel, or greenhouse—try 'Delta', 'Kwiek', or 'Magnet', all butterhead types. Butterheads take longer to mature than leaf lettuce—60 to 70 days—but when grown under protection they can be started in late winter for April and May crops.

5

Mizuna

Mizuna (*Brassica japonica*) is one of my favorite spring and fall greens. The toothed leaves of this Japanese mustard form a foot-high clump and bear vigorously all season long. Mizuna is not only

hardy but also mild flavored—superb for both soups and salads. And it rebounds quickly after cutting.

Get an early start with flats of seedlings started indoors six to eight weeks before the last spring frost date. Transplant to the garden three to four weeks before the last frost. Or plant seeds directly in the garden about a month before the last spring frost date. Sow thinly and shallowly, like lettuce. Gradually thin the plants to 12-inch spacing.

Tyfon

This leafy, turnip-Chinese cabbage cross is mild flavored, vigorous, and very hardy. Like mizuna, tyfon (*Brassica rapa*) is easy to grow, nutritious, and quick to regenerate.

The mild flavor of tyfon, *top,* and the tangy taste of mizuna, *bottom,* are welcome additions to spring salads. These fast-growing greens don't mind a little cold and can go into the ground a month before last frost. Pick young leaves as needed.

6

Plant seeds of tyfon greens directly in the garden four to five weeks before the last spring frost date or, for an earlier crop, start seeds indoors and set out seedling transplants a month or so before the frost-free date. Sow seeds thinly and shallowly. Thin to 10 to 12 inches apart.

Choose the Right Wildflowers for Your Yard

Some years ago, when we were living in our first house, our neighbors handed a pie pan back to us in an imaginative variation of the old custom of "never return a plate empty." Instead of a pie, the glass dish was crammed with a densely textured arrangement of wild plants: dainty, pink-striped spring beauties; budding violets; coils of new ferns nudging above a mossy surface; unfurling umbrellas of mayapples; flat, heart-shaped leaves of wild ginger with a silky sheen. There it was—a wild garden on a plate, an artful slice of woodsy landscape.

But the plants hadn't been dug from the woods. They came from the backyard of a semidetached house on a city lot in northwest Philadelphia. We planted the wildflowers in our backyard, and they grew and multiplied. By the time we sold the house to move to another state several years later, our introduced wildflowers had formed thriving colonies under the trees and along the hedges.

Match the Plant to the Place

Many wildflowers adapt very well to life in the average yard. Some, in fact, flourish when protected from competition. The secret of making adopted wildflowers happy is understanding their needs and providing for them. Unlike zinnias, marigolds, and other bedding plants that have been bred to accept a wide variety of conditions, many wildflowers have evolved in more specialized situations—in light shade, perhaps, or in acid soil, or in damp ground. These preferences can be used to your advantage when landscaping the difficult corners that most of us have on our grounds. Those shady spots on the north side of the house and under trees, the rocky ledge, the soggy corner, the dry sunny slope—all are perfect homes for one wildflower or another. Just match the plant to the place.

In the years since we dotted those first wildflower transplants along the edges of our city lot, we've managed to tuck at least a few wildflowers into each yard we've owned—suburban, small town, and now in the country. I've planted Virginia bluebells and ferns along the north side of a garage, forget-me-nots by a pool, bloodroot in a shady nook by the house, cardinal flower near a small stream, Jacob's-ladder and columbine along a rock wall. These natives have faithfully reappeared each year, and in some cases they've multiplied.

Before you reach for the catalogs to order wildflowers, take some time to observe actual conditions on your home grounds. Notice which spots are shady, and for how long: morning, all day, all year, only in summer? Look for different qualities of shade too, from the deep, dark shadowed recesses under pines to the light, dappled shade cast by slender birches. Identify wet spots and find any dry, bare patches that could be transformed into miniature wildflower meadows. Then, check "Adoptable, Adaptable Wildflowers" on page 12,

8

and your catalog collection, for plants that stand a good chance of thriving under the particular conditions you have to offer.

SPOILING THE LAND

It's easier than you might think to contribute to the extinction of a wildflower species. Good wildflower habitats—where soil and shade and moisture conditions are just right—are lost every day to suburban sprawl. Overgrazing by domestic animals, heavy use of off-road vehicles, and acid rain all help to spoil the land for native plants. Overcollecting of wildflowers, both by commercial dealers and misguided gardeners, is another reason that some wildflowers are getting scarcer all the time. Even un-witting introduction of competitive weeds like purple loosestrife and water hyacinth can choke out native growth.

When miles of a wildflower's natural growing territory are wiped out, colonies of plants become increasingly isolated. This restriction in numbers and range causes one of the most serious threats to the continued health of our native wildflowers: the loss of genetic variety caused by continued inbreeding. Wild-flowers have survived to this day because they've been able to transmit a wide range of genetic material. Some of the more adaptable ones produce seedlings that vary widely in height, blooming time, hardiness, and other traits. When plants exist in small or separated pockets, they can't receive new genes from other colonies of their kind. So you can see what careless dig-ging can do.

9

Be a Responsible Collector

Unless you have a neighbor or friend to supply you with roots or divisions from established wildflower plantings, you'll probably order plants from a mail-order nursery. Deal only with nurseries, like those listed in Resources beginning on page 337, that propagate their wild-flower offerings themselves. It is a sorry fact that some wildflower dealers sell plants that have been collected in the wild. Wild collecting, especially on a commercial scale, can quickly wipe out even a large colony of wildflowers. Nurseries that propagate their own wildflowers are proud to say so; read the catalogs closely. If you're lucky enough to live near one of the wildflower preserves that offer started plants for sale, you can buy potted plants in person and pop them in the ground the same day.

It is part of a gardener's honor to always ask permission to dig wildflowers from the woods or wayside. Even seemingly "wild" land belongs to *someone,* and in state and federal parks it is illegal to uproot plants. When you do have permission to dig, or when transplanting wildflowers from one spot to another on your own land, be sure to take only a few specimens, and only from well-established and abundant colonies. Only when outright destruction of the wildflower habitat is imminent—as when bulldozers are about to skin off the topsoil to make a road—is the wholesale digging of complete flower colonies defensible, and, again, only with the permission of the landowner.

Planting Wildflowers

The best time to plant or transplant wildflowers is when they're dormant or just starting into growth. Plants bought from a reputable nursery have been toughened by growing in outdoor beds and will be well rooted, usually in pots, when you receive them. Plant them promptly in the spots you've chosen for them.

Water the new plants well and keep the soil around them moist for the first week or two after planting. Provide light shade for a few days if the trees haven't leafed out yet. It's a good idea to mark the site and also to make a note of the planting in your garden records. Leaves of many spring-blooming wild plants—Virginia bluebells, bloodroot, spring beauties, and others—die back in summer. It can be embarrassingly easy to forget that spring planting and shove a summer annual in on top of it.

Should you add fertilizer when setting out wildflowers? Wildflowers have done just fine for millions of years without any help from us. They're accustomed to living on what's naturally available, and they don't need the special stimulation of a concentrated feeding. Fertilizer can encourage other less desirable plants that might crowd out your chosen plantings. After planting woodland plants, I often mulch with compost or duff, the leafy debris gathered from the forest floor. Most wild natives seem to suffer less damage from insects and disease than the average bedding plant, so you're not likely to have too much trouble with such infestations.

If they are happy where they are, your wildflowers will start to multiply after a few years—either by seed or spreading roots, sometimes both. Reproduction is a sign of an established colony. To extend your plantings, dig up the extras from a large clump, or gather and plant seed (a slower but immensely satisfying process).

Starting Wildflowers from Seed

Your own established plantings may yield enough seeds for wildflower "starts" to spread throughout your neighborhood. You can also introduce new kinds of wildflowers by growing them from seeds offered by mail-order companies.

Unlike cultivated bedding plants, wildflowers haven't had human help in producing the next generation of their kind, so they've developed some protective mechanisms to ensure that their seeds have a good chance to germinate. Many wildflower seeds go dormant after they ripen. Such seeds will not sprout until they've been chilled—the equivalent of the natural process in which the seed falls to the ground, waits out the winter, and germinates in spring when conditions are right for it to grow. If all wildflower seeds could sprout as soon as they ripened, those tender young plants might not make it through the winter. Accept the inconvenient trait of dormancy as part of the plant's natural protective system, and work around it.

The process of giving seed a chilling period in order to promote germination is called stratification. It's not as complicated as it sounds.

- The easiest way to stratify seeds is to plant them in the fall in a well-prepared nursery bed of fine, light soil. Then watch for tiny sprouts in the spring. (A few wildflowers enter such deep dormancy that they may not germinate until the second spring after planting.)
- Or plant the seeds in labeled flats and keep them in a cold frame or on an unheated porch or garage.
- Or, for spring planting, press the seeds into a small flat or pan of damp peat moss, shredded sphagnum moss, or vermiculite, encase

the flat in a plastic bag, and keep the whole shebang in the fridge (at 33° to 40°F) for a month or so. Then put the planted flat under fluorescent light, in the greenhouse, in a cold frame, or on a porch, to encourage germination.

Many wildflower seeds grow slowly. If seedlings you started in spring are still tiny as summer approaches, keep them in the pot or nursery bed for another year to let them develop further. Perennial wildflowers begin to bloom in their second or third season from seed.

Adoptable, Adaptable Wildflowers

Whether you start with seeds, potted plants, or transplanted clumps, you have a rainbow of native plants from which to choose. The following pages include wildflowers of many colors, all of them easily adaptable to the home garden. Blooming times suggested are for Zones 5 and 6 and will be a few weeks earlier in warmer zones. (See Resources beginning on page 337 for nurseries and seed catalogs that feature wildflowers.)

Wildflowers for Shade

If your intended wildflower spot leans toward the shady side, wildflowers found naturally in woodsy places will be most happy there.

Bloodroot (*Sanguinaria canadensis*)

Starry, white, eight-petaled bloodroot blossoms appear while the leaf is still furled around the stem. A lovely double-flowered form is also available. Large leaves open after blooming, forming a ground-cover, but they wither away by early summer.

Growth habit:	Perennial; single-stemmed; 6 to 9 inches tall.
Color of flowers:	White.
Bloom time:	April through May.
Where to grow:	Partial shade; moist, rich soil.
How to start:	Purchase plants.
Spacing:	Space plants 6 inches apart.
Growing tips:	Plant roots 1 inch deep in soil; mulch around plants. Increase your stock by slicing the thick root, or rhizome, into divisions; allow the cut roots to dry overnight before replanting.

Columbine (*Aquilegia canadensis*)

The dainty blossoms of wild columbine nod on wiry stems over attractive lobed foliage. In the wild, they grow in open woods and on rocky ground, sometimes sprouting improbably from rocky ledges.

Growth habit:	Perennial; 1 to 3 feet tall.
Color of flowers:	Red with yellow.
Bloom time:	April through May.
Where to grow:	Partial shade; well-drained soil.
How to start:	Purchase plants or start from seeds.
Spacing:	Space plants 1 foot apart.
Growing tips:	Seeds need light to germinate; do not cover.

Dutchman's-Breeches (*Dicentra cucullaria*)

The arching stems of Dutchman's-breeches are strung with white flowers resembling tiny, inflated "britches," over small clumps of attractive, ferny foliage.

Growth habit:	Perennial; 6 to 10 inches tall.
Color of flowers:	White.
Bloom time:	April through May.
Where to grow:	Partial shade; rich, humusy soil.
How to start:	Seeds or plants.
Spacing:	Space plants 10 inches apart.
Growing tips:	To increase your planting, dig up your mature plants and separate some of the tubers into smaller kernels. Plant the kernels ½ inch deep and mulch the ground lightly.

Foamflower (*Tiarella cordifolia*)

Allegheny foamflower is a fine groundcover or edging plant. It bears spikes of small white flowers.

Growth habit:	Perennial; 6 to 12 inches tall.
Color of flowers:	White.
Bloom time:	April through May.
Where to grow:	Partial to full shade; moisture-retaining, rich soil.
How to start:	Seeds or plants.
Spacing:	Space plants 6 inches apart.
Growing tips:	Foamflower has shallow roots, so it needs to be watered during dry spells. Mulch to retain moisture.

Jack-in-the-Pulpit (*Arisaema triphyllum*)

The "Jack" under the hooded green canopy is the flower column. It turns into a stalk of red berries in fall.

Growth habit:	Perennial; 1 to 2 feet tall.
Color of flowers:	Green, maroon.
Bloom time:	April through May.
Where to grow:	Partial to full shade; rich, humusy, moisture-retaining soil.
How to start:	Seeds or plants.
Spacing:	Space plants 6 inches apart.
Growing tips:	Don't fertilize during the growing season; wait until winter to feed.

Solomon's-Seal (*Polygonatum biflorum*)

The creeping rhizomes of small Solomon's-seal produce arching stems decorated with pairs of dainty bell-shaped flowers dangling beneath alternate leaves. Small Solomon's-seal is good for shady slopes or woodsy corners and is nice planted with ferns.

Growth habit:	Perennial; 1 to 3 feet tall.
Color of flowers:	White.
Bloom time:	June through July.
Where to grow:	Partial shade; moisture-retaining, humusy soil.
How to start:	Purchase plants.
Spacing:	Space plants 1 foot apart.
Growing tips:	Fall planting is best. Plant the rhizomes in a horizontal position, 1 to 2 inches deep.

Wild Ginger (*Asarum canadense*)

The heart-shaped leaves of wild ginger often conceal brownish-burgundy, bell-like flowers, which are borne near the ground. Wild ginger makes a good groundcover, especially under trees.

Growth habit:	Perennial; 4 to 6 inches tall.
Color of flowers:	Reddish brown.
Bloom time:	April through May.
Where to grow:	Partial to full shade; ordinary garden soil.
How to start:	Purchase plants.
Spacing:	Space plants 6 inches apart.
Growing tips:	Expand your plantings by division or by rooting a pair of leaves that you've cut from the plant with a small piece of root attached.

Wildflowers for Sun or Shade

These plants will adjust to a wide range of light and soil conditions.

Blue-Eyed Grass (*Sisyrinchium angustifolium*)

This grasslike plant is actually in the iris family! It bears small, starry, blue flowers with yellow centers amid clumps of grasslike foliage. Use blue-eyed grass to enliven sunny meadows.

Growth habit:	Perennial; 8 to 10 inches tall.
Color of flowers:	Blue.
Bloom time:	May through June.
Where to grow:	Full sun to light shade; ordinary garden soil.
How to start:	Seeds or plants.
Spacing:	Space plants 6 inches apart.
Growing tips:	To prevent crown rot, do not mulch. Separate the clumps when they become crowded. The pealike seeds are larger than you'd expect from such small flowers.

Forget-Me-Not (*Myosotis scorpioides*)

Often found near streams, the scalloped, china-blue flowers seem to reflect the blue of the sky. Our city neighbors planted these sprawlers around a sunken-bathtub pool in their yard, where they clambered engagingly over the rim.

Growth habit:	Perennial; sprawling mats; 6 to 15 inches tall.
Color of flowers:	Light blue.
Where to grow:	Full sun to part shade; ordinary soil with plenty of moisture.
Bloom time:	May through August.
How to start:	Seeds or plants.
Spacing:	Space plants 6 inches apart.
Growing tips:	Keep forget-me-nots well watered, or plant near a pond or pool.

Jacob's-Ladder (*Polemonium reptans*)

Jacob's-ladder bears clusters of medium-blue, bell-shaped flowers above clumps of airy, paired-leaflet foliage that resemble ladders. This wildflower is lovely when planted with spring-flowering bulbs, or along a rock wall with coralbells (*Heuchera sanguinea*).

Growth habit:	Perennial; 10 to 12 inches tall.
Color of flowers:	Blue.
Bloom time:	May.

Where to grow:	Full sun to partial shade; ordinary garden soil.
How to start:	Seeds or plants.
Spacing:	Space plants 10 inches apart.
Growing tips:	Found in open woods in the wild, it won't flower much in heavy shade.

Mayapple (*Podophyllum peltatum*)

Mayapples are charming plants that look just like wide-open um-brellas. Some are single, others a pair of leafy parasols. Peek under the leaf canopy to find the waxy white flower that later develops into an edible fruit. Mayapples are best planted under trees, along a drive-way, or in a shady corner, for they spread vigorously and can be hard to contain in a flower bed.

Growth habit:	Perennial; 12 to 15 inches tall.
Color of flowers:	White.
Bloom time:	May.
Where to grow:	Full sun to full shade; moisture-retaining soil.
How to start:	Purchase plants.
Spacing:	Space plants 6 inches apart.
Growing tips:	Plant mayapples where they can roam; they spread to form colonies.

Shooting-Star (*Dodecatheon meadia*)

The flowers of common shooting-star look like little rockets poised above a neat rosette of ground-hugging leaves.

Growth habit:	Perennial; 10 to 15 inches tall.
Color of flowers:	Pink, lavender, or white.
Bloom time:	May through June.
Where to grow:	Full sun to partial shade; rich, humusy soil.
How to start:	Purchase plants.
Spacing:	Space plants 6 inches apart.
Growing tips:	Shooting-stars need moisture during their blooming period but tolerate drier conditions when dormant. Foliage dies back soon after blooming.

Spring Beauty (*Claytonia virginica*)

Treat yourself to a look through a magnifying glass at the delicate flowers decorated with fine, deep pink stripes. The corms, sometimes called fairy spuds, are edible.

Growth habit:	Perennial; 4 to 6 inches tall.

Color of flowers: White or pale pink.
Bloom time: April through May.
Where to grow: Sun to partial shade; humusy soil.
How to start: Seeds or corms.
Spacing: Space plants 3 to 6 inches apart.
Growing tips: Spring beauties need moisture during blooming period but tolerate drier conditions when dormant. The grasslike foliage dies back after blooming.

Virginia Bluebells (*Mertensia virginica*)

One of my favorites, Virginia bluebells has sprays of sky-blue, bell-shaped flowers that dangle over oval leaves. Even a single plant is an eyecatcher, and a drift of them along a stream is an unforgettable sight. In the wild, this lovely flower likes moist woods and stream edges and open bottomlands, but it adapts well to the home garden.

Growth habit: Perennial; 1 to 2 feet tall.
Color of flowers: Pink buds open to blue flowers.
Bloom time: April through May.
Where to grow: Sun to partial shade; rich, humusy, moist but not wet soil.
How to start: Purchase plants.
Spacing: Space plants 1 foot apart.
Growing tips: Moisture is especially important in early spring. The leaves die back after blooming.

Wild Geranium (*Geranium maculatum*)

Rosy, five-petaled flowers make this easy wildflower a desirable addition to a shady border or woodland path. It self-sows readily.

Growth habit: Perennial; 1 to 2 feet tall.
Color of flowers: Lavender-pink.
Bloom time: April through May.
Where to grow: Full sun to shade; ordinary garden soil.
How to start: Purchase plants or grow from seeds.
Spacing: Space plants 1 foot apart.
Growing tips: Self-sows freely. Seed pods split suddenly and forcefully, dispersing the seeds far and wide. Bag some pods to be sure of getting some seeds. Mulch plants exposed to full sun. Protect flowering plants from strong winds; the blossoms shatter easily.

Wildflowers for Sun

If the sun shines on your wildflower patch most of the day, these sun lovers will make themselves right at home.

Black-Eyed Susan (*Rudbeckia hirta*)

These meadow and roadside charmers multiply fast in your home wildflower garden. The flowers last a long time in bouquets.

Growth habit: Self-seeding biennial; 18 to 30 inches tall.
Color of flowers: Golden yellow with dark brown center.
Bloom time: June through September.
Where to grow: Full sun; well-drained, lean to ordinary garden soil.
How to start: Purchase plants or start from seeds.
Spacing: Space plants 18 to 24 inches apart.
Growing tips: Technically a biennial. Cut back after blooming to encourage another year's growth. Self-sows freely. Plants grown in rich soil develop taller stems that may need staking for support.

Bright orange butterfly weed (*Asclepias tuberosa*) and rosy purple coneflowers (*Echinacea purpurea*) add a splash of color to a sunny wildflower garden. Clip faded flowers to keep coneflowers blooming until frost.

Bluebell (*Campanula rotundifolia*)

Bluebells on wiry stems dance in the breezes on rocky or sandy sites. The ground-hugging leaves are heart-shaped; those along the stalk are slender and sparse. Sometimes called harebells, the flowers are almost an inch long.

Growth habit:	Perennial; 6 to 18 inches tall.
Color of flowers:	Blue.
Bloom time:	June through August.
Where to grow:	Full sun; well-drained, average to poor soil.
How to start:	Purchase plants or grow from seeds.
Spacing:	Space plants 1 to 2 feet apart.
Growing tips:	Bluebells like cool weather. In the South, plant where they'll receive afternoon shade. Excellent drainage is essential. Mulch to keep roots cool.

Butterfly Weed (*Asclepias tuberosa*)

The flat-topped clusters of bright flowers attract hummingbirds and butterflies.

Growth habit:	Perennial; 1 to 3 feet tall.
Color of flowers:	Bright orange; yellow, pale orange, and pink cultivars are also occasionally available.
Bloom time:	June through July.
Where to grow:	Full sun, but will tolerate some light shade; well-drained, ordinary to poor soil.
How to start:	Purchase plants or grow from seeds.
Spacing:	Space plants 2 to 3 feet apart.
Growing tips:	Butterfly weed likes it hot and dry. To prevent plant crowns from rotting, do not mulch.

Purple Coneflower (*Echinacea purpurea*)

A favorite herbal healing plant, purple coneflower has daisylike flowers. In the wild, you'll find it in meadows or on sunny slopes.

Growth habit:	Perennial; 2 to 4 feet tall.
Color of flowers:	Lavender-pink with purple, bronze, or orange centers.
Bloom time:	June through August.
Where to grow:	Full sun; well-drained, ordinary garden soil.
How to start:	Purchase plants or grow from seeds.
Spacing:	Space plants 18 inches apart.
Growing tips:	Coneflowers will tolerate light shade.

CHAPTER THREE

Try These Herbs in a Shady Corner

20

The sun can't be everywhere. There's shade in every yard—small patches of it, anyway. If you have a few trees, some shrubs, and perhaps a boundary fence, you have a variety of semishady sites. You needn't settle for planting these spots with ferns and letting it go at that. Instead, transform one of them into an herb garden. While many popular herbs do require full sun, some prefer and others adapt happily to partial shade. The herbs described in this chapter will all do well in a shady or partly shady spot.

Begin by spending a day pacing around your place. Notice when and where the shade falls, so you'll have a feeling for the conditions your plants will experience. A north or west side of the house may be in shade part of the day, with a few hours of afternoon sun. Partial shade can also be found in the shifting shadows and sunlight filtered through branches of a small-leaved, open tree, such as a birch.

PLANTING TIPS

- Most plants can be started from seed, but some must be propagated from cuttings or division to make sure the flavor comes true. Buying a plant or two of each herb is nearly as economical as seed—and will give you instant and reliable results.
- Don't plant near trees, because roots close to the surface can impede digging and compete with plants for nourishment.
- If soil is poor or very compacted, make a raised bed. Bring in new soil and add compost and other organic matter to create a 6- to 10-inch-high mound on top of the soil surface. (Don't make a raised bed right next to a tree trunk; changing the soil depth around a tree can harm or kill it.)
- Check plant heights. Plant taller herbs at the back of a border or corner bed, or at the center of a circular bed.
- Feel free to pick your new herbs. Frequent pinching of the growing tips helps make them bushier and sturdier.

Angelica (*Angelica archangelica*)

Angelica is a stately plant with large leaves and impressive white flower umbels. The flower clusters turn into open-spoked globes of seeds 4 to 8 inches in diameter. Don't collect this herb from the wild: It's very similar to the extremely poisonous water hemlock and can easily be confused with it.

Description:	Biennial; 3 to 5 feet tall.
Where to grow:	Prefers partial shade; moisture-retaining soil. Hardy to Zone 3.
How to start:	Grow from seeds or purchase plants.

Spacing:	Space plants 3 feet apart.
Growing tips:	Plant fresh seed; old seed has very poor germination. Seeds need light when planting; do not cover them with soil. Stake plants to keep them standing upright.
Uses:	Angelica leaves, seeds, stalks, and roots taste like licorice and are all edible. They add a sweet flavor to salads, soups, and stews. Stems are often candied. In medieval times, angelica was used as an antidote to magic spells and poisons.

Chervil (*Anthriscus cerefolium*)

A mass planting of chervil with its host of small white flowers is a pretty sight at blooming time. Chervil does well in the shade of taller plants in the open garden. It makes a good groundcover around large shrubs, or tall herbs like angelica.

Description:	Annual; 6 to 8 inches tall.
Where to grow:	Prefers partial shade; rich, well-drained but moist soil.
How to start:	Start seeds in staggered plantings for continuous supply.
Spacing:	Space plants 9 to 12 inches apart.
Growing tips:	Does best in cool weather. Sow where it is to grow. Spring plantings go to seed in summer. Plants may reach 1 to 2 feet tall when setting seed. Chervil self-sows readily.
Uses:	The delicate anise flavor of chervil leaves is good in soups, salads, and casseroles. Flavor of the leaves is best before flowering; seeds are edible, too.

Lemon Balm (*Melissa officinalis*)

The scented leaves of lemon balm are pretty as well as fragrant. A member of the mint family, it spreads vigorously, though not rampantly. The white flowers attract bees.

Description:	Perennial; 18 to 24 inches tall.
Where to grow:	Full sun to shade; ordinary soil. Tolerates dry soil. Hardy to Zone 5, Zone 4 with protection.
How to start:	Grow from seeds or purchase plants.
Spacing:	Space plants 10 to 12 inches apart.

Growing tips:	Leave seeds uncovered when planting; light promotes germination. Lemon balm self-sows freely. Keep the plant bushier and more shapely by regular shearing.
Uses:	Lemon balm adds a delicate lemon flavor to tea, potpourris, and salads.

Lovage (*Levisticum officinale*)

Lovage is a handsome, hollow-stalked plant for the back of the garden. The leaves and umbels of greenish-yellow flowers resemble a giant-size celery plant.

Description:	Perennial; 5 to 7 feet tall.
Where to grow:	Full sun to partial shade; moist but well-drained soil.
How to start:	Grow from seeds or purchase plants.
Spacing:	Space plants 3 feet apart.
Growing tips:	Use fresh seed and plant in the garden in late summer or early fall. Lovage does best in areas with cold winters; it seems to need a winter freeze to encourage it to break dormancy in spring. New shoots appear early in spring.
Uses:	Lovage has a flavor similar to celery. It's good in soups, green salads, and potato salads. Seeds may be used like celery seeds to add flavor to pickles, stews, and breads.

Mints (*Mentha* spp.)

Mints vary in size and shape, but all have in common a diagnostic sign anyone can recognize: a square stem. Some species have smooth leaves; others, hairy. Flowers are white, lavender, or pink. All have fragrant foliage.

Description:	Perennial; size depends on species; plants range from low and creeping to 3 feet tall.
Where to grow:	Full sun to partial shade; ordinary soil. Many mints like plenty of moisture. Hardy to Zone 5.
How to start:	Buy plants or root stem cuttings. Seeds do not always come true.
Spacing:	Space plants 1 to 2 feet apart.
Growing tips:	Mints spread voraciously. Give them their own bed or plant in a bottomless bucket with the rim

23

1 or 2 inches aboveground, to control spreading. Shear them two or three times a season for a more pleasing shape and better-flavored leaves.

Uses: Mints are used for tea and in jelly and cold drinks. They also add an aromatic touch to a table bouquet.

Parsley (*Petroselinum crispum*)

For intense flavor, choose Italian parsley. It has plain, flat leaves and a looser growth habit than the familiar curly-leaf parsley, whose perky, tufted-looking leaves may be a bit harder to chew.

Description: Biennial; 6 to 10 inches tall.
Where to grow: Full sun to partial shade; ordinary garden soil.
How to start: Grow from seeds or purchase plants.
Spacing: Space plants 6 to 8 inches apart.
Growing tips: Parsley seeds are notorious for slow germination. Soak them overnight before planting and discard the water, which contains leached-out compounds that inhibit germination. Be sure to cover the seeds; they germinate best in darkness.
Uses: Parsley adds flavor and color to soups and salads. It also is an attractive garnish.

Sweet Cicely (*Myrrhis odorata*)

This tall, licorice-scented plant has finely cut leaves that resemble ferns. Black seeds, ¾ inch long and held in upright clusters, follow the broad, flat umbels of white flowers.

Description: Perennial; 3 to 4 feet tall.
Where to grow: Prefers partial shade; moist but well-drained soil. Hardy to Zone 3.
How to start: Grow from seeds or purchase plants.
Spacing: Space plants 2 to 3 feet apart.
Growing tips: Plant fresh seed; old seed germinates poorly if at all. Established sweet cicely plants self-sow readily.
Uses: All parts of the plant are edible. Leaves are sweet and may be used to flavor baked goods and stewed fruits. Seeds are good snacks or pastry garnishes.

Sweet Woodruff (*Galium odoratum*)

Clusters of starry white flowers help light up those dark, shaded areas of your yard. Sweet woodruff is a low-growing plant with small, deep green, pointed leaves surrounding the stem in a whorl. It makes an excellent groundcover under tall shrubs and around spring-blooming wildflowers.

Description:	Perennial; 6 to 10 inches tall.
Where to grow:	Full or partial shade; rich, moist soil. Sweet woodruff will not do well in dry soil.
How to start:	Purchase plants.
Spacing:	Space plants 1 foot apart.
Growing tips:	Spreads rapidly when growing conditions are right.
Uses:	Sweet woodruff has a pleasant, vanilla-like scent when dried. It is a good ingredient in potpourris.

Tarragon (*Artemisia dracunculus* var. *sativa*)

People grow French tarragon more for its flavor than its looks; although not unattractive, tarragon can be straggly at times. Flowers are whitish green. It is a low-growing plant, with narrow leaves on drooping stems.

Description:	Perennial; 12 to 15 inches tall; sprawly.
Where to grow:	Full to partial shade; rich, loose, well-drained soil.
How to start:	Purchase plants. Break and rub a bit of leaf when buying plants to make sure you get true French tarragon, with its aromatic licorice flavor, rather than the tall, coarse, almost flavorless Russian tarragon.
Spacing:	Space plants 12 to 15 inches apart.
Growing tips:	Tarragon must have good drainage. In cold regions, tarragon survives winter better if planted in very well-drained soil: A raised bed is perfect. Mulch the plants to prevent winterkill. Divide plants regularly to stimulate root growth.
Uses:	A superb culinary herb, the leaves are used to flavor sauces, soups, salads, and vinegars.

25

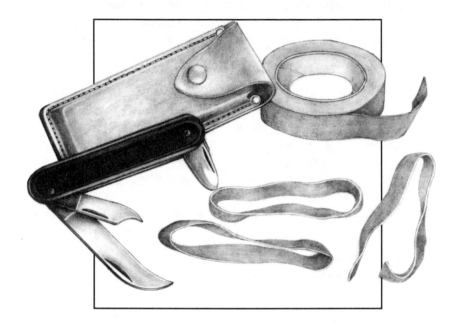

Make a Simple Graft

26

ntil you've tried it, grafting seems mysterious, a special skill that only wizards can perform. After I watched my husband learn to make simple grafts, I began to realize that grafting is just another growing process. Like the seeds and plants you nurture in the ground, your grafts will grow if you do them carefully and give them the conditions they need.

Grafting is the process of uniting parts of two (or more) plants, making them grow together as one plant. When we say that a graft has taken, we mean that the formerly separate parts have fused and begun to produce new growth.

There are many good reasons to graft. Let's say your neighbor has a wonderful apple cultivar you'd like to add to your crop, but you don't have space for another tree. Graft a branch from his tree to one of yours and you can have some of this special fruit for yourself. Here are some other reasons for grafting.

- Graft multiple cultivars to a single rootstock to sample many types of fruit, or attach a pollinating branch to a fruit tree that is not self-fruitful.
- Graft full-sized cultivars to a dwarf rootstock to start your own dwarf orchard, or an extra-hardy root to encourage better winter survival in cold climates.
- Graft to improve the branching pattern of an awkwardly structured tree or to repair winter damage to an injured tree.
- Graft a branch of an heirloom pear tree from your grandfather's farm to a tree in your own yard, hundreds of miles away. You'll perpetuate the cultivar—and the memories.

Grafting Basics

Ready to try? Before you put your coat on, take a minute to learn the rules and lingo.

For your first efforts at grafting, stick to attaching apples to apples, plums to plums, peaches to peaches, and so on—trees within the same species. Successful grafts are possible, for the most part, only between closely related plants. Two different species within the same genus may also give good results—sour to sweet cherry, peach to nectarine, English walnut to black walnut.

Although it's tempting to try to break the rules, it's a waste of time to try to unite such unrelated trees as hickory and walnut or cherry and pear. Their genetic heritage is too different.

Even experienced grafters report their success rate varies between 50 and 70 percent. My husband has had as many as five out of six apple grafts take, but in some cases, only one out of ten English to black walnut grafts were successful. Even with perfect technique, weather and other variables can interfere. It's always wise to make more grafts than you need, so at least some will take.

Before you start, practice on scrap twigs to gain assurance in making smooth cuts at the correct angle and in the right shape. Once you develop some skill in cutting and wrapping, you'll find you can make quite a few grafts in an afternoon.

WHY GRAFTS FAIL

Grafting is not foolproof; always make more grafts than you need. Here are some common reasons why grafts fail to take.

- The scion dried out before the graft was made.
- The scion and stock were incompatible.
- Cut surfaces dried too much before being joined.
- Insect infestation or fungus interfered.
- The graft was made too early, before the sap started to flow.
- The graft was made too late in the season.
- Inaccurate cut, loose binding, or wind contributed to a poor union of the cambium layers.

The Language of Grafting

The vital element—the true heart of the graft—is the bonding of the cambium layers of the two plants. *Cambium* is a thin tissue layer just beneath the bark, sandwiched between the outer bark of the tree and the inert wood at the center, which isn't capable of growth. Cambium, crucial to the life of the tree, lays down new growth at the outer rim of the tree's woody core. It's a vascular system that carries nutrients from roots to stems. Grafting places the cambium layers of the parts to be united in close contact with each other, and keeps them in that position until they start to form common tissue.

28

The *scion* is the newcomer, the piece of branch or the bud to be grafted to an existing plant. The rootstock, often simply called the *stock*, is the rooted plant to which the scion will be grafted. The stock may be a slender year-old tree seedling, or it may be an established tree (or bush or vine). It is already living on its own, in the ground or in a pot. In grafting, the healthy scion is placed in contact with carefully prepared stock, in a season favorable for growth. The union is then sealed to keep out air and immobilized to prevent breakage.

Grafting Supplies

Many successful grafts have been made with the simplest of tools: a pocket knife and plastic electrical tape. Some cuts are easier to make with a special grafting knife, though, and it's helpful to have on hand a variety of binding and sealing materials, specially purchased or makeshift. For binding, try electrical tape, raffia, rubber grafting bands, cut strips of bike inner tubes, wide rubber bands, or nursery tape; for sealing, use grafting wax, asphalt emulsion, beeswax, or petroleum jelly. Now let's do some grafting.

Collecting the Scionwood

Cut scionwood while the tree is completely dormant, and either graft immediately or store for later use. Choose healthy, one-year-old branches near the top of the tree, where growth is the most vigorous. Or look for an upward-growing, rather than horizontal, branch.

Cut scions from the middle of the branch, rather than from the tip. Allow seven to nine buds on each piece; you'll be trimming it later. If you're grafting immediately after cutting, make your scionwood 3 to 5 inches long, with about three buds. It's vitally important to keep track of which end of the scion is which—it won't grow if attached to the rootstock in reverse. Make a straight cut at the top of the scion (the end furthest from the tree) and a slanting cut at the bottom (the end you'll graft to the rootstock).

Label the scions right away with the name of the scionwood—it's easy to get them mixed up. To store the scions for later use, bundle them together, keep them cool so they'll stay dormant, and cover them so they won't dry out. Wrap bundles in plastic and bury in the ground layered in leaves or sawdust for easy retrieval. Or stash bunches in deep snow on the north side of the house. Mike keeps his scions from February pruning in plastic bags in the refrigerator. (Open one end of the bag now and then to discourage mold formation.)

Making the Graft

29

Graft in late winter or early spring, before the trees begin to leaf out. In most northern states, February and March are a good time. Do your grafting on a cloudy day, so the sun won't dry the cut wood surfaces. Before doing anything, nip the bottom inch of the scionwood off to expose moist wood. That last inch or so near the end will have dried too much to make a good graft.

Whip or Splice Graft

This is just about the easiest kind of graft you can make. It unites two slender branches in a simple splice, and works well for branches up to about ¾ inch in diameter. It's easier to line up the cambium of the scion with that of the rootstock if both branches are about the same size, but if you're matching up thin scions with somewhat thicker stock, don't worry. Keep the cambium layers in good contact at one edge, and protect the graft from drying out.

For best results, follow the steps below.

1. Cut both the stock and scion at matching angles of about 60 degrees.
2. Fit stock and scion together, taking care to line up the cambiums, and bind them firmly. Be sure the two cut ends don't slip out of position while you're wrapping them. The wrap keeps the cambium layers in close contact until they grow together, and helps to keep out air, preventing the cut ends from drying out.
3. To further exclude air, seal the graft. If you don't want to go to a lot of trouble, just wrap the entire grafted area and 1 to 2 inches up each side of the graft with plastic tape. Or wrap with a sheet of plastic and tape that on. My husband, Mike, has had good results with this easy, if nonprofessional, procedure, and we know of other people who have, too.

   The traditional method is to paint or smear grafting wax or another sealer over the bound-together graft, making sure to cover the edges where the binding meets the wood. Be sure to seal the cut end at the top, too, to reduce moisture loss.
4. For extra security tie on a splint outside the wrapping to keep the joint stable.

Tongue Graft

The tongue graft is performed in the same way as the splice graft — the same angled cut, the same wrapping and aftercare. The difference is you make two extra cuts into the woody tissue of both scion and stock, then mesh them together. This forms a stronger joint that's less likely to be dislodged.

It works best if stock and scion are equal in diameter. If the stock is wider than the scion, cut the end of the stock at a sharper angle, leaving a smaller exposed surface, so the pieces will match more closely. In either case, make your cuts slightly off-center, closer to the longer edge of the slanted cut, so the angled surfaces will match more closely. Tie on a splint, a stick, or wire outside the wrapping, to keep the joint stable.

Making Good Connections

Grafting is an ancient art. It was practiced in the first century A.D. and probably well before that. I like to imagine that, like seed planting, the process of grafting was filled with meaning and performed, perhaps, with certain rituals that confirmed the sacred possibilities of new life. We can make our grafts with a sense of participating truly in a rite of

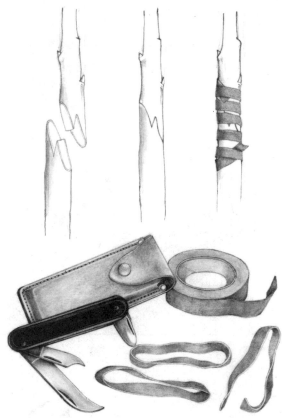

Simple tools for a simple graft: a pocketknife to make the cut, a roll of plastic tape or a few wide rubber bands for wrapping and sealing. The tongue graft shown here is an easy way to join scion and stock securely. A cloudy day in early spring is a good time for experimenting.

spring—fostering new growth, preserving old cultivars, encouraging diversity, making good connections so the sap can flow.

Plan On Iris for Spring Color

O f all the plants you can add to your home landscape, bearded irises have one of the widest color ranges. Name any pastel or primary shade, except for clear, true red, and you'll most likely find a bearded iris of that hue—apricot, mauve, pink, maroon, lavender, blue, purple, bright and pale yellow, white, cream, light green, bronze, and near-black. Many kinds have blended colors or two separate colors—gold and white, purple and yellow, peach and rust, just for a sample.

In addition to their glorious color and beautiful form, bearded irises have other features. They bloom after most spring bulbs have finished and before many summer perennials and annuals begin to flower—just when your garden needs a splash of color. They also are among the most adaptable members of the genus, which contains more than 200 species. They're hardy, easy to grow, and last for years if conditions are to their liking.

A Weekend of Planning

Such dependable and beautiful additions to the garden are worth a couple of days of careful planning. If you already have a flower border, bearded irises will contribute height and color. Or, start a bed composed entirely of irises, using early, midseason, and late cultivars for a longer blooming period.

For a special treat, visit an iris garden when the plants are in bloom. You'll meet irises in colors and combinations you never knew existed, and it will help you choose just the right plants for that special spot. Late spring, from May through June, is the peak of the season in most areas, but since bloom time depends on weather conditions, call ahead when planning your visit.

A trip to the Presby Memorial Iris Gardens in Montclair, New Jersey, gave me a good case of iris fever. This collection of more than 6,000 iris cultivars is well organized in a series of beds that sweep in a pastel blur across a greensward, on a street of elegant houses. Each plant is labeled with name, date of origin, and name of breeder. We saw a rainbow of luscious irises, from the fragrant blue and white sixteenth-century Florentine variety to modern bearded iris hybrids with names like 'Gold Galore', 'Angelic Light', and 'Count Cobra.'

Catalogs from growers that specialize in bearded irises are full of gorgeous choices. Your only problem will be limiting your list to what you have room for and what you can afford. Keep bloom time and height in mind when selecting your favorites. To find growers in your area who show and sell bearded iris plants, check newspaper ads and ask your local garden club.

33

Care and Feeding of Bearded Iris

When I first planted bearded iris, I lost some because I planted them too deeply and they rotted. Plant shallowly, placing the rhizome on

DECIPHERING AN IRIS CATALOG

Iris fanciers have their own language, words that describe the parts of the flower and its colors. The "beard" is the chenillelike strip of fuzz on the upper part of the iris's falls. Some cultivars have beards the same color as the falls; others have contrasting beards, such as bright orange on a pure white flower. Bearded irises are further classified into types according to height: from the miniature dwarfs, only 6 to 8 inches tall, through the standard tall beardeds, which may reach 40 inches or more. Since most catalogs can't show you a picture of every flower, you'll need to know the difference between a "blue and white plicata" and a "blue and white bicolor."

Bicolor: a flower with standards of one color and falls of a different color; for example, yellow standards with purple falls.
Bitone: a flower with falls and standards in two different shades of the same color; for example, lavender standards with purple falls.
Blend: a flower with two colors, shaded, in the same part of the flower.
Falls: the three outer sepals of the flower that arch downward.
Plicata: a yellow or white flower with speckled margins.
Standards: the three upright petals of the flower.

a mound of loose soil and spreading the roots around it. Cover the roots with soil, but make sure the tops of the rhizomes are exposed. Space plants depending on cultivar, from 6 inches apart for dwarf types to 18 to 24 inches for tall bearded cultivars. Bearded irises must have full sun to flower well, and a neutral or slightly alkaline soil with plenty of organic material. They are hardy to Zone 3.

Irises need a good supply of water while they're in bloom, but they don't mind dry soil after that. They definitely dislike wet soil over winter, or waterlogged soil at any time. Feed with an organic fertilizer in early spring and about a month after bloom. Stake tall plants if they are exposed to the wind.

Bloom time varies according to cultivar. Some of the miniature

Frilled and fancy or classically simple, bearded iris fill the late spring border with almost every color of the rainbow. Plant the rhizomes shallowly in groups of at least three of the same kind. Good drainage is a must.

dwarfs bloom at daffodil time; late-season tall bearded cultivars bloom with peonies. Individual plants have a relatively short bloom period: around two weeks for an established clump of plants, but sometimes less than a week for a single plant in hot weather. Remove the bloom stalks after flowering so the plant doesn't put its energy into seed production. Stretch out the blooming season by planting early, mid-season, and late cultivars. Some tall beardeds are rebloomers, producing a few flowers in late summer.

Dividing Bearded Iris

About three years after you plant them, your bearded irises will have produced a knotted mass of rhizomes and will need dividing. Divide them right after flowering, before mid-August, so the new plants have a chance to form roots before cold weather. Cut back the leaves of the clump you're dividing to 6 to 8 inches, cut through the tangle of rhizomes with a garden spade, and dig up part of the clump. Using your hands and a knife to help things along, cut sections of

35

BEYOND THE BEARDEDS

When they think of iris, most people think of the tall bearded irises that bloom in May. Besides those wonderfully varied favorites, there are other excellent kinds of irises, some of which thrive in difficult conditions. Japanese iris (*Iris kaempferi,* now listed as *I. ensata*) and Siberian iris (*I. siberica*) are two adaptable species, both largely untroubled by pests or diseases.

The early- to midseason flowers of Japanese irises are wide, flat, and large—up to 8 inches across. Colors range from white to red-purple, with a wide selection of blues and purples. The standards are small and the falls extend more horizontally than those of bearded irises. Often planted beside pools, they grow best where the soil remains evenly moist but is well drained; they will do fine in the garden if kept well watered. Because they are not true bog plants, they do not appreciate standing in waterlogged soils, especially in winter. Japanese irises prefer full sun and an acid soil and are hardy to Zone 5. Plant the rhizome 1 inch below the soil surface. They grow to 24 to 40 inches tall and multiply more slowly than bearded types.

Easy-to-grow Siberian irises (*I. siberica*) produce a satisfying amount of bloom in less than ideal soils and part shade or sun. Hardy to Zone 2, they thrive in ordinary soil, high-moisture or dry sites alike; they do not like waterlogged soil, especially over winter. Siberian irises have slender, arching foliage—a contrast to the stiff, upright leaves of the beardeds—and smaller, simpler flowers about 3 to 5 inches across and open in arrangement. Flowers bloom in early to midseason in white, red-violet, and a wide range of blues and purples. The plants reach 24 to 36 inches tall and multiply rapidly. Fully cover the rhizomes with soil when planting. These irises seldom need division, which is a good thing because the rhizomes and roots are so densely packed together that they are difficult to separate.

rhizomes from the cluster. Each should have one or two leaf fans, a sturdy rhizome, and good, healthy roots. Discard any hollowed, dried-out rhizomes, or any mushy ones. Then replant by settling the rhizomes with the leaf fan in the direction you want the plants to grow. Settle the rhizome on a mound of soil and spread the roots around it. Cover only the roots with soil, leaving the top of the rhizome exposed.

An Ounce of Prevention

Bearded iris needs some preventive care to ward off pest and disease problems. Leaf spot is a fungal disease that begins as brown spots on the leaves and eventually progresses to dead, brown leaves. To help prevent it, cut the leaves back before winter. At the first sign of leaf spot, promptly remove affected leaves. Do not compost them. The fungus overwinters on infested leaves; destroying them gives it no place to hide.

Iris borers are moth larvae. Soon after hatching, in early spring, the tiny borers work their way through the leaf, down through the center of the leaf fan, and into the rhizome. Their tunneling weakens the plant, leaving it open to infection by bacterial soft rot, a disease that rots the rhizomes and may eventually kill the plants. The best defense against borers is prevention. Remove and destroy the plant's old leaves in the fall. Divide the plants regularly, inspecting the rhizomes carefully and discarding any portions that appear diseased. Irises growing in beds with other kinds of plants are less likely to be attacked by borers than those in beds composed only of iris. Monoculture always makes things easier for the bugs.

Start a
Sweet Potato Patch

Learning to grow sweet potatoes is a new venture for many gardeners. Although "sweets" require no more care than tomatoes or lettuce, they're often overlooked when garden plans are made. I don't know why, for sweet potatoes are delicious and easy to grow. If you want to find out what you've been missing, start by planting a crop of these heat-loving delicacies. Harvest the tubers in fall, and store the sweets to keep all winter. Next spring, complete the cycle by starting new plants from sound roots you've kept over from the fall harvest.

Easy to Satisfy

Consider, first, what sweet potatoes require. Members of the morning glory family, sweet potatoes (*Ipomoea batatas*) are essentially undemanding plants. They produce well even in dry weather and poor soil. Insect problems are not common. In southern climates, some diseases are more troublesome in neutral or alkaline soil, so in the South, sweets are traditionally grown in acid soil (pH 5.2 to 6.7).

Native to the tropics, sweet potatoes have one absolute requirement: a minimum of 150 days of warm weather. The vines grow best at air temperatures between 65° and 95°F; soil temperatures between 75° and 85°F. At 60°F the vines stop growing; prolonged temperatures below 50°F retard the plants. Sweet potatoes are very tender and can't tolerate the slightest touch of frost.

Sweet potatoes aren't raised commercially much above the latitude of New Jersey, but they are grown successfully in home gardens as far north as Michigan, Wisconsin, Connecticut, and Massachusetts. Use these suggestions to make a warm spot for sweets.

- In cold, borderline climates, plant in sandy soil, which warms quickly in spring.
- A raised bed or ridge of loose soil is warmer than the surrounding ground.
- Black plastic mulch boosts heat retention in the soil.

Lean Soil Is a Plus

An excess of nitrogen makes sweet potatoes mature late, especially in a rainy reason. Go lightly on the manure when preparing the bed. Tubers harvested from plants grown in high nitrogen soil tend to be long and thin rather than chunky. Potassium deficiency causes spindly roots, so dig in some wood ashes, greensand, granite dust, or spoiled hay at spring planting or fall clean-up time to help supply needed potassium, or potash.

Contrary to popular opinion, you can grow sweets in clay soil, as long as your garden isn't afflicted with severe hardpan, a layer of impervious, compacted soil under the garden's surface.

39

Which Sweet For You?

Sweet potatoes come in all shades of orange, and in dry-fleshed and moist-fleshed varieties. Skin color of the tubers may be anywhere from light yellow to purplish red; the meaty flesh varies from near-white to deep orange. Most cultivars for the home garden are the moist-fleshed type; those grown for industrial use or livestock feed are dry-fleshed. Popular cultivars for the home garden include 'Centennial', 'Georgia Red', 'Gold Rush', and 'Velvet'.

Start with Slips

For your first sweet potato row, buy rooted slips either from a mail-order supplier (see Resources beginning on page 337) or a farmers' market. If your family eats a lot of sweets, like ours does, you'll find that 100 plants provide plenty of tubers for a family of four to eat fresh and store for winter use. Follow these steps to an ample crop.

1. Cold weather retards the growth of sweet potato plants; frost will kill them entirely. Don't take chances: Wait to plant until two weeks after your last spring frost date. Here in southcentral Pennsylvania, our last spring frost occurs about May 14, and I plant sweet potatoes over Memorial Day weekend.
2. The slips you receive in the mail will look most unpromising, to put it kindly. In fact, they may look close to dead. Don't worry, though—they're more alive than they look. Submerge the roots in water for a day before planting.
3. Prepare the row while the slips are soaking. The vines will ramble, so allow 4 feet between rows, 12 to 16 inches between plants. Rototill or dig and rake the soil to a fine tilth. Then rake or hoe down each side of the row to draw soil into a ridge along the planting line.
4. Now to plant the slips. Start with the largest, strongest ones in case you run out of room. Use a long-bladed trowel to settle the rooted slips in the soft, ridged-up soil about 12 inches apart. If your soil is good and loose, use the short-forked end of a stick to push the roots 4 to 5 inches into the ridge.
5. At the end of each row—or, better yet, as each plant is settled into the earth—water the slips thoroughly into the soil to help settle the roots.
6. Toss a light sprinkling of straw over the plants to protect them from the bright summer sun. By the time the vines grow high

enough to peek over their light protective covering, their roots are well established and they seldom need more watering.

7. Before the vines start to spread, I mulch the 4 feet of bare soil between the rows with old hay or coarse cut weeds, more for weed control than for moisture retention. From then on, the sweet potatoes are on their own, except for a weeding or two, until harvest time.

Harvest and Storage

In warm tropical climates, sweet potato plants are allowed to remain in the ground until the leaves turn yellow, indicating that the plant is mature. Most North American gardeners, though, must harvest them as soon as frost hits the vines. We enjoy snitching some tubers early in September to confirm the approach of fall, but we try to hold off on the main harvest as long as possible, for the tubers will double in size every week throughout the month of September. They'll continue to grow in October, providing frost is late, but at a somewhat slower rate.

Dig the sweet potatoes immediately after frost darkens and wilts the leaves, for continued cold nights will damage them if they're left in the ground. Using a spading fork, dig from the side of the row to avoid damaging them. Bruised potatoes rot readily, and it doesn't take much to bruise a sweet, so handle them gently. Lay them carefully in the wheelbarrow rather than tossing them in from a distance. Brush the loose dirt from the sweets and pile them gently in baskets or crates. Take a few moments to gloat over the largest specimens you've unearthed. There's nothing uniform about homegrown sweet potatoes; some will be huge, some medium, some small. The tiny fingerling potatoes are tender and delicious cooked whole, in the skin.

The skin of a newly dug sweet potato is very thin, almost wispy when cooked. Because there is such a thin barrier between a sweet potato and the outside world, sweets spoil readily unless well cured. The curing process toughens the skin and reduces the internal water content. To cure your sweet potatoes, keep them in a hot place—80° to 90°F—for two weeks. We stack our crates of curing sweets near the wood stove in our kitchen and by the time we learn to avoid stumbling over them, the two weeks have passed and it's time to pack them away for the winter.

For winter storage, keep the potatoes in a dry, well-ventilated place between 55° and 60°F. As you've probably discovered if you've ever tried to store sweets in the refrigerator, cold, damp places encourage sweet potatoes to rot. I wrap each one individually in a piece of newspaper and pile them loosely in a basket, which spends the winter in a cool upstairs room. Some shrivel or mummify, usually the very small ones, but enough of them make it through till spring to go with the Easter ham. And I've had some last a full year.

Completing the Circle

If you harvest your sweet potatoes carefully, cure them well, and store them cool and dry, you should have no trouble keeping a good supply over the winter. Having accomplished this feat, you're ready to start this year's from last year's tubers.

1. Begin about two months before planting-out time to root slips from several of your best potatoes: chunky, sound ones that have kept well. A medium-sized sweet potato has about 50 eyes, each of which will sprout into a new plant.
2. Stick a few toothpicks around the waistline of a tuber, and suspend it in a jar of water. Keep it warm until you see sprouts forming. I have kept my sprouting sweets on the pilot light of a gas stove and, more recently, on a counter near the warm wood stove. Some gardeners bury the sweets in damp sand or vermiculite and keep them in a warm spot.
3. Twist off the sprouts from the potato before the roots tangle.
4. Plant directly in the ground or in a container. I set my new slips 3 inches apart in good potting soil in a 4-inch-deep container (an old refrigerator crisper or dishpan works well). They spend a few weeks growing roots and leafy green tops in a protected setting, under fluorescent lights, or in the cold frame, before being planted out.

You'll probably find, as I have, that the homegrown slips take hold and grow at least two weeks ahead of purchased plants and have a much lower mortality rate. Growing your own has other intangible advantages—the satisfaction of having learned a new technique and the assurance that, come what may, you need never lack for sweet potatoes, as long as you keep tending them.

Get a Head Start on Early Tomatoes

We don't buy supermarket tomatoes because they're so inferior to our homegrown fruits, so it's a long stretch from the last shelf-ripened tomato in early winter to the first red, vine-ripened fruit of summer. Every day we can manage to advance that first picking adds that much more tomato pleasure to our plates. We don't settle for a first tomato in late July. With some planning and a bit of effort, we can move that first picking back to early June, here in south-central Pennsylvania.

43

Choose an Early Ripener

Planting the right cultivar makes a big difference in early tomato yields. The average tomato won't set fruit when night temperatures dip into the lower fifties, because the pollen loses vigor at such low temperatures. Cold-tolerant cultivars like 'Sprint', 'Subarctic Maxi', 'Subarctic Plenty', 'Oregon Spring', 'Gem State', and 'Stokesalaska' have been bred to set fruit at lower than normal temperatures. Most of these early cultivars are *determinate;* that means they stop growing after bearing fruit. *Indeterminate* tomatoes, on the other hand, continue growing until killed by frost. Unlike indeterminate tomatoes, determinate plants are bushy and seldom need staking or pruning; in fact, they need all their leaves to nourish an early load of fruit.

Consider your early crop a bonus. Don't count on extra-early plants for season-long production. I even plant my super-early tomatoes in a separate part of the garden and till them under when they finish, about the time midseason plants start to bear well. Cold-tolerant, extra-early bearing tomatoes tend to have lower disease resistance than main-crop cultivars. Plant them in soil where diseased tomatoes have not been grown recently. A heavier-than-usual dose of fertilizer early in the season will help support their early fruit load.

Flavor of the newer cultivars is better than that of earlier introductions like 'Siberia'. Although they don't quite measure up to full-flavored midseason tomatoes, the flavor of the extra-earlies beats supermarket tomatoes by a mile. Most of the super-early tomatoes are on the small side—1½ to 2 ounces. But it's the flavor and color that matter more than size when you're hankering for fresh tomatoes to go with your garden lettuce.

Off to a Good Start

Traditional seed-starting times for indoor planting range from six to eight weeks before the average date of your last spring frost. Use the earlier date if you'll be raising the plants under fluorescent lights or in a greenhouse or sunroom with plenty of light. Start a bit later if you plan to keep your seedlings on a windowsill, where they'll receive less light. Plants that spend too long indoors under low light conditions tend to grow tall and spindly. Because you can plant out the special cold-resistant tomatoes as much as two to three weeks earlier than regular cultivars, you can move the indoor seed-starting time for these back to eight to ten weeks before the last spring frost date.

Tomato seeds germinate better in the dark, so cover the planted flats with opaque material such as a dark cloth or a section of newspaper. After germination, give the seedlings a maximum day length of 8 to 12 hours. Long days—16 hours or more of light—in the seedling stage can delay fruit maturity.

Selecting a well-warmed spot can speed the fruiting and ripening of both extra-early and main-crop tomatoes by as much as a week. Look for a favorable microclimate: a southern slope; a raised bed, where soil warms faster; a spot protected from wind; a wall that reflects heat. It's worth a try, even if there's room for only a plant or two in that sunny nook. Well-drained soil and full sun are also essential to early harvests. Plant roots stay cold in soggy soil, and shade delays both fruit formation and ripening. Phosphorus in the soil promotes tomato plant growth by building strong stems and leaves, so be sure your garden has a good supply of this nutrient.

For robust growth, plant your tomatoes horizontally. If you bury part of the stem, rooting hormones will be stimulated by the darkness. Roots then form along the stem, producing a stronger plant. But don't plant the seedling straight up and down in a deep hole, where its roots would be far down in cold soil beyond the reach of the warming sun. When it's time to set transplants out, scoop out a shallow trough about 2 inches deep, and lay each tomato plant in horizontally. Pinch off any leaves on the lower stem and cover the roots and stem with soil, leaving only a tuft of leaves protruding. Firm the soil carefully around the plant.

Wait to mulch the ground around your tomatoes until settled warm weather arrives. Mulch applied too early will keep the soil too cool. For an extra head start, prewarm the soil in your tomato patch by covering the ground with clear plastic mulch, which can raise soil temperature by 20°F.

Once your plants have begun to bear, try to provide conditions that favor the retention of the blossoms: no blossoms, no fruit. Blossom drop in tomatoes can be caused by disease, high soil nitrogen, low soil moisture, and sudden changes in weather. Blossoms may also fall off when temperatures are higher than 74°F at night and in the high nineties during the day. But by that time, your main crop should be going strong.

Protection against the weather permits earlier planting and helps to stabilize temperatures during those occasional chilly nights that occur well after safe planting-out time. Ideal soil temperatures for tomatoes are 70° to 75°F by day; 60° to 65°F at night. (Tomatoes are native to the mountainous regions of South America near the equator, where days are warm and nights are on the cool side.)

To protect extra-early plantings made a week or two before the usual planting-out time, try spun-bonded row covers like Reemay or Harvest-Guard, well secured at the edges to keep out cold winds. Be sure to remove the filmy row covers when weather moderates and blossoms form, because they can raise temperatures high enough to interfere with fruit set.

Wallo' Water, a cylinder of water-filled tubes, which act as miniature solar collectors, not only wards off cold air but also retains warmth during cold nights. Although not practical for large plantings—filling them can be an awkward and time-consuming job—Wallo' Water tubes are effective plant protectors when well supported by two or three stakes so they don't collapse on the plant. The umbrella greenhouse, a dome-shaped, clear umbrella, is handy to pop over tomato plants or other early crops. It has an anchor shaft that plunges into the ground for stability, and it seems to be nearly windproof.

A master gardener in our area puts old tires around his early tomato plants to retain heat and shield them from wind. Wire cylinders wrapped with clear plastic also can act like mini-greenhouses to bring on an earlier crop. Even a tall juice can placed on the east and west side of each plant, with an old shingle on the north side, will speed things along. Use your creativity to keep your tomatoes warm.

Enjoy the Fruits of Your Labor

Even if you only try the easiest of the early-tomato strategies—planting seed of cold-resistant cultivars—you should be able to knock several weeks off that long-awaited first-tomato date. If you also take the trouble to prewarm the soil and provide extra protection, you might even set a neighborhood record. Keep notes, so you'll have the satisfaction of knowing how much tomato time you've gained. And enjoy that first big red one.

Plant a Snacking Garden

47

If you're already growing all the vegetables you need for your dinner table, why not grow your own snacks, too? Popcorn, peanuts, and sunflower seeds are nutritious garden-grown treats. None are at all difficult to raise, and they'll more than return the little effort they require with delicious, taste-tempting treats. Any one of them would be a good project for a child's garden, with a bit of adult help.

Popcorn

If you can grow decent sweet corn, you should be able to raise a fine crop of its close relative, popcorn. Experience is not necessary for success, though. Picking time is less critical than for sweet corn, which must be snatched promptly when it reaches its brief moment of perfection. Since popcorn should dry on the stalk anyway, your only picking concern will be to leave the ears on the stalk long enough to allow them to cure sufficiently. In order to pop, you see, the kernels must develop skin hard enough to contain the internal moisture until it builds up enough steam-generated pressure to burst the kernel.

Popcorn has shorter ears and smaller kernels than sweet corn. Some cultivars, like 'White Cloud Hulless Hybrid', 'Tom Thumb', and 'SnoPuff', have pointed, white, ricelike kernels that pop to high volume and excellent tenderness. Yellow-kernelled cultivars, some with rounded kernels, are also available. 'South American Hybrid', for example, produces creamy-colored kernels that, when popped, look as if they've already been buttered. 'Strawberry' popcorn is a double-purpose cultivar grown for both its plump little 2-inch ears, which make attractive table and door decorations, and its pop-able kernels.

Almost every seed catalog carries at least one cultivar of popcorn. Since, in our experience at least, there is less flavor difference between cultivars of popcorn than sweet corn, you'll find it hard to go wrong on even a random choice. Naturally, cultivars grown especially for popping are often more tender and pop to a higher volume than those that are also advertised for their ornamental qualities, but you'd have to be a real popcorn connoisseur to find an objectionable difference.

Planting Popcorn

Plant popcorn about the time of your last frost in spring. Most cultivars need 90 to 100 days to mature. Space seed of dwarf types 4 inches apart; larger kinds 8 to 10 inches apart. Rows should be 2 to 3 feet apart depending on expected stalk height, which usually ranges from 3 to 5 feet. To avoid cross-pollination with nearby sweet corn or field corn, plan your garden so that your popcorn is no closer than 500 feet to other tasseling corn. (Kernels that are the result of a cross will not pop well.)

Like sweet corn, popcorn likes hot weather, well-fertilized and limed soil, and good drainage. It is less particular about moisture and rich

48

soil than sweet corn and, in fact, often produces especially good popping kernels in a dry season.

Harvesting and Storing Popcorn

Let the ears remain on the stalk until the kernels are hard and dry. Then pick them, peel back the husk, and hang the ears, bunched together and tied by the husk, in a dry, airy place to cure for another week or two. As long as you can protect them from rodents, it is perfectly all right to leave the ears whole until you are ready to use them. Otherwise, flake off the kernels (put an old clean sock over your hand or rub two ears together to save your fingers). Store the kernels in a covered jar in a cool place. Avoid using artificial heat to dry the ears because the kernels will not pop well if overdried; they won't contain enough moisture to make them burst. If you find that a batch of stored corn doesn't pop well, it is probably too dry. Just shake a few drops of water into the jar and try again in a few days.

Peanuts

I don't know anyone who's gotten rich planting peanuts (*Arachis hypogaea*) north of Virginia, but what's wealth when the aroma of your own homegrown roasted peanuts fills the house? Although peanuts need at least 110 frost-free days, and thrive in really warm weather, they will bear as far north as Michigan, South Dakota, Massachusetts, and central New York State if planted on a southern exposure in sandy soil, which warms up fast. The crops we've grown in the gorgeous deep limestone soil of Lancaster County, while not outstanding, were definitely worth our while. Until you get to be an experienced peanut grower, it's best to opt for yield rather than size. The small, sweet Spanish peanuts will consistently outproduce the larger Virginia strain when grown in the North.

Planting Peanuts

Sow the seed when your last frost is safely behind you. Maple leaves should be at least the size of squirrel's ears. You can plant the nuts shelled or unshelled. Poke the peanuts about 2 inches deep into soft, deeply worked soil, in rows 2½ feet apart. If you leave the nuts in their outer, tan-colored shells, space about 8 inches apart. If you pre-

49

fer to remove the nuts from their casing, take care not to break the papery skin. Space the shelled nuts 3 to 6 inches apart. Thin the plants to stand 12 inches apart. Some seed will rot, and you may have a few gaps in the row. Peanuts do not transplant well.

If it is very important to you to raise peanuts, sow the seed in peat pots indoors a month or so before planting-out time. Then set the plants, pot and all, at 12-inch intervals in the row. Be sure to set them deep enough to cover the rim of the pots; otherwise, the pressed peat will dry out quickly and form an impenetrable barrier for the roots.

When the rather sprawling plants are about a foot high, hill up loose soil around them from either side of the row. You'll have more peanuts to pull at harvest time if you keep the soil loose and crust-free around the plants once flowers form. Peanuts have their own way of doing things, you see. As in other plants, formation of seed (peanuts) follows fertilization of the flowers, but with peanuts, there's an extra twist.

50

The perky, yellow-orange, pealike flowers form in the leaf axils. When they are pollinated, the stem begins to elongate. This lengthening shoot, called a peduncle, grows earthward, eventually burying the developing fruit at its tip in the soil. This process is called pegging. The pods complete their development underground. Hilling the plants with loose soil helps to facilitate pegging. The nuts form 60 to 80 days after the flower pegs go into the ground.

Growing peanuts gives you a close-up look at an unusual process: After peanut flowers are pollinated, shoots called peduncles grow to the ground, burying, or pegging, the developing fruit under the soil. The peanuts ripen underground.

PEANUT-GROWING TIPS

- Although peanuts are often grown in poor soil, they respond to light liming and adequate phosphorus and potassium. What they don't need is nitrogen, which promotes leafy growth and delays seed formation. Since peanuts are legumes, they're capable of utilizing atmospheric nitrogen, thanks to the nitrogen-fixing bacteria on their roots.
- Soil nematodes are often a problem in the South, but seldom in the North. But peanut plants are tasty to other pests, too: I have had to cover my plants with tunnels of bent wire fencing to ward off rabbits.
- To warm the soil, northern gardeners mulch the rows with black plastic until pegging time, and then remove it to allow the peduncles to burrow in the ground. Don't use organic mulch; it will cool the ground and slow the peanut's growth.

Harvesting and Storing Peanuts

In the South, peanuts are harvested when the vines turn yellow, but northern-grown peanut plants will quite likely still be green when frost hits. Immature peanuts have soft, pale, spongy shells, pale skins, and sometimes a rather bitter flavor. As they mature, shells dry and harden and the skins turn pink and finally red. Dig up an experimental peanut in September, and if it is still immature, wait until frost to harvest the plants so the nuts will have time to ripen.

A light frost that just nips the tops won't hurt the underground nuts, but dig them up before a heavy, killing frost. Most peanuts contain about 40 percent moisture when harvested. In order to keep well, they must be dried to a moisture content of around 10 percent. Cure the nuts on the vine by exposing them to the sun for several days and then hanging them in an airy place for several weeks.

Peanuts keep best in paper or cloth bags. Plastic-bag storage encourages dampness and spoilage. The good old southern practice of hanging burlap sacks of peanuts from the rafters can't be beat; it keeps them dry, well ventilated, and makes the odds better against marauding mice and squirrels.

Peanuts are especially good candidates for seed saving. Select seed

51

from the best-performing plants each year, and you'll gradually develop a strain adapted to your growing conditions. When saving seed, leave the nuts in the shell until spring, and take care not to split the nut when removing the hull.

Roasting Peanuts

Roast and shell the peanuts as you need them. We've found a temperature of 350°F for 20 to 30 minutes to be just about right. Peanuts are a good source of vitamin E and the B vitamins. Some of those vitamins are inactivated by heat, but the plain raw nuts taste a bit beany. We've discovered we can have our vitamins and that good nutty taste, too. We roast half the nuts and mix them with an equal amount of raw or lightly roasted nuts. The roasted flavor predominates, and we know the vitamins are there.

Sunflowers

The nutmeat of the common sunflower (*Helianthus annuus*) is somewhat less accessible than that of the peanut, but the plant is quite productive and extremely easy to grow. For snacking seeds, pass over the ornamental types listed in the flower sections of seed catalogs, and look in the vegetable section. 'Mammoth Russian' and 'Peredovik' are good cultivars, yielding large, plump seeds. Sunflower seeds have a delicious nutlike taste and a good supply of B vitamins and calcium, iron, and phosphorus. They contain 22 percent protein and 30 percent unsaturated oil. Although it is common practice to roast the bulk-shelled seeds purchased in stores, the kernels are good—and certainly more nutritious—eaten raw.

Planting Sunflowers

Sunflowers can be grown in any part of the United States or Canada where corn will grow. Although they require a long growing season— at least 120 days—they withstand light frost in the early seedling stage, and in fact often volunteer in midspring from crops grown the previous year. We plant our sunflowers around the time of our last frost. Drop a seed every 6 to 8 inches in rows 3 to 4 feet apart. Thin the seedlings later to stand 2 feet apart.

If your season is short, sow sunflower seed two weeks before your frost-free date, since it may take that long to germinate in cool weather. Or presprout the seeds indoors. Wrap them in damp paper towels and keep in a warm place to encourage germination.

Harvesting and Storing Sunflowers

A well-nourished sunflower is a spectacular plant—about 10 feet tall with large leaves, a 2-inch-thick stalk, and a bright yellow flower head. As the seeds develop, the head nods downward with their weight. Heads of 'Mammoth Russian' measure from 9 to 24 inches across.

Be sure to cut the heads before birds pick off the seeds or before the heads "shatter," scattering their seeds. Hang the seed-filled disks in a well-ventilated place to cure for several weeks. This drying helps to bring out their nutty flavor. Watch out for mice: Their idea of heaven is a barn festooned with easy-to-reach sunflower heads.

After curing, rub the seeds from the head and store them in cans or jars. Use the empty, rough-toothed circular base of the head as a disposable scrubber.

Cracking Sunflower Seeds

Now, how do you extract the seed from the shell? If you grew up in Poland, as my husband did, or in any other Slavic country, the answer is that you don't. You pop the seeds in one side of your mouth, split the shell with your teeth, chew the kernel, and eject the shell, all the while introducing new seeds and relishing them in the same way. This kind of sleight-of-tongue remains completely beyond me. After having admired my husband's performance for 34 years, I can only say that I still haven't the slightest idea how to do it. I split the seeds one by one, the slow way, either biting off a thin side or poking it open with my thumbnail. Still, despite our uneven mastery of this Slavic art, we find a pocketful of sunflower seeds a necessary and companionable adjunct to a walk in our woods.

Other gardeners report they shell sunflower seeds by first whirling them in the blender or putting them through a coarse food grinder to crack them, then floating off the hulls and straining out and drying the heavier sunken seeds. This is far from the last word in kernel retrieval, though. For a simpler method, try roasting the seeds at 200°F until they're crisp, which makes them easier to shell manually. What we really need is a neat little gizmo that would do the job mechanically, so that more of us could take advantage of the 50-bushels-of-seed-per-acre potential of the sunflower plant. It will probably come from some dedicated freelance inventor, who will promptly become a hero to us sunflower-seed lovers. Meanwhile, we stuff our pockets with seeds and snack away as we hike.

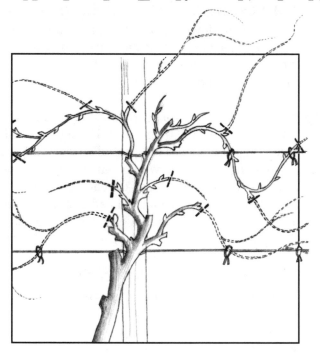

Grow
Your Own Grapes

E ating dessert in the garden patch is one of our favorite summer traditions. We start with strawberries in June and go on to raspberries in July. In August and September, we head for the grapevines. Since we don't spray the grapes, they need no washing. It's so easy to pluck them—no stooping or tangling with briars. And they're so beautiful, hanging in clusters of purple, green, bronze, tawny red—the very picture of abundance. All of this would almost be enough. But there's more: flavor. If you'd like to enjoy grapes so delicious that they evoke an involuntary 'mmm' of appreciation, take a weekend to plan for and plant a grapevine or two.

Starting Out Right

A little thought before planting time will help get your grapes off to a good start. Sun and good air circulation are a must, so plan your planting with care.

Since they grow well on a fence and spread in only two dimensions, grapevines fit neatly into yards that are too small for fruit trees. If you have a choice of sites, a southern slope is ideal for frost protection. Full sun also brings out all the sweetness the fruit can have. Friends of ours who garden on a long, narrow lot in northwest Philadelphia planted grapevines on the roof of their one-story kitchen addition—an excellent use of space and effective natural cooling for the living space beneath.

Grape blossoms are insignificant in appearance but very fragrant. The flowers are wind-pollinated, so set the vines no more than 50 feet apart. Closer together is better, but leave at least 8 feet between the vines for good air circulation.

A Grape for Every Taste

The standard Eastern grape, the customary dooryard variety, has long been 'Concord'. 'Concord' grapes are good—dependable, vigorous, productive—but there are scrumptious cultivars that aren't any more difficult to grow. Check your catalogs or ask at a local nursery for regionally adapted cultivars; grapes vary greatly in winter hardiness. All the grapes listed below are hardy to Zone 5 except 'Van Buren', which is hardy to Zone 4.

Outstanding cultivars to look for include 'Buffalo', an early purple grape; 'Himrod' and 'Interlaken', both fine-flavored green-golden seedless grapes that ripen in August; 'Van Buren', an extra-hardy purple grape with fine sweet berries of medium size; 'Canadice', a rich-flavored, red seedless grape that ripens in mid-August; and 'Sheridan', a sweet blue grape that ripens in late September or early October. Also consider 'Alden', 'Catawba', 'Concord Seedless', 'Delaware', 'Niagara', and 'Steuben'.

Planting and Care

Prune the roots lightly at planting time to encourage generous development of feeder rootlets. Cut the top of the vine back to a single branch with three buds. Drastic treatment, but good for the vine's long-term development.

The vines do not need permanent support their first year of growth, but they should have a stake for protection from breaking and for training in the right direction. In the meantime, you can decide on the system you want to use and prepare and set the posts accordingly.

Our vines are planted at cedar posts spaced 8 feet apart. Cedar railings on top of the posts and one heavy wire strung 2 feet below the railing support the vines. The posts are set with their ends 2 feet below ground level, extending below the frostline. End posts are deeper: 2½ feet, at least.

Overfertilizing can cause lush growth that winterkills easily, especially if air drainage isn't good. In the first few years after planting, we spread manure and wood ashes around the plants annually, working up to a bushel of manure into the soil for a three-year-old plant. We fertilize our 14-year-old vines less frequently: every 2 to 3 years.

A well-developed grapevine has roots extending several feet out from the trunk, so extend all soil enrichment offerings 2 to 3 feet beyond the main stem; more, in the case of old vines. The feeder roots are near the soil surface, so mulch for weed control instead of using mechanical cultivation. Grapes thrive in even very dry seasons since their roots penetrate very deeply, as much as 8 feet, into the subsoil.

Pests and Diseases

If air drainage is poor, mildew may be a problem. For this reason, it's best not to plant rows of grapes closer than 8 to 10 feet. You want sun and air to reach the plants. The wire supporting the canes should be at least 3 feet above the ground, with no tall undergrowth. (Mowed grass is all right.) "Mummified" grapes that shrivel on the vine are a sign of black rot. Control this fungus by removing and burning any affected bunches. Japanese beetles show great enthusiasm for grape foliage, and in a bad year the leaves can look like lace curtains, though the effect doesn't seem to harm the grapes or the vine. Prevent damage to the fruit from stinging insects and birds by enclosing the grape clusters in paper bags when they begin to ripen.

Pruning

No matter how natural your garden may be, and we lean to shagginess rather than total control, you won't get far with grapes if you let them ramble on their own. They'll form a wild tangle that produces only a few small berries.

Pruning is a process of selection and of training the best new shoots. Good pruning develops a proper balance between cane growth and fruit yield. To prune judiciously, you need to know how a grapevine grows. It is the last season's growth, each year, that produces the fruit. A new cane grows in spring from a bud at each leaf node and bears a bunch of grapes the following year. By fall of its second year, the cane will have hardened and grown a fibrous bark, and will not bear fruit anymore. Year-old canes—the previous year's growth—tend to have reddish-brown, fairly smooth surfaces. Older canes are a duller gray-brown and slightly shaggy with shreds of partly shed bark. My husband prunes our vines in March or April. Vines pruned in very cold weather are more susceptible to chilling injury.

Step-by-Step to Bountiful Bunches

Let's take a vine from planting to maturity and see when and where it should be pruned. There are several good methods of training grapes. The one described here works for us.

1. Plant the dormant vine in spring. Prune it to three buds and loosely tie it to a post with a piece of strong twine or strip of cloth. Let the vine grow over the first season so it can develop good roots. (See top-left illustration on page 58.)
2. The following winter or early spring, while the vine is still dormant, cut off all but the best cane. This shoot will develop into the main trunk of the vine. Reduce the single remaining cane to three buds and tie it to a stake or an arbor. (See top-right illustration on page 58.)
3. Let the vine grow, training and tying the best branches so they grow out along the wires. Tie one of the most vigorous branches to the wire on one side of the post and a second-best branch to the wire on the other side.
4. During the second winter, trim all shoots from these two main "arms," cutting them off close but being careful not to injure the buds on the arms. Leave only two or three buds on each main arm. Cut back the top of the vine to the second bud, cutting through

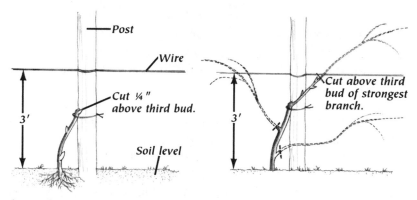

Left: At planting time, prune the new vine to 3 buds and loosely tie it to the post with a piece of strong twine or strip of cloth. *Right:* At the end of the first winter, cut the strongest cane back to 3 buds. Remove all other branches. As the vine grows during the next spring and summer, tie the most vigorous branches to the supports to form the arms of the vine.

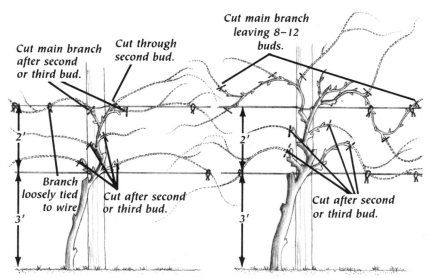

58

Left: At the end of the second winter, cut back the main arms to 2 or 3 buds. Cut back the top of the vine to the second bud, cutting through the bud to prevent further growth. Remove all other branches. *Right:* At the end of the third winter, cut back the top main arms to 8 to 12 buds. Cut back the lower arms and another pair of branches to 2 to 3 buds each. Remove all other branches. Get ready to enjoy your grapes in the summer!

the bud to prevent further growth. There will be no fruit in the following summer; you're still shaping the vine at this point. (See bottom-left illustration on page 58.)

5. During the third growing season, tie the two most vigorous branches along the wire, one on each side of the post. These branches will be the main fruit-bearing parts.

6. During the third late-winter pruning, leave two main branches with 8 to 12 buds each. Also, to get more fruit you may want to select about four next-best new-growth branches, originating from the previous year's growth close to the trunk, and cut them down to spurs of 2 to 3 buds each. Remove other branches. (See bottom-right illustration on page 58.)

7. During each succeeding spring (a grapevine can keep going for 60 years!), remove all extra second-year canes and any nonstructural canes that have borne fruit. Retain the strongest shoots that are close to the central stem, keeping 8 to 12 buds, and tie them to the wire. These will become the next year's fruiting canes. Try to keep the vine as compact as possible by retaining shoots that are close to the main trunk of the vine.

In other words, you're always thinking two years ahead—developing budded spurs that will bud out the following year into fruit-producing canes. Look for a decent sampling of grapes by the fourth growing season and enough to boast about within the following two to three years.

Renovation and Propagation

If your vine gets out of hand, or if you're renovating an old vine, feel free to cut off an errant branch of thick, old wood. The vine will renew itself by forming buds on old wood.

To increase your stock of vines, root the clippings you have pruned off. Select good mature canes, about ¼ inch in diameter, from your most vigorous vines. Plant them in a nursery row, with one to two nodes buried and the top one exposed. Label them, or make a garden diagram. Select the best-rooted canes that take and plant them in a permanent place, letting them grow unclipped until they are year-old field-grown plants. Then start the pruning and training process.

Plot Your Weeding Strategy

I t has taken me years to come to terms with garden weeds—to learn when to pull them, when to live with them. In my early gardening days, I found weeds intimidating. When I first saw a thick stand of lamb's-quarters take over a corner of my vegetable patch, I thought all was lost. Gradually, though, I realized that I could redeem a weed-choked plot by working at it steadily. Persistence, I found, does give the gardener the last word—for a week or so, until the next batch of weed seed germinates.

Developing a weed strategy involved reconciling positives and negatives. As I gained confidence that my efforts could indeed hold weeds at bay—for a while—I discovered that weeds are ever ready to heal over the breaks we make in the soil. Weed seeds are scattered in astounding numbers throughout the soil. There may be as many as 5,000 weed seeds in a square foot of cultivated ground. One lamb's-quarters plant can produce 70,000 seeds! In addition to numbers, many weed seeds have the advantage of longevity; some can sprout after decades underground.

On the Way to Weed-Free

"Weed-free" is a relative term that, if you've been diligent, occasionally applies to a certain part of your garden on a Monday, after rain, in May, but never to the whole plot.

In overcoming weeds, prevention is easier than cure. Here are some measures that will help decrease the number of weed seeds that fall on your garden.

- Compost barn manure to kill the many weed seeds it contains before putting it on your garden.
- Don't use fresh hay mulch, which is full of ungerminated weed seeds. Let it rot for a season or two.
- Try to pull weeds before they go to seed. You know what grandmother said: "One year's seeding makes seven years weeding." And cut that thistle plant on the hedgerow before it can produce seeds that will blow over to your garden.
- Before introducing soil to your garden from other gardens, screen it to make sure that it is free of roots of quack grass, witch grass, and other invasive pest plants.
- Above all, hoe weeds while they're young.

Timing Is Everything

Good timing can be one of your most effective weed-control strategies. If you grub out weeds while they're still small, you'll spare your seedlings unnecessary competition, and the job will be much easier.

For most vegetable plants, the critical time for weed control is in the first few weeks. Corn is especially vulnerable to weed competition during its first three weeks after the leaves appear. If you remove weeds early, they don't seem to significantly decrease the corn yield later in the season. With asparagus, too, early-season weediness in a new planting can interfere with later production if it lasts more than a few weeks. Fall weeds in established plantings are less serious. Onion plants are most susceptible to competition from weeds during their first two to ten weeks, while they are in the two- to four-leaf stage.

My approach to garden weeds has been most strongly influenced by the advice of market gardener Mort Mather, who takes a preventive approach. Mather's ten-day cultivation rule really works (even if you fudge it a bit, as I do). In exchange for keeping a weeding schedule at the beginning of the season, you earn freedom later on.

1. Till the soil ten days before planting. Weed seeds will sprout, and you can rake or hoe them out before you plant. Rake the ground even if weed seedlings are not visible; they may be sprouting below the surface.
2. Cultivate the soil ten days after planting, before those tiny weeds look as though they'd ever amount to anything (be careful to avoid the roots of germinating garden plants). Weeds are easy to uproot at this stage.
3. Work the ground a third time ten days after the second cultivation. For fast-growing and late-season crops, Mather maintains, the third is often the final cultivation.

Diligence, Not Perfectionism

I've found that it's important to remove the weeds while they still look too small to matter. Don't wait until they're large enough to yank up by hand. The job is so much easier while they're small, and the advantage for your seedlings in being free of competition is greater at that tender age, too.

For the past few years, I've used a swan-neck hoe to cultivate those early-spring vegetable beds. This superb tool is angled perfectly for easy chopping. The long handle makes the job go smoothly, with no back strain, and even permits me to reach into an adjacent row. Later in the season, I use a rotary tiller to catch up on weeds between unmulched rows after returning from a trip. But I much prefer the swan-neck hoe in early spring when, as Charles Dudley Warner wrote in *My Summer in a Garden* (1871), "Hoeing the ground on a bright, soft

May day, when you are not obliged to, is nearly the equal of going trouting."

Later, when I start to can tomatoes and pickle cucumbers, more weeds escape my hoe, and some pop up at the edge of the mulched crops, but by then the sturdy, maturing plants can cope with a bit of competition, as long as it's not rampant. By then, too, I've outgrown my early-season illusion that I'll be able to keep things shipshape in every row all season long, and I'm ready to settle for a more achievable notion of perfection: a steady, plentiful harvest.

WHAT IS A WEED?

A weed is sometimes defined as "a plant in the wrong place." Weeds can lower your vegetable yields considerably by competing with them for vital nutrients—moisture, space, and sun. Crowding by weeds can encourage fungal disease by interfering with the free circulation of air around plants. And some weeds— notably redroot pigweed, velvet leaf, yellow foxtail, and lamb's-quarters—contain hormones that inhibit the growth of other plants, such as corn and soybeans, when the weeds' residues are mixed into the soil.

Ralph Waldo Emerson had another definition of a weed: "a plant whose virtues have not yet been discovered." Weeds do serve a number of useful purposes in the garden. They keep disturbed ground from washing away in the rain. Deep-rooted weeds like dandelions, Queen Anne's lace, and prickly lettuce absorb buried soil minerals and then release them when they decay; they can break up hardpan in the soil, too. Some weeds repel insects; for example, milkweed discourages wireworms. Others are trap crops, like lamb's-quarters, which attracts leaf miners away from beets and spinach. Lamb's-quarters is also a delicious, nourishing potherb.

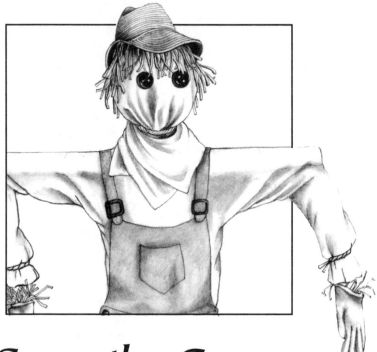

Scare the Crows, Amaze Your Friends, Amuse Your Children

Gardening is pleasurable work—and it is also play. The spirit of playfulness has its place in the garden. If you have a child or a young neighbor or relative for whom you can do some of these perfectly useless pranks, you'll have a ready-made alibi. If you don't have a child, just enjoy the luxury of doing something simply for fun.

Scare the Crows

People have been making scarecrows for hundreds of years, and for much of that time, they have depended on these figures to discourage crows and other garden predators. Scarecrows are still made for this reason, and they work as well as they ever have. But many are also created as a spring ritual, for the fun of concocting a character out of odds and ends and occasionally, perhaps, even for some silent companionship in the garden.

We make scarecrows out of things we find in the shed, old clothes, kitchen discards, and other assorted whimsies. They're always more than the sum of their parts. As we assemble them, they develop a personality of their own—perhaps mysterious or threatening, often genial, sometimes wacky. Most scarecrows are on the spare, gaunt side. We don't flesh

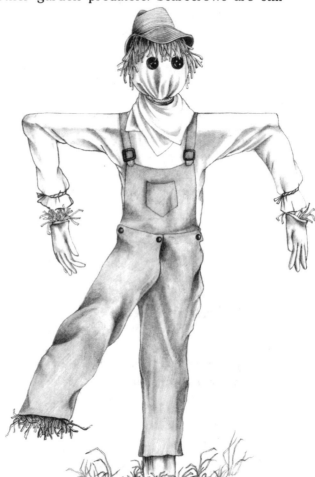

Concoct a scarecrow from odds and ends of clothing and a pair of crossed sticks. Don't try too hard; the fun is seeing just who emerges.

them out as much as we do the more rotund and complete "harvest figures" that sit on our porch in fall. Scarecrows are shorthand for the human figure. A pair of eyebrows painted on a shingle can sug-

65

gest a face, a derelict hat can make a head, an undulating cape can form a body. Use the following steps to help you create a scarecrow that is uniquely your own.

1. Most scarecrows begin with two crossed sticks: you can use pieces of lath, spare 2-by-4's, old broom handles, or retired fence posts. Choose a longer stick for the upright that forms the body, a shorter stick for the crossbar that forms the arms.
2. Collect an outfit for your scarecrow: When it comes to clothing, your creation can be as dignified, rustic, or offbeat as your attic discards permit.
3. Cut the bottom of the longer stick to a point, so it can be easily stuck in the ground.
4. To make dressing easier, insert the shorter crossbar into the sleeves of that old flannel shirt—or whatever you're going to use to cover the top—before you attach the crosspiece to the upright. Then nail, wire, or tie the crossbar securely to the longer upright in at least two places.
5. Many scarecrows are faceless, and no less effective for it. But if you want to make a stab at realism, attach a saucepan, a shingle, a Halloween mask, a plastic jug, or any other facsimile of a head to the top of the basic crossed sticks. Hair may be an old mop, a wad of rope, a rug scrap, or what have you.
6. Finish your scarecrow's costume, tying or stapling to the frame as necessary.
7. If you really are trying to spook the crows, tie on dangling aluminum pie pans, foil strips, and other eyecatching or noisy appendages that will flutter and clang in the breeze.

The thing about making a scarecrow is not to try too hard at it. Use whatever silly stuff comes to hand, let your materials lead you on, and see what (or who) emerges. In traditional gardens, scarecrows are often left in place to weather over winter. These storm-tossed effigies molder into wraithlike presences that look as though they have been guarding the garden for hundreds of years. You never know what will happen with a scarecrow. Wrens built a nest in a scarecrow's hat in a friend's yard. And we once visited a farm where the buxom, hay-stuffed scarecrow at the edge of the garden was host to a colony of bees. Start and see what develops.

Cuke in a Bottle

This trick is easy. Anyone can do it, even a child.

1. Select a young, straight cucumber growing on a healthy vine. Leaving the cucumber attached to the vine, carefully insert it into a narrow-necked bottle or canning jar.
2. Tuck the bottle under leaves to avoid the sun's heat.
3. Leave the trapped fruit undisturbed for several days, and then check it daily or every other day.

You will have a mystifying exhibit of a large cucumber filling the seemingly impossible confines of a narrow-necked container. You can even pour in your favorite vinegar/spice solution and pickle the cucumber right in the jar. To get it out for eating, you'll have to commit mayhem, but meanwhile you can have a lot of fun amazing your young visitors and nongardening friends.

Personal Pumpkin

Children enjoy having a pumpkin personalized with their name or carved with fanciful or realistic faces, complete with hair, ears, and facial features. When the fruit is about half-grown, carve a message or design in the still-tender skin, using a sharp knife. The cut must be more than a mere scratch, but not so deep or wide that rot sets in; make a pattern of V-shaped cuts about ¼ inch deep and ⅛ to ¼ inch wide. The growing pumpkin will heal over the cut, forming a scar-tissue outline of your design.

Butterbean Tent

Lucky the child who can remember hiding out in the tent formed by the bean vines and their poles! The buzzing warmth of a summer day, the small secret hideout, the green of the sheltering vines, all blend in memories of that dreamlike world where days were long and summers endless. Here's how to create those special memories for your youngsters.

1. The number of poles and the spacing between them depends on the size and shape of the tent. Allow a 2- to 3-foot gap between two poles for a doorway. For a one-person, three-pole tent, space

67

poles 3 to 4 feet apart to form a circle. Ram the thick end of each pole about 12 inches into the ground.
2. Tie or wire the top ends of the bean poles together.
3. Tie a 1-inch-thick stick horizontally, a little lower than head height, between the two doorway poles.
4. Plant five pole bean seeds at the foot of each pole.

Pole beans are traditional, but you might prefer morning glories, climbing nasturtiums, moon vine, gourds, scarlet runner beans, or a

Children of all ages love a secret hideout all their own. A few poles and some bean seeds are all it takes to make a summerhouse of greenery.

mixture. The vines will form a leafy canopy by midsummer.

To make a somewhat roomier hideout, yet one that costs much less than a wooden playhouse, set poles in the ground in either a circular or rectangular shape. (For a 5-by-7-foot structure, you'll need about 18 poles.) Place two of them a bit farther apart than the others to form a doorway space. Then wire or staple wire-mesh poultry netting to the poles to form the walls of the structure, leaving space for the doorway. If you want a roof, tie strings across the top. Finally, plant seeds of any quick-growing vine at the base of each pole. The vines will transform the bare string and wire into a lovely, leafy teahouse—ephemeral but perfect while it lives.

Put Some Flowers in the Soup

T he use of flowers in cookery is an ancient tradition. The flowers we plant in our gardens as ornamentals today were often grown especially for culinary purposes in centuries gone by. Extracts of certain blooms—notably roses and orange blossoms—were used 200 to 300 years ago as extensively as we use vanilla today. Early eighteenth-century cookbooks offer recipes for soups and salads that include marigold, primrose, and violet flowers, along with strawberry leaves, lettuce, and spinach.

Does eating blossoms still seem strange? Consider the broccoli you had for dinner: What you ate was really a tightly packed mass of flower buds.

Chances are you already have some edible flowers in your garden, since many of them are time-tested favorites. It's not a very big jump to planting a few calendulas for cooking, growing some violets and daylilies especially for their flowers, or collecting the fragrant petals of roses. Start small with flower foods by snipping just a blossom or two into a dish, and work up to the most pleasing proportion.

Guidelines for Flower Eaters

Don't use just any flower to embellish your meals. Not all that bloom are good to eat. Take care to identify the flower accurately; check its botanical name. And be aware that individual allergic reactions can occur after eating flowers that are generally considered safe. Although daylilies have been eaten for centuries, there are reports of diarrhea after daylily ingestion, and large amounts of chive blossoms can cause digestive upsets. Eat only flowers, not leaves, seeds, or bulbs. Follow these guidelines for safe and tasty treats.

- Use only clean wild or garden flowers that have not been sprayed. Flowers from the florist have been treated with chemicals.
- Pick flowers around noon on a sunny, dry day if possible.
- To dry flowers for winter use, spread them on a sheet-covered screen or large piece of cardboard in a hot, dry, dark, well-ventilated place. Dry violets whole. Daisy-family flowers like calendulas dry more quickly if petals are plucked off. For best results, individual petals should not touch each other.
- For flecks of color in soups and muffins, grind dry blossoms with a mortar and pestle.

Safe and Tasty

The flowers in this chapter are not the only edible ones: They're some of the easiest to grow and most familiar. Use only flowers that you *know* are edible. If you have any question about these or other flower suggestions you might find in cookbooks, check with your local poison control center, listed inside the front cover of your phone book. Better yet, stick to flowers like these, which are widely recognized as safely edible.

SERVING SUGGESTIONS

- Use flowers as a garnish: tucked next to the meat, arranged around a vegetable dish, floating in a cool drink.
- Stuff larger edible flowers like daylilies and tulips with chicken salad or cheese spreads.
- Toss flowers and individual petals in salad.
- Float flowers or petals in soup.
- Steep flowers in teas.
- Make jam or syrup of rose petals or violet blossoms.
- Include flowers in a sandwich: rose petals and cream cheese, nasturtiums with tuna or mashed sardines.
- Freeze flowers in ice cubes or ice rings to add interest to cold drinks and punch bowls.
- Put petals in cake or muffin batter.

Borage (*Borago officinalis*)

Borage has been useful in the kitchen since Roman times. The star-shaped flowers, borne in profusion, are a beautiful clear blue—the color of forget-me-nots and Virginia bluebells, which are also members of the borage family. Use borage blossoms to garnish a cool drink or an upended cup of custard. Float the flowers in a punch bowl or freeze them in an ice ring. If you're short of salad ingredients, borage leaves are good to eat, too. Chop them finely because they're rather hairy.

Growth habit:	Annual; 2 to 3 feet tall.
Where to grow:	Full sun; ordinary to poor garden soil.
How to start:	Seeds.
Spacing:	Space plants 10 inches apart.
Growing tips:	Sow the seeds a week or so before the last spring frost date. You can transplant seedlings; older plants are difficult to transplant successfully. Borage self-sows readily.

Calendula (*Calendula officinalis*)

Calendula, or pot marigold, was a staple household medicine in medieval times, when the orange or yellow blossoms were considered an effective treatment for a wide variety of ailments. It appears

71

in eighteenth-century cookbooks as an ingredient in soups, stews, salads, and meat dishes. Calendula petals are a homegrown substitute for saffron, adding appetizing color, but lacking the rich, musty saffron flavor. Just pluck the petals from the flower head and discard the central button.

I like to sprinkle a handful of fresh calendula petals into tossed salads, soups, and stews. They give a rich golden shade to noodles and egg dishes. Dried petals may be stirred into most any recipe, including muffins, fish chowder, chicken potpie, or paella.

Growth habit:	Annual; 15 to 18 inches tall.
Where to grow:	Full sun; ordinary to poor garden soil.
How to start:	Seeds.
Spacing:	Space plants 10 inches apart.
Growing tips:	Seeds sprout best between 60° and 65°F. For early June bloom, sow seeds indoors in March and set out plants in late April or early May. They don't mind light frost. Calendulas put on a good show during early summer, but look a bit straggly during the hotter days of July and August. They come into their own again in fall. Cut back after first bloom to encourage new buds. Calendulas self-sow readily.

Daylilies (*Hemerocallis* spp.)

Orange daylilies often grow unbidden in old perennial borders. They bloom in June and July along roadsides or around the crumbling stone cellar holes of burned-down farmhouses. Newer hybrids extend the blooming season through August, and flower colors include orange, yellow, pink, maroon, and peach. You can use either buds or day-old spent blossoms, and the flavor is mild and good, not unlike green beans. Braised with beef, batter-fried, or steamed and buttered, daylily flowers are a delicacy most people enjoy at first taste; they're everyday fare in the Orient. The first time you serve them, simply steam the flowers in a covered pot for about 5 minutes in order to discover their true flavor. Then try adding them to soups, stews, casseroles, or your favorite oriental-style dinner along with thin slivers of meat, peppers, onions, and a sweet/sour sauce.

Growth habit:	Perennial; 24 to 40 inches tall.
Where to grow:	Full sun to part shade; ordinary, well-drained garden soil.

How to start:	Purchase plants or divide existing clumps.
Spacing:	Set plants 18 to 24 inches apart.
Growing tips:	Daylilies will grow almost anywhere. They are hardy, disease-free, and not preyed upon by any important insect pests. Don't mow down foliage after bloom; the plants need those green leaves to nourish their roots.

Nasturtium (*Tropaeolum majus*)

The bright, clear orange or yellow blooms of garden nasturtiums have a place on the dinner table as well as along the garden path. Some of the most spectacular beds of nasturtiums I've ever seen were growing in what looked like pure sand near a weather-beaten ocean-front cottage in Maine—an extreme example of the truism that nasturtiums bloom best in poor soil. They bloom well, but not outstandingly, at the edge of my kitchen garden, which has pretty good soil. Nasturtium flowers, leaves, and seeds are fairly well-known table fare.

Cook both flowers and leaves in soup and toss them in salad. I like the color and peppery tang this flower food adds to mixtures of bland ingredients—rice dishes, leaf lettuce salads, chicken soup. Or, surprise your family by serving nasturtium blossoms stuffed with chicken salad!

Growth habit:	Annual; dwarf, tall, or climbing, depending on cultivar; 1 to 3 feet tall.
Where to grow:	Full sun; ordinary to poor soil.
How to start:	Seeds.
Spacing:	Thin to 1 foot apart.
Growing tips:	Nasturtiums bloom best in poor soil. They have tender, sappy stems and don't transplant well, so plant the seeds right in the garden after danger of frost has passed.

Squash (*Cucurbita* spp.)

Zuni Indians, and presumably other tribes as well, often picked the orange-yellow male blossoms from their squash plants to add to soup. Nature provides prodigiously for the dissemination of pollen, so there are plenty of male blossoms to enjoy without spoiling the crop. How to tell the difference? Male blossoms appear at the end of a relatively long stem, and there is no swelling at the base of the bud. Female

73

blossoms have a swollen area—an actual tiny fruit—at the base of the blossom, and often (but not always) have shorter stems as well. To serve squash blossoms in soup, add them during the last 5 minutes of cooking. The blossoms may also be dipped in batter and fried.

Growth habit:	Annual vine; 3 to 8 feet long.
Where to grow:	Full sun; rich garden soil high in organic material.
How to start:	Seeds.
Spacing:	Space plants 2 feet apart.
Growing tips:	Be sure to leave a few of the male pollinator blossoms so you don't interfere with vegetable production.

Sunflower (*Helianthus annuus*)

The common yellow sunflowers we grow for their robust, cheerful appearance were interrupted in the blossoming stage by early American colonists and their sixteenth-century English forebears, who cooked their buds as a vegetable. Try a sunflower cultivar like 'Sunburst Mixed', with many small heads instead of a single large flower, and cook the flower buds until tender. Then either pickle or serve them with a lemon-butter sauce.

Growth habit:	4 to more than 12 feet tall.
Where to grow:	Full sun; ordinary garden soil.
How to start:	Seeds.
Spacing:	Space plants 1 foot apart.
Growing tips:	Sow the seeds where the plants are to grow after the last frost date. Plants may need staking in a windy site.

Violets (*Viola sororia; V. pubescens* var. *eriocarpa*)

Many of the violets I pick for eating never get as far as the kitchen; they make a piquant nibble that can be gathered along the way on an early spring walk. I use the purple, yellow, or white blossoms that remain when my rambles have brought me back to my front door as a garnish for a salad of early green garden lettuce. Fresh leaves can be added to salads, too. Or, embed freshly picked violet blossoms, along with cucumber slices, chopped chives, and super-thin shavings of spring radishes, in a gelatin salad made with lemonade or a light-colored herb tea as a base. Concoct a violet syrup by cooking violets with sugar and lemon. The culinary and medicinal use of violet blossoms dates back at least as far as the writings of Homer and Virgil. Medieval and Victorian cooks dipped individual blossoms in beaten egg white and then in sugar, dried the confections in a warm place, and used them to garnish puddings and cakes.

Violet blossoms are not only beautiful, but they are also a good source of vitamin C. According to studies done at Penn State University at the suggestion of wild foods expert Euell Gibbons, and tabulated in his book *Stalking the Healthful Herbs,* 100 grams of violet blossoms contains 150 milligrams of vitamin C.

Growth habit: Perennial; clump; 6 to 10 inches tall.
Where to grow: Part shade; ordinary garden soil.
How to start: Purchase plants.
Spacing: Space plants 6 inches apart.
Growing tips: Violets often spread to form a groundcover. Try tucking some in rocky pockets to keep their roots cool.

More Edibles

Here's an additional sampling of flowers you can sink your teeth into.

Bee balm (*Monarda didyma*)
Chives (*Allium schoenoprasum*)
Dandelion (*Taraxacum officinale*)
Forget-me-not (*Cynoglossum amabile, Myosotis scorpioides*)
Gladiolus (*Gladiolus* × *hortulanus*) flower, not bulb
Hollyhock (*Alcea rosea*)
Lavenders (*Lavandula* spp.)
Mints (*Mentha* spp.)
Orange (*Citrus sinensis*)
Pansy (*Viola* × *wittrockiana*)
Pinks (*Dianthus* spp.)
Rose-of-Sharon (*Hibiscus syriacus*)
Redbud (*Cercis canadensis*)
Tulips (*Tulipa* spp.) flowers, not bulbs
Yuccas (*Yucca* spp.)

BEAUTIFUL BUT DANGEROUS

Take great care not to include any of the following flowers in your kitchen bouquet. Note that this list is not a complete list of all toxic flowers. If you do not know *for sure* that a flower is edible, do not eat it.

Anemones (*Anemone* spp.)
Bleeding-hearts (*Dicentra* spp.)
Buttercups (*Ranunculus* spp.)
Cardinal flower (*Lobelia cardinalis*)
Clematis (*Clematis* spp.)
Delphiniums (*Delphinium* spp.)
Foxgloves (*Digitalis* spp.)
Hydrangeas (*Hydrangea* spp.)
Lantanas (*Lantana* spp.)
Larkspurs (*Consolida* spp.)
Laurels (*Kalmia* spp.)
Lily-of-the-valley (*Convallaria majalis*)
Lupines (*Lupinus* spp.)
Monkshoods (*Aconitum* spp.)
Narcissus (*Narcissus* spp.)
Rhododendrons (*Rhododendron* spp.)
Rose periwinkle (*Catharanthus roseus*)
Star-of-Bethlehem (*Ornithogalum* spp.)
Wisterias (*Wisteria* spp.)

CHAPTER THIRTEEN

Plant Wisteria
for Future Pleasure

77

Wisteria has always seemed to me a romantic and hauntingly beautiful plant, with its drooping panicles of pastel blossoms, often seen draping old porches or arbors. Much as I love wisteria, I've never had a blooming vine. I planted a seedling from a friend's vine in the shady yard of the Philadelphia weaver's cottage that was our first house, but it didn't bloom before we moved away. I was in my twenties and impatient with a plant that I thought, at the time, must take ten years to flower, so I failed to plant a vine in our next home.

Now that I'm older, ten years no longer seems so long to wait. Besides, I've found that wisterias sometimes flower at a younger age. So I decided to learn all about wisteria, and in the process I became more smitten than ever.

Wisterias are deciduous climbers that reach upward by twining around the nearest support. The spring-borne blossoms resemble sweet peas and are carried in long, pendent racemes. They range in color from white through lilac, violet, mauve, and rose; white and blue-violet are most common. The fruits, which are pods up to 7 inches long, have prominent seeds and tend to remain on the vine over winter. Despite its delicate appearance and its occasional reluctance to bloom, wisteria is not a fragile plant. Its vines grow gnarled and thick with time, it is a strong climber, and some species can survive cold northern winters to Zone 5.

Some Choice Wisterias

Botanists recognize eight to ten species of wisteria. Of these species, four are widely available and commonly grown in the United States.

Chinese wisteria (*Wisteria sinensis*) bears lilac-blue flowers in May, and is hardy to USDA Zone 6 (5 with protection). The foot-long racemes of blossoms are slightly fragrant and bloom all at once before the leaves emerge. The compound leaves usually have between 7 and 11 leaflets, occasionally 13. It's the strongest climber of the wisterias, easily reaching 100 feet. 'Alba' is a white cultivar.

Japanese wisteria (*W. floribunda*) is hardy to Zone 5 (4 with protection), and usually more fragrant than Chinese wisteria. Blossoms appear along with the leaves, with florets on each raceme opening gradually from the top down. Flower clusters are longer—12 to 18 inches—and the compound leaves have 13 to 19 leaflets. There are several cultivars. 'Macrobotrys' bears 2- to 3-foot-long flower racemes. 'Ivory Tower' is a very fragrant white-flowered cultivar. 'Violacea Plena' has double reddish-violet blooms. 'Rosea' bears rose-pink and 'Carnea' pale pink flowers.

Two native species are especially good choices for southern gardens, where, according to Robert McCartney of Woodlander's Nursery, in Aiken, South Carolina, the Asiatic wisterias "grow like a weed—in some places like kudzu. The native wisterias are a lot less aggressive."

W. frutescens, native from Virginia to Florida and west to Texas, bears ½-inch-long lilac flowers in racemes 2 to 5 inches long. Leaves have 9 to 13 leaflets. It is hardy to Zone 7, but with a protected location, to Zone 5.

W. macrostachya, a native to Kentucky and the Midwest throughout the lower Mississippi Valley, is hardy to Zone 5. It is the species latest to bloom and has lilac-purple flower clusters.

Planting and Care

Wisteria vines accept a variety of soil types and quality. Deeply dug, loose soil with plenty of humus is ideal, but it needn't be extra rich; as legumes, wisteria vines are good nitrogen producers. Full sun is best. However, there are plantings in the South that flower in light shade.

Many choice wisteria cultivars are grafted, and graft union between scion and rootstock should be covered with soil when planting so the scion forms its own root. The rootstock often sends up suckers that can crowd out the more desirable grafted shoot. For this reason, some wisteria growers prefer to work with rooted cuttings. Horticulturist James Erbaugh of Wayside Gardens in Hodges, South Carolina, advises, "Those suckers should be removed promptly. It's just one of those little chores that needs to be done. If you see any suspicious shoots coming from below the soil line, just scrape away some soil to determine whether the shoot is from the grafted scion or the base." Once your main vine stem is established, remove all suckers regardless of origin.

Although young plants need a steady supply of water, mature specimens may be surprisingly drought-tolerant. But if you find that the wisteria sheds its blossoms unopened, it probably needs a thorough soaking. Protect young plants from strong winds until they become established, and if you plant a vine near a building, watch for overhanging eaves or a very sheltered corner that might block the rain. Make sure rain actually reaches the plant. Stake the plant until it grows tall enough to lean on its permanent support. Just-planted wisteria can be slow to get off the ground; newly planted vines may not leaf out until as late as August. In the northern states and Canada, protect the stem of a young wisteria with burlap or paper wrap or a plastic spiral for the first few winters.

Strong Support Is a Must

Because wisteria is a vigorous climber, selection of a site requires some thought. If you want the vine to drape the side of a building, a southern exposure is best. Provide a sturdy trellis, pipe, or wire for support. The ideal support for a wisteria vine is probably an arbor or pergola, which keeps it accessible and allows for good air circulation and exposure to the sun. The flowers can cascade through the open roof at eye level, intensifying their impact. If you have a dead tree to disguise, wisteria will do the job. Just don't allow the vine to climb on a live tree that you value; it will eventually strangle the tree.

Given support, wisteria climbs quite high. The vines will also exert great force, and have been known to pull gutters and even entire porches off houses. The trunk of an older wisteria vine is often 4 to 6 inches in diameter. One of my favorite wisterias grew over a wrap-around porch on a big old gray house with oval glass in the front door and hosta lining the front path. When the clusters of lavender flowers tumbled down from the roof in May, that porch was a special place.

Although my preference is for wisteria vining gracefully on an arbor or house, I must admit that wisterias trained as trees have certain advantages. They don't need architectural support, nor do they threaten porches or chimneys with their vigorous growth. They stand by themselves on the lawn. To do so they must be carefully trained and pruned.

Landscape architect William Frederick of Wilmington, Delaware, trains his wisterias to an upright steel pipe to straighten the stem for a good standard form. The White Flower Farm (Litchfield, Connecticut) catalog recommends threading the young shoot through a 4-foot-long cardboard tube and supporting the tube with a 1½-inch-diameter pipe. The shoot grows up rapidly, and because there is no stake to twine around, it remains straight. Remove the tube when the shoot is over 4 feet long, taking care not to damage the brittle growing tip. Then gently secure the straight shoot to the pipe. Wisteria grower Don Shadow leaves his plants unstaked. "It takes longer," he says, "but you have a better plant. I prune to keep side and top branches in proportion until the stem is strong enough to support a heavy top. Then I allow the top to build."

Coaxing Flowers

No one grows wisteria solely for its leaves, although they are attractive; wisteria is grown for its blossoms. Don't expect flowers the second year, however. "Flowering usually starts when the trunk is about an inch in diameter," says Frederick. "I haven't had any problem getting wisteria to flower as long as the vines are planted in full sun. When I first plant them I put good topsoil and usually some peat moss in the hole. But I never feed them. Avoid high-nitrogen fertilizers, which promote vegetative growth at the expense of flowering."

The key to wisteria's occasional yet sometimes persistent refusal to bloom is that the plants grow vegetatively as long as conditions are favorable. If the roots become restricted or nutrients are depleted, the plant usually switches from vegetative growth to the reproductive or flowering method of renewal. Feeding plants heavily or allowing rampant growth of vines and roots to go unchecked hinders the flowering process.

Clarence Hubbuch, horticulturist at Bernheim Arboretum in Clermont, Kentucky, recommends avoiding seed-grown stock: "I try to get two-year-old plants that are vegetatively propagated, and they'll usually bloom in three to four years." Erbaugh at Wayside Gardens, which propagates cultivars from flowering wood, says some specimens still take as many as seven years to flower. At the Brooklyn Botanic Garden in Brooklyn, New York, Ed Moulin maintains that "there's no timetable for flowering. Wisterias vary tremendously, even from a given source; and even if a plant has flowered in the nursery, it may not always flower the next year. Root pruning works to shock them into flowering. The addition of phosphate fertilizer also works."

Hal Bruce, horticulturist at Winterthur Museum and Gardens in Winterthur, Delaware, concurs: "Root pruning really works. I've gone all the way around the vine about 2 feet out using a spade to cut a lot of the surface roots about 1 foot down."

81

Pruning to Keep Control

Once the vine is established, prune to direct and control its growth. Wisteria flowers are borne on last year's wood, so it's important to avoid pruning off the flower buds. "You should leave two or three basal buds of last year's growth there," Moulin says. "That's where the flower buds are. We prune ours in winter. You can top-prune in the summer if the growth is too rampant. Watch the top-pruning, though; don't prune so much that you stimulate too much top growth." It's best to avoid pruning heavily less than six weeks before frost.

Down in Kentucky, Hubbuch finds that "it takes two prunings a year to keep our wisteria in shape. It's a pretty rank-growing plant." If you prune regularly, beginning when the plant is young, you will be less likely to face the prospect of drastic shearing of the sort that would encourage too much vegetative growth.

Not a Fragile Beauty

Late to bloom but long-lived, slow to break winter dormancy but cold-hardy, softly appealing in bloom yet tenacious—even aggressive—responsive to sun and reflected warmth though not to rich feeding, wisteria doesn't always behave as you think it would or should. But in May, when the lavender blooms cascade from the arbor and shimmer, slightly out of focus, in the gentle air, I regret only my impatience and my failure to find a place to plant one of each color. Wisteria casts a spell.

PART TWO

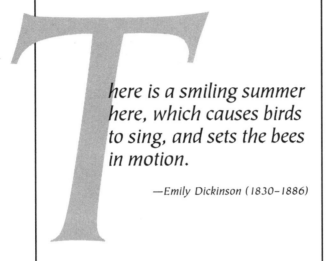

There is a smiling summer here, which causes birds to sing, and sets the bees in motion.

—Emily Dickinson (1830–1886)

SUMMER

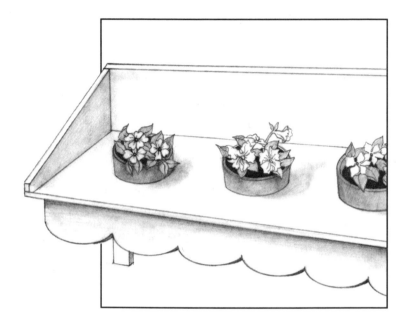

CHAPTER FOURTEEN

Work Magic with Window Boxes

W herever you live—city apartment, suburban ranch, or country farmhouse—window box plantings will add charm to your home. Artfully filled with bright flowers and cascading greenery, these small planters add a cheerful touch anywhere they're used. Window boxes have an impact far out of proportion to their modest size. Flowers raised to eye level seem more significant somehow, demanding special notice and apprecia-

85

tion. Remember, too, that you can enjoy a window box from indoors as well as out.

Plan your window garden to follow your own whims. You don't *have* to plant geraniums and petunias! These old standbys are lovely indeed, and for color impact and abundance of bloom, you certainly won't go wrong with them. But, for an interesting scene, experiment with plant arrangements and color schemes. Include plants that have different growing habits—some bushy, forming neat low mounds; some that grow upright; and a few vining or trailing plants to spill over the edges. Look for different textures—frothy alyssum blossoms with smooth waxy-leaved begonias, for example. Choose plants of varying heights, from 4 to 15 inches high—taller plants tend to look awkward unless "faced down" with lower-growing ones in front. Many little-known plants may prove to be worthwhile additions to your arrangement. Give them a chance.

Selecting a Box

Wood is still the most-used material for window boxes. A well-made wood box will last for many years. Wood boxes are heavy, insulate well, and may be custom-made to fit your space. Fiberglass window boxes are also a good choice. They are durable, lightweight, and easy to clean. Stay away from metal boxes: They conduct heat readily and can cause plant roots to overheat.

The deeper the box, the better for encouraging healthy root growth. Make sure your window box is at least 6 inches deep; a depth of 8, 10, or 12 inches is even better. The width of the box should be between 6 and 10 inches. A foot-wide box is very heavy and too ungainly to attach to a house.

Waterlogged plant roots soon die from lack of oxygen. Make sure your window box has drainage holes at each end. Add another drainage hole or two in the center for a box longer than 36 inches. If you use a metal liner in your wood box, make sure the drainage holes of box and liner match up.

Line the bottom of the box with a piece of screen to prevent soil from washing out. Or use an inch or two of shredded sphagnum moss as a liner. The moss will also help keep the box from drying out and provide air spaces to encourage healthy roots.

MAKE IT LONG-LASTING

Whether you make it or buy it, your window box will last longer if you follow these suggestions.

- Cheap lumber is no bargain. Redwood, cedar, or cypress, all naturally resistant to decay, are best. One-inch boards make a sturdy box.
- Treat pine with a preservative to help extend its useful life. Apply preservative to the inside surface of the box, where the wood will be in contact with wet soil. Don't use creosote, which is toxic to plants. Use Cuprinol, a widely available wood preservative.
- Unless the box is made of slabwood, which still has an outer surface of bark, or of naturally rot-resistant wood like redwood, protect the outside with a good grade of exterior paint or a clear exterior sealer.
- Soil in the box exerts considerable outward pressure. Use screws rather than nails to join the box parts together. Brass screws won't rust.

Mounting the Window Box

Mount the box—before filling and planting it—so its top fits just under the windowsill. (If the top is flush with or above the windowsill, water may not drain away properly from the house, and your windowsill may rot.) If you are attaching the box directly to wood siding, don't mount it flush against the house. Protect the siding and provide for ventilation by attaching a ½-inch-thick wood spacer between the box and the house. Attach the spacer to the framing lumber below the sill or to strong wood siding, using a pair of galvanized wood screws every 24 inches. The screws should extend at least an inch into the lumber. Attach the box to the spacer in the same way. Use at least four screws to attach a 36-inch-long box. If your box is long, you may want to attach screws at closer intervals to make it sturdier.

To mount a window box on a brick house, drill holes in the mortar between the bricks and drive a lug in each hole. Then drive the screw through the back wall of the box into the threaded lug.

(continued on page 90)

BEST BETS FOR WINDOW BOXES

LIGHT	HABIT OF GROWTH	
	Vining/Trailing	**Sprawling**
Full sun	Chrysanthemum (*Chrysanthemum* × *morifolium*) English ivy (*Hedera helix*) Euonymus (*Euonymus fortunei*) Ivy geranium (*Pelargonium peltatum*) Periwinkle (*Vinca minor*)	Butterfly flowers (*Schizanthus* spp.) Lantana (*Lantana camara*) Nasturtium (*Tropaeolum majus*) Oregano (*Origanum vulgare*) Petunia (*Petunia* × *hybrida*) Sweet marjoram (*Origanum majorana*) Verbena (*Verbena* × *hybrida*) Wishbone flower (*Torenia fournieri*)
Some sun	Achimenes (*Achimenes* spp.) Asparagus fern (*Asparagus setaceus*) English ivy (*Hedera helix*) Euonymus (*Euonymus* spp.)	Forget-me-not (*Myosotis sylvatica*) Petunia (*Petunia* × *hybrida*) Wishbone flower (*Torenia fournieri*)
Light shade	Achimenes (*Achimenes* spp.) Euonymus (*Euonymus* spp.) Fuchsias (*Fuchsia* spp.) Periwinkle (*Vinca minor*) Strawberry begonia (*Saxifraga stolonifera*)	Cupflowers (*Nierembergia* spp.) Wishbone flower (*Torenia fournieri*)
Deep shade	English ivy (*Hedera helix*) Periwinkle (*Vinca minor*)	

Bushy Mounds	Upright
Ageratum (*Ageratum houstonianum*)	Calendula (*Calendula officinalis*)
Annual phlox (*Phlox drummondii*)	Celosia (*Celosia cristata*)
Artemisias (*Artemisia* spp.)	Dusty millers (*Centaurea* spp., *Senecio* spp.)
California poppy (*Eschscholzia californica*)	English daisy (*Bellis perennis*)
China aster (*Callistephus chinensis*)	Geraniums (*Pelargonium* spp.)
Edging lobelia (*Lobelia erinus*)	Marigolds (*Tagetes* spp.)
Globe candytuft (*Iberis umbellata*)	Nicotiana, dwarf (*Nicotiana alata*)
Marigolds (*Tagetes* spp.)	Pinks (*Dianthus* spp.)
Pansy (*Viola* × *wittrockiana*)	Sage (*Salvia officinalis*)
Parsley (*Petroselinum crispum*)	Sage, scarlet (*Salvia splendens*)
Rose moss (*Portulaca grandiflora*)	Snapdragon, dwarf (*Antirrhinum majus* 'Nanum Compactum')
Sweet alyssum (*Lobularia maritima*)	Sweet basil (*Ocimum basilicum*)
Thyme (*Thymus vulgaris*)	
Viola (*Viola cornuta*)	
Zinnia, dwarf (*Zinnia elegans*)	
Ageratum (*Ageratum houstonianum*)	Balsam (*Impatiens balsamina*)
Browallia (*Browallia speciosa*)	Coleus (*Coleus* × *hybridus*)
Cupflowers (*Nierembergia* spp.)	Dusty millers (*Centaurea* spp., *Senecio* spp.)
Edging lobelia (*Lobelia erinus*)	English daisy (*Bellis perennis*)
Johnny-jump-up (*Viola tricolor*)	Heliotrope (*Heliotropium arborescens*)
Nemesias (*Nemesia* spp.)	Impatiens (*Impatiens wallerana*)
Pansy (*Viola* × *wittrockiana*)	Sage (*Salvia officinalis*)
Parsley (*Petroselinum crispum*)	Wax begonias (*Begonia Semperflorens-Cultorum hybrids*)
Sweet alyssum (*Lobularia maritima*)	
Viola (*Viola cornuta*)	
Browallia (*Browallia speciosa*)	Caladiums (*Caladium* spp.)
Impatiens, dwarf (*Impatiens wallerana*)	Coleus (*Coleus* × *hybridus*)
	Ferns
Pansy (*Viola* × *wittrockiana*)	Impatiens, tall (*Impatiens wallerana*)
Parsley (*Petroselinum crispum*)	Rex begonias (*Begonia Rex-Cultorum hybrids*)
Sweet alyssum (*Lobularia maritima*)	Tuberous begonias (*Begonia Tuberhybrida hybrids*)
Hostas (*Hosta* spp.)	Caladiums (*Caladium* spp.)
Lily-of-the-valley (*Convallaria majalis*)	Ferns
	Rex begonia (*Begonia Rex-Cultorum hybrids*)

TRY A PLANT SHELF

A board shelf reinforced at the corners with wedges of wood makes a simple plant holder. Measure the diameter of your selected flower pots just below the rim. Cut holes in the shelf for flower pots. Fill pots with soil and plants, then insert them, up to the rim, in the shelf.

This arrangement exposes the plants to drying from sun and wind, especially if porous clay pots are used. Use humus-rich soil to hold moisture and water frequently. A semishady location helps, too.

A simple shelf holds potted plants in a charming variation of a window box. It's easy to change plants with this display—try pastel impatiens one week, trailing ivy the next. Use plastic pots to minimize water loss.

To help support the weight of the box, it's a good idea to nail small pieces of wood to the siding directly below the box. You can also use brackets—one on each end of a short box, one every 2 feet for a long box. Be sure the window box is level. If it slopes, plants at the high end may not receive enough water.

Filling with Soil

Fill with a balanced planting mix, because the confined plant roots can't range far in search of nutrients. Don't use garden soil alone. No matter how rich it may be, garden soil will pack into a dense, air-

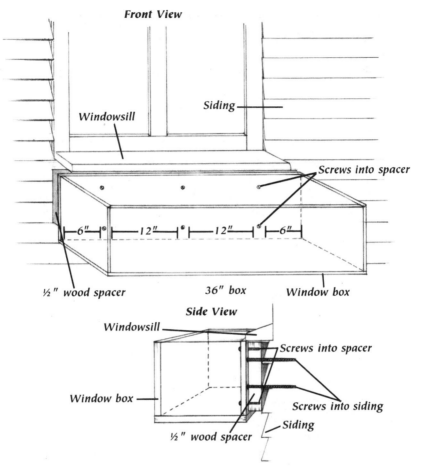

Front View

Windowsill

Siding

Screws into spacer

6″ — 12″ — 12″ — 6″

½″ wood spacer   36″ box   Window box

Side View

Windowsill

Screws into spacer

Window box

Screws into siding

½″ wood spacer   Siding

Use a spacer board between house siding and window box to allow air to circulate. Center the box under the window, and mount just below the sill to allow water to drain and prevent rot. Add more support screws for an extra-long box.

excluding, root-suffocating mass when used for container plantings. A good formula is equal parts of compost, topsoil, and sharp sand, perlite, or vermiculite. (Remove all old soil and start fresh when re-planting a window box from a previous season.)

Put 2 to 3 inches of potting soil into the window box before adding well-rooted larger plants. For smaller plants, fill the box with soil to within 1 inch of the top, and use a fork handle or other slender tool to dibble planting holes.

Planting and Growing Tips

Put plants that grow upright, such as dusty miller, geraniums, salvia, or dwarf nicotiana, at the back of the box. In the foreground, dot a few sprawling plants, such as lantana, verbena, alyssum, or nasturtiums, that will tumble over the edge of the box. Use vining plants, such as vinca, ivy, or strawberry geraniums, to soften the edges of the box.

Strive for an effect of fullness. Set plants closer than you would plant them in the garden and water them in well. It's better to transplant a few crowded plants out of the box later than to start with a skimpy arrangement and wait for it to fill in.

To keep window box plants growing well, water them every second or third day in summer unless it rains. If overhanging eaves block rainfall, water even in rainy weather. In extremely hot, sunny weather, water daily. There should be enough nourishment in the soil mix for the first two weeks. After that, feed every 10 to 14 days, using an all-purpose liquid fertilizer diluted according to package instructions.

Mulch your window boxes to help retain moisture and prevent mud from splashing on flowers. Spread a ½- to 1-inch layer of wood chip mulch or dried grass clippings on the soil surface.

Encourage an abundant and long-lasting display of flowers by picking off faded blooms before they produce seeds. For bushier plants, pinch back the growing tips of leggy stems. Remove any plants that die or look diseased.

Your window box can be interesting all year round. In early spring, plant it with an arrangement of pansies, forget-me-nots, and violas. Later, when summer heat slows the pansy bloom, replace with any of a myriad of summer-flowering annuals, supplemented by green vines and house plants. Most annuals bloom until frost. If yours finish early, replace them with chrysanthemums. By late October or early November, when killing frost has put an end to even the mums, fill the boxes with bittersweet, teasel, and Chinese lanterns. In December, decorate with stray evergreen prunings and pinecones, and leave them until spring.

CHAPTER FIFTEEN

Grow
Great Hot Peppers

Hot peppers are the firecrackers of the vegetable kingdom. Some, like 'Ring of Fire' and 'Cow Horn', are Roman-candle hot. A few, including 'Peperoncini' and mild 'Hungarian Wax', are more like sparklers, adding a tingling touch of piquancy to an otherwise bland meal.

Before I started to grow them, I assumed one hot pepper was pretty much like another. I've since learned that they vary almost as much

Hot peppers come in all sizes, shapes, and sizzles, from tiny fruits of three-alarm heat to big, mildly spicy peppers perfect for stuffing. Keep your hands away from your eyes after handling hot peppers!

as tomatoes do. They range in size from the tiny, pointed, 'Thai Hot' to medium-sized 'Ancho', which is big enough for stuffing (and makes super *chiles relleños*), to the appropriately named 'Big Jim'.

Color, in most cases, progresses from green to red as the fruits ripen. A few, like 'Goldspike' and 'Santa Fe Grande', go through a yellow stage before turning red. 'Pusilla', 'Mulato', and some others turn brownish-black when ripe. And one, 'Aurora', goes from lavender to orange to red. Hotness varies, too, from a mild, warm sensation in 'Mulato' through the full-bodied, three-alarm heat of 'Chimayo', to the incendiary 'Long Red Cayenne'. A few named cultivars, like 'Hungarian Wax', are available in both mild and hot strains. With so many cultivars of peppers to choose from, it's easy to find one (or two or three) to suit your taste. Read through the offerings in mail-order seed catalogs or make a visit to a local nursery and try out a few!

A recent visit to Mexico reminded me that I've just scratched the surface of hot-pepper possibilities. There, where people have been eating peppers for thousands of years, market stalls are heaped with straw baskets full of red, mahogany, and black dried peppers—samples of some of the hundred different kinds of chiles grown in Mexico. The wild *chiltepene* still grows here, too. Along with tomatoes, beans, corn, and sometimes squash, peppers are a staple of Mexican meals.

They are an exceptionally good source of vitamin C and contain significant of amounts of vitamin A, too.

The hotness in chili peppers comes from *capsaicin,* which is concentrated in the seeds and in sacs in the flesh between the lining and the inner wall of the pepper. Capsaicin in the seed probably helps protect it from destructive fungi during germination. Perhaps this antifungal action explains the time-honored use of hot peppers as preservatives for meats and other perishable foods.

Tips for Success

Hot peppers are easy to grow. Started plants of the most popular cultivars can often be found at your local garden center. For a wider selection, start from seed. Plant indoors 10 to 12 weeks before the last frost in spring. Here's how.

1. Sow the seeds in a light seed-starting mix.
2. Moisten the soil when planting the seeds, but don't overwater; pepper seeds can germinate in relatively dry soil.
3. Keep the planted seeds warm. They sprout as soon as a week after planting if soil temperature stays at about 80°F. In a cool spot, germination can take as long as three weeks.
4. When seedlings appear, lift them out into larger flats, spacing 2 inches apart each way.
5. Keep in a warm, sunny place—ideally, in a greenhouse or under fluorescent lights. I always use warm water to water peppers; cold water can chill young plants and retard their growth.
6. Two to three weeks before the last spring frost date, harden off seedlings by exposing them to gradually increasing amounts of sun and outdoor air for a period of seven to ten days.
7. Plant seedlings in the garden a week after the last spring frost date. I usually put out my pepper plants after I plant my tomatoes.

95

Wide spacing has been customary for pepper plants, but recent experiments have shown that yields per row (though not per plant) are higher with closer spacing of 12 to 15 inches. Sunscald occurs less often with this method, because the leaves shade the fruit.

Perhaps because they are closer to the ancestral wild form of the plant than the large bell peppers, most hot peppers produce well in garden soil that is not exceptionally rich. They accept acid soil, too, as low as pH 5.5. A sidedressing of manure tea or fish emulsion fertilizer about a week after planting helps form strong, bushy plants. Some gardeners wait to fertilize until after blossoms form. Pepper plants respond to large doses of nitrogen fertilizer by producing branches and leaves aplenty but setting fewer fruits, so don't over-fertilize. In order to avoid spreading the highly contagious tobacco mosaic virus, don't handle pepper plants after touching tobacco.

Cool Nights for Hot Peppers

There's a common misconception that chili peppers thrive in very hot weather. A quick look at their ancestry helps us to understand why that assumption isn't valid. Peppers are native to the Andes Mountains, and although mountain days can be warm, evenings are cool. Peppers grow best in similar conditions—temperatures between 70° and 80°F by day and 60° and 70°F at night. In sizzling weather— much over 80°F by day and 70°F at night—flower buds tend to drop. Dry soil, cold nights, and windy weather can cause bud drop, too. Cultivars that produce small fruits are more tolerant of hot weather than large-fruited plants. Use mulch judiciously to keep the plants comfortable: Wait to apply it until the soil is thoroughly warm, then keep an insulating blanket of mulch around each plant to keep the soil cool.

Chili peppers grown in a warm climate taste hotter than those grown in cool weather. Hotness increases as fruits ripen. If your summers are cool, try medium-hot 'Espanola Improved' (available from Plants of the Southwest; see Resources beginning on page 337). It turns red even in cool climates.

Picking and Keeping Peppers

Hot peppers may be used when green, but they are highest in vitamin content when allowed to mature on the bush. It's best to cut the pods off: The branches are brittle and easily broken by pulling on fruits. Coat your hands with oil to reduce burning when working with hot peppers. And remember not to rub your eyes!

In addition to using them fresh, we pickle, freeze, and dry our hot peppers. 'Long Red Cayenne', 'Serrano', and other thin or small cultivars are easy to dry. Just thread them on a string and hang them up. These strung, drying peppers are the famous *ristras* of the Southwest, hung by doorways in the mellow days of late summer. Split fleshier cultivars like 'Hungarian Wax' and 'Ancho' and dry on screens in a hot or sunny place.

Plant a Cutting Garden

The flowers we bring indoors to put in vases do more than decorate. Each time I put together a simple bouquet for our table, I think of how glad we are to be here, to have each other, to be eating this meal together. Flowers convey sympathy, too, and friendship and welcome. (In Victorian times, each flower was assigned an emotion or a message, and it was possible to "read" a bouquet like a coded letter: Daisies signified innocence; forsythia, anticipation; jonquil, affection returned; and spider flower, "elope with me.") Many of my bouquets are small assortments of casually mixed

97

flowers, sometimes arranged in my hand as I pick them. Or I may use a single blossom, chosen for color or form or because it's the first of the season or because I accidentally broke its stem while working in the garden.

Growing flowers especially for cutting differs in several ways from planting flower borders to delight the eye. In a border, you strive for harmony, so you limit your planting to a careful scheme of color and texture. In a cutting garden, what you want is a whole crowd of colors and forms from which to choose.

Keep your cutting garden small at first, until you determine how much work it will take and how much time you want to spend on it. You can plant a row or two of flowers among the vegetables or plant a separate cutting garden, laid out in easy-to-reach rows with narrow paths between. If ordered rows aren't your style, a cottage garden crammed with a jumble of whatever you love serves just as well.

Choosing Cutting Garden Flowers

You don't need to balance colors and plant heights in a cutting garden. Include flowers hard to fit in a border: those lovely in arrangements but stiff in form; those with awkward or floppy stems; or those too exuberant for a neatly planted bed.

98

Annuals are the mainstay of a cutting garden. They are easy to grow and will reward you with plenty of bloom from summer through frost. Supplement bouquets of annuals

You don't have to snitch flowers from the border if you plant a patch just for cutting. Colorful annuals supply plenty of bloom for a bright bouquet. An unusual container adds interest to the arrangement.

with wildflowers, perennials, herbs, and roses, either planted in the cutting garden or snitched from other beds.

Annuals for the Cutting Garden

Let's start your cutting garden with annuals, which may be tucked into bare spots or planted in rows for easy access. Those suggested here produce especially pleasing flowers for cutting, arranging, giving, and even selling. This is not an exhaustive list, by any means, but a good beginning. Unless otherwise noted, all of the following plants thrive in ordinary garden soil, perform best in full sun, and will bloom from June or July to frost.

Bachelor's-Button (*Centaurea cyanus*)

These easy-to-grow favorites have shaggy, old-fashioned blossoms in gentle colors like true cornflower blue and purple, pink, and white.

Growth habit: Bushy; 12 to 30 inches tall.

How to start: Sow seeds where they are to grow.

Spacing: Thin to about 8 inches apart.

Growing tips: For earliest bloom sow indoors in individual pots six to eight weeks before last spring frost date. Or sow outdoors in early spring or in fall. Cover the seeds; darkness promotes germination. Seedlings do not like to be transplanted.

Celosia (*Celosia cristata*)

Celosia comes in crested and plumed forms, and flower colors run the gamut, including crimson, wine, gold, yellow, and orange. Fresh or dried, they are striking in arrangements.

Growth habit: Upright; 1 to 2 feet tall.

How to start: Sow seeds indoors in individual pots about four weeks before the last spring frost date.

Spacing: Space dwarf celosia 6 inches apart, taller cultivars 12 to 15 inches apart.

Growing tips: Leave seeds uncovered; light promotes germination. Water with lukewarm water and protect young plants from chills. Transplant with care to avoid disturbing roots.

99

China Aster (*Callistephus chinensis*)

Lovely daisy- or mum-like flowers in soft colors are long-lasting in bouquets. Flowers come in a range of colors, including rose, pink, lavender, crimson, white, and pale yellow.

Growth habit:	Bushy; 8 to 24 inches.
How to start:	For earliest bloom sow seeds in pots six to eight weeks before last spring frost date. Or sow outdoors where plants are to grow.
Spacing:	Thin to 12 to 15 inches apart.
Growing tips:	Germination rate is often low, so sow seeds thickly. Start indoor seedlings in individual pots; asters don't transplant well. Pinch back the plants in June to encourage side shoots and more flowers.

Cosmos (*Cosmos* spp.)

Airy cosmos adds a graceful touch to any bouquet. Cultivars of *Cosmos bipinnatus* come in single or double flowers in pink, rose, and white; *C. sulphureus*, in orange, yellow, and red.

Growth habit:	Tall and graceful (*C. bipinnatus*) or short and bushy (*C. sulphureus*); 1 to 6 feet tall.
How to start:	Sow seeds where they are to grow.
Spacing:	Thin to 1 foot apart.
Growing tips:	For earliest bloom, start seeds indoors two to three weeks before last spring frost date. Cover seeds with only a thin dusting of soil; some light aids germination. Tall-growing cosmos may need staking.

Dahlias (*Dahlia* spp.)

Dahlias come in the most luscious colors, from pale yellow on through peach and pink to copper and burgundy. Flowers may be tiny pom-poms or dinnerplate-sized giants. They grow best in rich, well-drained soil.

Growth habit:	Bushy; 1 to 3 feet tall.
How to start:	Purchase tuberous roots. Some species may be started from seed. Sow seeds either indoors, four to six weeks before the last spring frost date, or in the garden around the last frost date.
Spacing:	Space plants 12 to 18 inches apart.
Growing tips:	Taller dahlias may need staking. Dahlias are actually tender perennials; save the tubers in fall, store in peat moss in a cool place, and replant next spring.

PERENNIALS FOR CUTTING

Many perennials are lovely in bouquets, though they generally bloom for a shorter period than annuals. Add some of your favorite perennials to the cutting garden, where you can pick whenever you like without creating bare spots in the border. The following plants are all easy to grow.

Asters (*Aster* spp.)
Astilbe (*Astilbe* × *arendsii*)
Baby's-breaths (*Gypsophila* spp.)
Balloon flower (*Platycodon grandiflorus*)
Blanket flower (*Gaillardia* × *grandiflora*)
Chrysanthemum (*Chrysanthemum* × *morifolium*)
Coralbells (*Heuchera sanguinea*)
Delphinium (*Delphinium elatum*)
Feverfew (*Chrysanthemum parthenium*)
Globe thistles (*Echinops* spp.)
Peonies (*Paeonia* spp.)
Perennial phlox (*Phlox paniculata*)
Pinks (*Dianthus* spp.)
Shasta daisy (*Chrysanthemum* × *superbum*)
Tickseeds (*Coreopsis* spp.)
Yarrows (*Achillea* spp.)

Love-in-a-Mist (*Nigella damascena*)

Long-lasting in a vase, the feathery foliage provides a misty setting for unusual blue, white, or rose fringe-petalled flowers. Spidery seedpods are good in dried flower arrangements.

Growth habit:	Airy; 2 feet.
How to start:	Sow seeds in the garden where they are to grow in early spring or fall, while soil is cool.
Spacing:	Thin to 10 inches apart.
Growing tips:	Nigella blooms best in cool weather. Mulch to keep roots cool; start a second planting in fall. Nigella does not transplant well.

Marigolds (*Tagetes* spp.)

From the 6-inch dwarfs to the imposing giants, marigolds are easy and reliable. The pure yellows add a sunny touch to a vaseful of flowers, and the russet, gold, and orange shades are especially nice in fall bouquets.

Growth habit:	Dense, bushy; 6 to 36 inches, depending on cultivar.
How to start:	Start the tall types indoors four to six weeks before the last spring frost date, because they are late bloomers. Sow other types in the garden where they are to grow, or start indoors two to three weeks before last frost date for earlier bloom.
Spacing:	Space short marigolds 8 to 10 inches apart, taller ones 18 inches apart.
Growing tips:	Marigolds flower less in extremely hot weather, but recover when early fall nights turn cool.

Mexican Sunflower (*Tithonia rotundifolia*)

Mexican sunflower produces abundant, vivid orange or red-orange, 3-inch flowers on imposing plants.

Growth habit:	Tall, bushy; 4 to 6 feet.
How to start:	Sow seeds in the garden where the plants are to grow.
Spacing:	Thin to 2 feet between plants.
Growing tips:	Not bothered by drought or insects. Abundant water will bring on a good blossom crop.

Snapdragon (*Antirrhinum majus*)

Colors both bright and pastel, upright perky growth habit, and ease of growing make the common snapdragon an outstanding plant for the cutting garden. Purple, red, pink, yellow, orange, and white blooms are available.

Growth habit:	Erect; 6 to 36 inches, depending on cultivar.
How to start:	Sow seeds indoors for early bloom eight to ten weeks before last spring frost date. Sow seeds in garden where plants are to grow four weeks before last spring frost date.
Spacing:	Space plants 6 to 12 inches apart, depending on cultivar.

TIPS FOR
CUTTING AND PREPARING FLOWERS

- Cut flowers just before they are fully open for longest life in a bouquet.
- Not sure whether a blossom will make a good cut flower? Cut a sample bloom and keep its stem in a glass of water overnight. If the water level goes down, the flower absorbs water well and should last in a bouquet.
- As you pick, plunge flowers into a container of water.
- Watch out for daffodils, bellflowers (*Campanula* spp.), balloon flower (*Platycodon grandiflorus*), heliotrope (*Valeriana officinalis*), and lantana (*Lantana camara*). All are lovely in bouquets, but their sap contains toxins that can damage other blossoms. To leach out the offending substances, keep these cut flowers in water overnight before adding them to an arrangement with fresh water.
- To aid in water uptake, recut flower stems under water before arranging. Slice stems diagonally to expose more of the cut surface to the water. Make a 1-inch slit in the stem at the cut end, to help peonies absorb more water.
- Strip off all leaves that will be submerged in water in the container.
- Try one of these methods to lengthen the life of cut flowers: (1) Add 1 cup of lemon-lime soda and 2 drops of liquid chlorine bleach to each 2 cups of water; or (2) add 2 ounces of Listerine mouthwash to 1 gallon of water.
- Out of "frogs"? Those stem-holders made from wire mesh, glass, or needles are called frogs by florists. You can substitute a wad of crumpled chicken wire. Stick it to the bottom of the container with floral clay if necessary.
- Put the arrangement where it won't be in direct sunlight and spray daily with a plant mister to keep flowers fresher.
- Change the water every day to avoid buildup of bacteria and fungi.

Growing tips: Leave seeds uncovered; they need light to germinate. Snaps prefer cool weather. Plants may be set out two to three weeks before the final frost. They are a half-hardy perennial and may overwinter in a sheltered location.

Sweet Scabious (*Scabiosa atropurpurea*)

Some call scabiosa the pincushion flower: The stamens, with their pollen-heavy heads, look like pins inserted into the fully double blooms. Flowers are purple, blue, rose, wine-red, pink, or white. The perennial *S. caucasica* is also worth trying.

Growth habit: Open, erect; 2 to 3 feet.

How to start: Sow seeds indoors four to six weeks before the last spring frost date, or sow seeds directly in the garden about three weeks before the frost-free date.

Spacing: Space plants 10 to 15 inches apart.

Growing tips: Seedlings are hardy to light frosts.

Zinnias (*Zinnia* spp.)

Zinnias are the backbone of many a cutting garden. Their many-hued blossoms—red, rose, pink, orange, cream, white, salmon, even pale green—have good substance and last well in water.

Growth habit: Bushy; 8 to 36 inches or more, depending on cultivar.

How to start: Sow seeds in the garden where plants are to grow. For earlier bloom, start seeds in small pots three weeks before the last spring frost date.

Spacing: Space plants 6 to 12 inches apart, depending on cultivar.

Growing tips: Don't cover zinnia seeds too deeply—a bit of light will encourage germination. To prevent mildew, a common fungal disease, plant where air circulation is good and avoid getting the leaves wet when watering.

CHAPTER SEVENTEEN

Start a Patch of Trouble-Free Gooseberries

Supermarkets don't sell gooseberries, so they're sometimes considered a rare delicacy. Yet these tasty berries are among the easiest fruits to grow. They bear early, accept a wide variety of soil types, and, in our experience at least, are seldom bothered by insects or birds. Growing gooseberries is a good project for the weekend gardener because the little care they do require isn't complicated or time consuming.

Gooseberry bushes are short and shrubby. Their thorny branches grow 3 to 4 feet high and, if not pruned, form a dense thicket. Mature bushes spread to about 5 feet across. The leaves are attractively creased small fans, resembling those of the related currant bush.

The berries dangle from the undersides of the arched stems, and have an attractive, faintly striped translucence. They are crisp and juicy, with skin about the same texture as that of a grape; the flesh is a bit firmer. Some gooseberries bear fruit the size of a big grape; other kinds have smaller fruit, down to cultivated-blueberry size. Some older (and more tart) cultivars have berries that ripen to greenish-white, but berries of many of the sweeter forms turn pink or deep rose when ripe. Some cultivars are sweet and delicious eaten fresh; others need cooking and sweetening. All types of gooseberries are delicious in preserves and pies.

The small, white gooseberry flowers open early in spring, and the berries are ready in early summer. A mature gooseberry bush can yield as much as 10 pounds of berries. Most kinds of gooseberries ripen all at once, but a few will hold their berries for several weeks, providing a prolonged harvest. Gooseberries are self-pollinating, so a single bush will bear well. Try several different cultivars if you have the space.

Growing Gooseberries

Gooseberries grow best in cooler climates. The bushes are exceptionally hardy, surviving and producing well up into Canada and at high elevations, and the flowers seem to be frostproof. Like apples and some other fruits, they need the rest that freezing temperatures provide. They are long-lived bushes, too, producing for up to 20 years.

Although they grow well in many different kinds of well-drained soil, gooseberries thrive with regular applications of well-rotted manure or other fertilizer. Space the bushes 4 to 5 feet apart in rows 6 to 8 feet apart. Plant in an open area where air can circulate freely to prevent mildew. They start to bear the second or third year after planting. Mulch to retain moisture, control weeds, and protect the close-to-the-surface roots.

Pick with Care

Easy as they are to grow, gooseberries can be a challenge to pick. The branches are thorny and may tangle and grow close to the ground if not pruned. We often pluck small handfuls of our 'Poorman' berries from the tips of the branches to eat fresh, as we go about our garden work. When we want a bucketful of gooseberries, we arm ourselves with a left-handed leather glove. Using the gloved hand to lift the branches, we pick with our right hand. Some gardeners who have several gooseberry bushes and a lot of berries to pick put leather gloves on both hands. They use the gloved right hand to strip one branch at a time, sliding the hand up the branch to dislodge the berries, which fall into a waiting bucket. This picking method is quick but messy; leaves and twigs get mixed in with the berries. Some can be floated off when the berries are washed; the rest get sorted out as you go over the berries. I prefer to pick more slowly and to pick clean.

To prepare gooseberries for eating fresh or cooking, pinch off the stem and the remnant of the dried flower that clings to the blossom end. (For strained jelly, these parts may be left on.) To reduce the summer berry-cleaning workload, freeze the berries as picked and "top and tail" them in the winter just before you put them in a pie. The firmness of the frozen berries makes the cleaning job easier.

Give Your Bushes a Boost

Although gooseberries are troublefree plants, they will produce more food of higher quality if well maintained. Spread some compost or well-rotted barnyard manure around the bushes each spring. Use cow manure or other less-concentrated manure rather than chicken manure, which might contain too much nitrogen. High doses of nitrogen can produce abundant sappy growth that is prone to mildew.

Pruning is the other procedure to put on your calendar. Prune while the plant is dormant—late fall or late winter into very early spring, before the bushes start to leaf out. Gooseberry bushes produce their best fruit on one- or two-year-old canes. On a mild late-winter or late-fall day, put on your leather gloves and take up your pruning shears.

- Cut out all canes that are more than two years old to give the new productive stems a chance to grow and to improve air circulation.
- Remove spindly or misshapen stems and those that cross.
- Remove all hard-to-reach, ground-hugging branches to make picking easier.
- Leave 8 to 15 well-shaped bearing branches.

We've had no trouble at all with insect, mildew, or other disease problems—and, surprisingly, very little pilfering by birds. If you do

107

see signs of mildew, thin more often. Two other problems that hit some gooseberry bushes, somewhere, but have never afflicted ours, are currant worms and anthracnose. Nurseryman Lewis Hill, of Greensboro, Vermont, who has grown gooseberries for years, recommends rotenone for the currant worms, which eat the leaves off the plants. Anthracnose, a disease that causes brown spots on the leaves, can be controlled with bordeaux mixture or lime sulfur (both available from your neighborhood garden center).

Gooseberries and White Pine Disease

Gooseberry plantings were restricted for some years—and still are in some states—because they were considered a threat to the lumber industry. Gooseberries and some of their relatives in the genus *Ribes* are an alternate host to white pine blister rust, a fungus that damages white pine trees (but does not adversely affect the gooseberry bushes). Black currants and wild gooseberries are much more likely to harbor white pine rust than cultivated gooseberries and currants. If you live in a state that restricts gooseberry plantings, you must get a permit from your state's department of agriculture to purchase and plant gooseberries, stating that you will not plant the bushes within 900 feet of a white pine tree or within 1,500 feet of a nursery where white pine seedlings grow.

According to Dr. Kim Hummer of the USDA, the following states place no restrictions on the planting of gooseberries and other *Ribes* species: Alaska, California, Colorado, Connecticut, Georgia, Hawaii, Idaho, Illinois, Indiana, Kansas, Kentucky, Minnesota, Nebraska, Nevada, New Mexico, North Dakota, Iowa, Oklahoma, Oregon, South Dakota, Texas, Utah.

These states permit the planting of *Ribes* species with a nursery certificate stating the plants are free of specified diseases or organisms, or with other documentation specific to certain states: Alabama, Arizona, Arkansas, Florida, Louisiana, Maryland, Massachusetts, Michigan, Missouri, Montana, New Hampshire, Rhode Island, Tennessee, Vermont, Washington, West Virginia, Wyoming. Check with state departments of agriculture for specific requirements.

The following states restrict or prohibit the planting of *Ribes* species: Delaware, Maine, Michigan (check to see if gooseberries are allowed; black currants are prohibited), New Jersey, New York (*Ribes* may be brought into certain areas with written permission), Ohio (gooseberries allowed; black currants prohibited), Pennsylvania (check with the state plant pathologist for details; *Ribes* restrictions are on the books but are not enforced), North Carolina, South Carolina; Virginia and Wisconsin (gooseberries are allowed but black currants are restricted). Even if black currants are prohibited in some states, gooseberries might be permitted in certain areas. Check with state departments of agriculture for specific regulations.

The Best Berries

Superior types of gooseberries are so good that the slight effort of tracking down these special cultivars is well worthwhile. You don't need to settle for 'Pixwell', a common cultivar sold in nursery catalogs, which has smallish, tart berries. If you plant only one bush, plant 'Poorman', a productive, vigorous bush that bears deep rosy berries with excellent flavor in midseason. 'Welcome,' an early-bearing bush with fewer thorns than average and pinkish-red berries and 'Captivator', a vigorous, thornless cultivar with medium-size, pinkish-purple berries, are good contenders, too. 'Mountain' (also called 'Champion') is a vigorous plant good for hot summer areas. It has red fall foliage and medium-size, sweet berries that turn very dark when ripe. Other cultivars to look for include 'Clark', 'Downing', 'Fredonia', 'Glendale', 'Hinnomaki', and 'Sylvia'. To extend the picking season, buy an early and a midseason bush.

CHAPTER EIGHTEEN

Create a
Butterfly Garden

110

For most people, a mental picture of an idyllic garden includes a tracery of bright butterflies flying from one flower to another. Colorful, delicate, graceful in flight—butterflies are one of the most charming of our fellow creatures. Their visits may seem capricious, but butterflies are full of purpose. What appears a carefree, airy stitchery of flower hopping is, in fact, a quest for the necessities of life.

Last summer, I noticed we had more butterflies than usual around our farm. As curiosity led me to read up on butterflies and their behavior, I learned that I had, unwittingly, planted some of their favorite nectar plants in my garden, and that some of the conditions provided by the fields, woods, and dirt roads on our place were just what butterflies like best. The abundance of rain we had surely helped, too. Now I notice them more than ever and make purposeful plantings to attract and nurture them.

Your butterfly-attracting project can be as simple as planting more of the flowers they favor, or as ambitious as landscaping with specially chosen plants, building a windbreak, and allowing meadow areas to remain unmown.

Your butterfly garden will add—if only minutely—to the range of favorable habitat. Some species of butterflies—the monarch, the orange sulphur, and the cabbage butterfly, for example—are found across the United States; others have distinct regions that vary in size. Of the 700 butterfly species in North America north of Mexico, 10 are on the United States endangered species list and 31 others have been proposed for protected status. The dwindling species have, for the most part, grown scarce because their habitat has been destroyed—by building, draining of wetlands, or other alteration of the land. Even though saving a species is beyond the scope of a single gardener's efforts, we can do a lot of good for the beautiful creatures we hope to attract.

A Life Cycle of Changes

The beautiful designs on the butterfly's wings are formed by a mosaic of minute scales. In many species, male and female butterflies have different coloration—usually brighter in the male, as in birds. Each species has an individual flight pattern, and all butterflies perform a courtship "dance"—circling and touching antennae—in a way that is specific to the species.

The butterfly's life cycle, from egg to larva to pupa to adult, varies in length from several months to a year, according to the species, the climate, and the time of year. Soon after mating, the female begins to lay eggs and continues for several days—in some cases, even for a few weeks. She is very choosy about egg-laying sites, depositing eggs only on those plants that make good food for her larvae. The

A garden of tempting nectar plants is well known to attract butterflies. But a wilder, weedy spot is also favored by butterflies seeking nectar or shelter for the night. Wild plants, including asters, clover, nettles, willow, wild cherry, and many others, are used as food by caterpillars and attract egg-laying butterflies.

tiny eggs—most are less than one millimeter in diameter—hatch quickly, within a week. As the caterpillars eat and increase in size, they outgrow their skins and molt, or shed, their old skins. Most species molt four to five times between hatching and pupating.

112

Depending on the species and the time of year, the pupa may remain in its chrysalis for only several days before emerging. Or it may overwinter in its chrysalis, emerging as an adult in spring. Most temperate zone species spend the winter as pupae. The chrysalis undergoes marked color changes just before the butterfly is ready to emerge. When it first hatches, the butterfly has flaccid, wrinkled wings and a plump body. Then, as it pumps up its wings with stored body fluids, the body shrinks and the wings take shape.

Basic Butterfly Needs

To survive and multiply, butterflies require nectar for energy. Their sugar sensitivity is exquisitely fine-tuned. Butterflies even have nectar sensors in their feet. A monarch butterfly can detect sugar in a solution as dilute as 0.0003 percent—a sense of taste 1,408 times more sensitive than ours! Butterflies need water, too, and certain minerals and nutrients that aren't available in nectar. They find these in muddy puddles, manure piles, carrion, and rotting fruit, which explains the incongruous sight of a delicate butterfly perched on a pile of barn cleanings.

BUTTERFLY OR MOTH?

Butterflies are easily distinguished from moths, in most cases, by the following differences.

- Butterfly antennae have a little ball, or club, at the tip. Moth antennae are often feathered and lack the tip.
- When at rest, butterfly wings are upright; moth wings are flat.
- Most moths fly at night. Butterflies fly during the day.
- Most butterflies have slender bodies. Moths have thick bodies covered with short fine hairs.
- Most butterflies pupate in an uncovered chrysalis. Moths, on the other hand, spin cocoons.

Flowers for Nectar-Sippers

There are a few simple guidelines to help you select blossoms your butterflies will love. Plant flowers with single, not double blooms for easier access to the nectar. Most butterfly nectar sources have tubular flowers. Flowers that are pendant (hang down) or heavily ruffled are more difficult to sip from, and therefore less appealing. Include plenty of the favorite colors of butterflies. They are most attracted to purple flowers, and they like yellow a lot, too. Pink and mauve are also favored, but—contrary to what you might expect—bright red doesn't seem to be high on their list. Bicolored or speckled flowers aren't as inviting as those in solid colors. Medium to pale-toned flowers seem to be more attractive to butterflies than deep, dark colors.

Group your butterfly-attracting plants together in the garden whenever possible, so they'll have more impact. Butterflies are more likely to come to masses of attractive plants than to single individuals. Provide water in low, flat containers, like bird baths set on the ground. If you have a bumpy dirt lane as we do, you'll have plenty of natural puddles to attract butterflies.

Food for Future Generations

Crucially important to the adult butterfly, in order to provide for the next generation, are plants that will feed its larvae. Each species has certain larval plant preferences. Some are exclusive—for example, monarchs lay eggs only on milkweed plants. The yellow-black-and-green-banded caterpillar that later turns into a black swallowtail butterfly will thrive on parsley or dill—but starve on basil or rosemary. On the other hand, there are a good many plants, such as clover, thistles, elm trees, and willows, that serve as host plants to larvae of a number of species.

To attract this year's adults, who know favorable conditions when they see (and smell) them, grow some food plants to nourish the larvae. Wild plants are the natural foods of butterflies and their caterpillar larvae, and they appreciate the shelter offered by tall grasses and other meadow plants. If possible, leave some areas of your property unmowed, and encourage wildflowers.

Learning about Your Garden Guests

You'll be most successful in hosting butterflies if you find out what kinds are known to frequent your area, and then plant the nectar sources and larval food plants preferred by these species. Spend time observing those that do come to your garden, and use a good field guide to identify them. To find out about other species you might expect to have in your area, get in touch with a butterfly organization or talk to the naturalist at a local park or natural area.

Keep records. Depending on how involved you want to become in your study of butterflies, you might jot down the names of butterflies you see in your garden, dates of first sightings of different species, which nectar flowers seem to be the most popular, where you notice egg laying taking place, and the location of night roosting spots.

A Butterfly Menu

Plant some of these proven nectar plants and see what comes to sample them. For your first efforts, try butterfly weed (*Asclepias tuberosa*), butterfly bush (*Buddleia* spp.), lantanas (*Lantana* spp.), and asters (*Aster* spp.). Here are some other good nectar sources to bring more butterflies to your garden. Those marked with an asterisk (*) are also eaten by caterpillars.

Garden Flowers

Ageratum	(*Ageratum houstonianum*)
Baptisia	(*Baptisia australis*)
Black snakeroot	(*Cimicifuga racemosa*)*
Blanket flowers	(*Gaillardia* spp.)
Clematis	(*Clematis* spp.)
Cosmos	(*Cosmos bipinnatus; C. sulphureus*)
Daylilies	(*Hemerocallis* spp.)
Hollyhock	(*Alcea rosea*)*
Lobelias	(*Lobelia* spp.)
Mallows	(*Hibiscus* spp.)
Marigolds	(*Tagetes* spp.)*
Nasturtium	(*Tropaeolum majus*)*
Nicotianas	(*Nicotiana* spp.)
Phlox	(*Phlox* spp.)
Pinks	(*Dianthus* spp.)
Purple coneflower	(*Echinacea purpurea*)
Salvias	(*Salvia* spp.)
Sedum	(*Sedum spectabile*)
Sunflowers	(*Helianthus* spp.)
Sweet alyssum	(*Lobularia maritima*)
Sweet scabious	(*Scabiosa atropurpurea*)
Tickseeds	(*Coreopsis* spp.)
Verbenas	(*Verbena* spp.)
Zinnias	(*Zinnia* spp.)

Wild Plants

Bee balms	(*Monarda* spp.)
Buttercups	(*Ranunculus* spp.)
Joe-Pye weed	(*Eupatorium maculatum, E. purpureum*)

Milkweeds	(*Asclepias* spp.)*
Oxeye daisy	(*Chrysanthemum leucanthemum*)
Pearly everlasting	(*Anaphalis margaritacea*)*
Sorrels	(*Rumex* spp.)*
Thistles	(*Cirsium* spp.)*
Vetch	(*Vicia* spp.)
Violets	(*Viola* spp.)*
White clover	(*Trifolium repens*)
White sweet clover	(*Melilotus alba*)

In addition, having wild plants such as crabgrasses (*Digitaria* spp.), field mouse-ear chickweed (*Cerastium arvense*), grasses, Queen-Anne's-lace (*Daucus carota* var. *carota*), ragweeds (*Ambrosia* spp.), stinging nettle (*Urtica dioica*), and tick trefoils (*Desmodium* spp.) nearby will increase your butterfly population. Adult butterflies will be attracted when it's egg-laying time because their caterpillars relish the taste.

Annuals and perennials aren't the only plants that attract butterflies. Shrubs, such as glossy abelia (*Abelia* × *grandiflora*), hawthorns (*Crataegus* spp.)*, lilacs (*Syringa* spp.), privets (*Ligustrum* spp.), spicebush (*Lindera benzoin*)*, and viburnums (*Viburnum* spp.) are also butterfly favorites. Don't forget the trees either. Try planting a few beeches (*Fagus* spp.), dogwoods (*Cornus* spp.), elms (*Ulmus* spp.), lindens (*Tilia* spp.), poplars (*Populus* spp.), sycamores (*Platanus* spp.), wild cherries (*Prunus ilicifolia*), or willows (*Salix* spp.) for a butterfly haven.

In the food garden, plant beans*, cabbage*, carrots*, celery*, chives, dill*, fennel*, or parsley to tantalize butterfly taste buds.

Try Container Gardening

ontainers are a handy way to surround yourself with green growing things when you're short of garden space and digging time. A container planting can be shifted as needed to bask in full sun or to take refuge in shade. At the back door, a pot of herbs, surrounded by tumbling nasturtiums, brings mealtime snipping within reach. Plants in containers can grow on balconies and rooftops, screen out an undesirable view, and shelter a porch from sun and wind, too. On a deck or at the edge of a patio, container gardens serve as instant landscaping.

A plant in a pot can go with you across town or across the country. During the course of six household moves, I discovered that a pot of flowers on the front step cheered us in new surroundings and helped us feel settled. Tender perennial herbs, flowers, and trees are easier to move indoors in winter if planted in pots. I've kept potted rosemary, lemon grass, and lemon verbena alive all year by moving them from patio to greenhouse.

Here's how to discover for yourself the many joys of container gardening.

Keep a pot of cooking herbs near the kitchen to make it easy to snip some seasonings for dinner. A terra-cotta pot spilling over with thyme, parsley, and other favorites is simple and attractive.

Container Garden Basics

118

One of the pleasures of container planting is the freedom to use almost any interesting object as a planter. Halved whiskey barrels, strawberry jars with multiple pockets, baskets, stone troughs, and clay drain tiles make handsome planters. I've seen whimsical planters: wheelbarrows, wagons, stovepipe sections, old sinks, wicker wastebaskets, an ancient metal clothes boiler, old dishpans, worn-out shoes, a toy dump truck. One arrangement I especially liked was a series of olive oil cans in different sizes, each printed with a different design, grouped on a short flight of steps. Slipcover a practical but unattractive pot by setting it inside another, more pleasing container. I have an old bottomless earthenware crock that makes a perfect cover-up for plants in black plastic nursery pots. Still, the most common porch and patio plant containers are clay or plastic pots and wooden enclosures of various kinds, from bark-slab boxes to custom-made cubes big enough to hold a small tree.

Strictly utilitarian are bushel baskets or wash baskets lined with plastic, plastic buckets, and plastic bags of potting soil, as is—with several plants set in slits in the top of the bag.

Choose a Pot to Fit the Plant

Whether you're using conventional or offbeat containers, they must provide drainage for water and hold enough soil to support the plant or plants that you intend to put in them. Small plants like thyme and lobelia can get along in small pots, but vegetable and most flower plantings should have soil at least 8 inches deep. Smaller pots dry out too quickly if left exposed. A standard 8-inch-diameter pot holds 1 gallon of soil. In it, you can grow 2 looseleaf lettuce or spinach plants, 20 radishes or green onions, 14 to 18 carrots, or 10 to 12 small beets.

A 12-inch pot holds 3½ gallons of soil; a 14-inch pot, 6 gallons. A half whiskey barrel, holding about 15 gallons, can be planted with three tomato plants, or four to five peppers, or two to three zucchinis. For single plantings of tomatoes, eggplants, or zucchini, use a 3- to 5-gallon pot, depending on the cultivar.

Good Drainage Is Vital

Good drainage is vitally important to the prosperity of container-grown plants. Roots need air in the soil in order to thrive, and in waterlogged soil, with all the air spaces filled by water, plant roots soon rot. It doesn't take long for this to happen. I've seen changes in plant health after only two days of living in swampy soil.

If there is no drainage hole in the planter you intend to use, drill a hole in the center of the bottom—or several holes, along midline, in a long planter box. Use a can opener to make holes in the bottoms of decorative cans.

Careful Care

Container plantings can help you grow a variety of plants in a variety of places, but they do require attention to certain details. Because the amount of soil is limited in a container, the drying effects of sun and wind are more severe. Confined roots are unable to range freely in search of nutrients, so these plantings need more frequent feeding than those in the garden.

If you're grouping different plants in a single container, be sure they all have similar needs of sun, soil, and water. Cactus, ferns, and petunias, for example, are too different in their requirements to make good companions in a pot. Try instead ferns, lobelia, and impatiens (all like part shade and plenty of water); petunias and geraniums with dusty miller (sun lovers). Plant drought-defying cactus alone.

When potting your container garden, to prevent excess soil from washing away, cover the holes with pieces of screening, or a layer of gravel, broken pot shards, or long-fiber sphagnum moss. When setting a plant in a pot, I spread an inch of potting soil on the moss and top that with 2 inches of compost (more in a big, deep pot). Then, after adding another inch or so of potting soil, I set the plant in, spread its roots, and fill in around it with more fine potting soil. I firm the soil around the plant and water. Usually I keep the newly potted plant in the shade for a day before exposing it to full sun. If you're planting a large, immovable pot or tub, fill and plant it where you want it to remain or set it on a wheeled plant stand after filling it. It will be heavy and difficult to lift when it's full.

Fertilizer

The soil mix nutrients will last for several weeks, but to keep your plants thriving, especially if they're producing fruits, start regular fertilizer applications three to four weeks after planting. Use your favorite all-purpose fertilizer, or try diluted fish emulsion concentrate or compost tea. A mixture of 4 parts blood meal, 2 parts bone meal, and 1 part kelp, rock phosphate, or greensand (dry mixture) is effective, or try a tablespoon each of fish emulsion concentrate and liquid kelp, plus a teaspoon of blood meal in 1 gallon of water.

If you use liquid fertilizer, give your plants more frequent but weaker feedings—half strength every two weeks, for example. Vegetable plants in full production can use weekly or biweekly full-strength feedings, but flowering and foliage plants will be satisfied with a fertilizer boost every three to four weeks.

Water

Your container plantings will be at their best if they're not allowed to dry out and wilt. Potted plants need frequent watering—as often

POTTING SOIL RECIPES

Here are several formulas for soil mixes from my book *The New Seed Starters Handbook*.

Home-Style Potting Soil

1 part finished compost
1 part loose garden or commercial potting soil
1 part sharp sand, perlite, or vermiculite—or a mixture of all 3

Thalassa Cruso's Potting Soil

1 part commercial potting soil or leaf mold
1 part sphagnum or peat moss
1 part perlite or sharp sand

Rich Potting Soil

1 part leaf mold
2 parts loose garden or commercial potting soil
1 part compost or rotting, sifted manure

Amended Potting Soil

4 parts loose garden or commercial potting soil
2 parts sphagnum or peat moss
2 parts leaf mold or compost
2 parts vermiculite
6 teaspoons dolomitic limestone (the limestone helps to
    neutralize the acids in the leaf mold and peat moss)

as daily in hot weather. Group pots to moderate the drying power of sun and wind and make watering easier.

My herbs and flowers with an eastern exposure are protected from much of the afternoon sun, and for them, watering every third to fourth day is enough. The eggplants in daylong sun on the south side, on the other hand, need daily watering in the full flush of summer.

Try to avoid splashing water on leaves while the sun is shining. Droplets can act as lenses that burn them. Pansies, lettuce, and other cool-weather crops don't mind a shot of cool water (truly cold water is a shock to any plant's roots). But for heat-loving plants like eggplants and peppers, use lukewarm water.

Plants in clay pots dry more quickly than those in plastic. If a lot of bare soil is exposed—as in a tree or single-stemmed herb planting—mulch the surface with fine material like shredded bark or cocoa hulls, or plant a creeping groundcover. Mulch reduces water loss and prevents soil craters and splashing mud at watering time.

Set the Theme

When landscaping a deck, you'll want some stately plants and bushy ones with substance, plus some that are bright and perky, and perhaps a few fragrant ones. For a note of welcome by the front door, a mix of blooming annuals and interesting foliage plants works well. A convenience garden of potted herbs near the kitchen door saves time and adds zest to meals—you'll more likely snip rosemary into the stew if it is near at hand. If garden space is skimpy and you crave fresh vegetables, devote container space to food crops. Perhaps you want to delight a child with a strawberry barrel or jar. Even a single potted plant can set a theme, provide an accent, offer a memory.

In one of my favorite pieces of garden writing, *Green Grows The Garden*, Margery Bianco refers to the Italian poet Pascoli, who spoke of a verbena bush that grew in the doorway of his home. When he went away to school, his mother put a sprig of it into things she sent him. "In one of his stories," Bianco writes:

> Pascoli tells how, many years later when he came to leave home, he took a rooted slip from his same doorside bush and kept it on his windowsill wherever he lived. He called this little pot of verbena his house and garden, for the earthen flowerpot was made of the same clay from which are made the bricks and roof tiles of a country house, and the earth inside was the earth of the field and vineyards. For many years, it was the only land, the only house that he possessed, but for him it was the symbol of home, for he had only to touch the leaves with his fingers and their fragrance brought back to him his early home, the faces of those he loved, and all his vanished years of childhood happiness.

Solve Landscaping Problems with Daylilies

D aylilies provide pure enjoyment as accent or border plants, filling in those hard-to-landscape areas beautifully. The graceful, trumpet-shaped flowers come in cheerful colors that have considerable impact, even from a distance: every shade of yellow, orange, and pink; rose, purple, even greenish yellow and near-black. They bloom for a longer period each year than most other perennials, and they even flower in partial shade.

An old favorite carried across America by homesteaders, the orange daylily (*Hemerocallis fulva*) has left the dooryard garden to become a familiar sight along country roadsides.

All that beauty can be practical, too. Daylily plants are very hardy, drought-resistant, and easy to care for. A planting of daylilies shades out most weeds, and plants last a long time before they need division. What's more, they spread readily without being invasive and seldom have problems with pests or diseases.

These easy-care plants make good groundcovers for areas you don't want to mow—especially slopes. Plant daylilies to prevent or control erosion—for example, to hold soil on steep banks, to pave the path of runoff in yards and fields, or to fortify streambanks against the force of running water. Use their arching leaves to hide the fading foliage of early-blooming spring bulbs. Try clumps on either side of a gate or doorway, or perhaps by the mailbox. For a great sweep of color, plant a whole swath of them along a fence or rock wall. Fast-spreading, vigorous daylilies like the common orange-flowered daylily species, *Hemerocallis fulva,* or a more recently introduced ultra-fast spreader, 'Nashville', are especially good choices for covering ground.

Most people are familiar with the orange daylily (*H. fulva* 'Europa'), an old garden favorite that has become naturalized along roadsides all across rural America. Daylilies were not native to America. Two species were brought to this country by the early colonists—*H. fulva* and the slightly smaller, yellow-flowered *H. lilioasphodelus,* fondly called lemon lily. As people pushed westward, settling homesteads throughout the Midwest and West, they took starts of *H. fulva* with them. These adaptable daylilies took hold and spread where they were introduced and came to be known as homestead lilies.

The orange daylily, or homestead lily, and the lemon lily are only 2 of at least 13 daylily species that originated in China. The ancient Chinese used them for food and medicine. Fields of daylilies are still grown in modern China, where the flower buds are eaten both fresh and dried.

In the twentieth century, and especially in the last 50 years, those original wild daylily forms have been bred and crossbred into an explosion of new cultivars. There were less than 200 different daylily cultivars registered in the late thirties, and 400 in 1954. Today there are approximately 12,000 registered cultivars on the market, with hundreds of new ones introduced each year.

A Daylily for Every Garden

While no one species or cultivar is ideal for all areas, there are daylilies suitable for conditions that prevail wherever you live. The daylily could be our national flower. This immigrant will grow in every one of our 50 states—some hardy cultivars even brave Alaskan winters!

Daylilies come in all sizes, too—from dwarfs not much over 8 to 10 inches in height, through short, midsize, and up to the extra-tall *H. altissima,* with flower stems up to 6 feet high. Most popular daylily types range from 2½ to 3½ feet tall. Flower size varies, too, from miniature flowers under 3 inches across to full-blown beauties 6 inches and more.

Many daylilies go dormant in winter, their clumps of leaves dying back to the ground. There are also evergreen daylilies that hold their leaves year-round. And we now have many semi-evergreen daylilies, products of a cross between the evergreen and the dormant lines. In general, dormant daylilies are the hardiest and do best in cold areas where they get a winter rest. Evergreen and semi-evergreen daylilies are most often planted in the South, but some of them perform well in the North, too.

Scientific Marvels

New plant-chemical treatments have given us even more choices—between diploids, daylilies with the conventional two sets of chromosomes per cell, and tetraploids, which have four sets of chromosomes in each cell.

Tetraploid daylilies are usually obtained by treating seedlings with colchichine, a plant extract. They produce larger flowers with more intense colors, and often more flowers in relation to the amount of foliage. The flower petals and the foliage are thicker, more leathery, and the stems are stiffer. Tetraploids tend to be extra-vigorous plants, though not as graceful as the more flexible diploids.

ALL-AROUND FAVORITES

Cultivars are introduced each year. Consult any of the reputable catalogs (see Resources beginning on page 337 for a list) for descriptions of some of the thousands of wonderful kinds. Here's a sampling of a few proven favorites.

'Eeenie Weenie'. Dwarf, 12-inch plants with abundant, light yellow, 2½-inch flowers that last till evening. Dormant, very hardy, heat-resistant.

'Hyperion'. Old cultivar, introduced in 1924, with fragrant, lemon-yellow flowers on vigorous 48-inch plants. Dormant.

'Mary Todd'. Early-blooming tetraploid with 6-inch yellow flowers on 26-inch plants. Semi-evergreen, reblooms.

'Ruffled Apricot'. Large, fragrant, apricot-shaded flowers in early midseason on 28-inch plants. Dormant.

'Shari Harrison'. A 22-inch-tall cultivar with a long blooming period and violet-purple 5½-inch flowers. Semi-evergreen, reblooms, very hardy.

'Stella d'Oro'. A mass of small, gold flowers and a long season of bloom; 24-inch plants. Reblooms. Dormant.

Flower for a Day, Bloom for a Season

Daylilies have blossoms that last a single day. That's the meaning of their botanical name, derived from the Greek words *hemera* (day) and *kallos* (beauty). The flowers usually open in the morning and close around sunset. The schedule varies with variety, exposure, weather, and season. Some extended bloomers stay open all day until around 10 P.M. A few, like *H. citrina* and its descendants, are nocturnal, opening just before sundown and closing the following afternoon. Some daylilies are pleasantly, though not strongly, fragrant.

Although the individual flowers are beautiful for just a day, the plant as a whole can bloom for up to six weeks. A single daylily plant has as many as 12 flowering stems, or scapes. Under ideal conditions, especially floriferous cultivars produce up to 30 flowers on a single scape. Stem and flower counts are, of course, more modest on the average plant.

By selecting cultivars that bloom early, midseason, and late, you can have bright daylilies nodding along your fence from June until frost. Repeat-blooming daylilies, called remontants, flower a second time in the North, and often a third time in the South.

Getting Off to a Good Start

Daylilies may be planted almost any time the ground is fit to dig. We planted our daylilies in October, because the nursery had a half-price sale on them, and they sprouted on schedule the following spring. I've known clumps that continued to bloom and thrive even after being moved in full flower (generous watering after the move helped ease the transition). In the North, it's best to get plants in the ground at least six weeks before the ground freezes solid, so the roots can grow and anchor the plant.

Daylilies are sun lovers, but they'll accept and, in hot climates, even appreciate some afternoon shade after a good dose of morning sun. Pink- and red-flowered plants, especially, fade less if sheltered somewhat from the full brunt of the afternoon sun. In all-day light shade, the plants produce fewer flowers in a slightly shorter display.

Daylilies thrive in just about any decent soil and even grow and bloom on some poor soils, as long as drainage is good. They are at their best in deeply worked soil with a good supply of humus. Technically, they like a soil pH around 6.5, but they obligingly bloom away on near-neutral soils and on soils that are more highly acid. Graceful daylilies blend well with many other perennials, including tall garden phlox, chrysanthemums, delphiniums, and coreopsis, to name only a few. Butterfly bush (*Buddleia davidii*) and roses make good shrub

127

STEPS TO SUCCESS

The American Hemerocallis Society recommends taking the following steps when planting daylilies.

1. When mail-order plants arrive, soak them in a weak liquid fertilizer solution for several hours before planting.
2. Plant roots in a mixture of 1 part good garden soil, 1 part peat moss, and 1 part compost or well-rotted manure, with bonemeal added.
3. Make a small mound of soil in the planting hole, and set the crown of the plant on it, spreading the roots around the sides of the mound. Cover the crown with about 1 inch of soil. Avoid too-deep planting (more than 2 inches).
4. Water thoroughly at planting time and mulch to conserve moisture, control weeds, and protect plants over winter.

companions. Dwarf forms of daylilies are good in rock gardens and as edging plants.

If you want to just set the plants and walk away without tinkering with them, plant medium-height daylilies about 3 feet apart. If it's quick results you're after, and you don't mind doing some thinning and transplanting in a few years, space roots as close as 2 feet. Plant shorter cultivars—those up to 18 inches tall—1 to 1½ feet apart. Tall ones need plenty of space—at least 3 feet.

Label your plants, both in the garden and on a planting diagram. Then, if you want to reorder a favorite or a plant that failed, you'll know what name to request. And you'll be able to identify the plants for visitors who want to grow the same thing. Knowing a plant's name is part of the pleasure of growing it.

To give a daylily planting more impact, plant at least three of a kind together, ideally in a triangular arrangement. A single color, or definite blocks of single colors, are more eyecatching than a spotty mixture. Our planting is a mixture, simply because I couldn't resist all those sumptuous choices in the catalog.

Easy Care and a Long Life

Caring for daylilies is easy: There's not much to do. Until they close ranks and cover the ground with their foliage, pull any weeds that encroach on their territory. Once established, the thickly knotted roots and heavy shade of their leaves crowd out most weeds. We give our daylilies a shovelful of compost per plant each spring. You can also feed them with diluted fish emulsion or manure tea. Overfeeding encourages exuberant foliage growth at the expense of flowers.

Daylilies are surprisingly droughtproof, because they store water in their fleshy roots. Still, they respond well to a steady supply of water, especially while flower scapes and buds are forming. Daylilies are self-supporting and need no staking.

Many gardeners regularly remove dead blossoms from plants they'll be enjoying up close, both to manicure the display and to conserve energy the plant might otherwise use on seed formation. If you have a large daylily planting, you'd need a hired gardener or ten children to keep up with this task. I deadheaded mine casually during their first year or two, but I seldom get around to it once they're established, and it doesn't seem to matter.

A winter mulch of loose, nonpacking organic material is recommended for evergreen and semi-evergreen daylilies in cold areas. Remove the mulch in spring when the new shoots are about 6 inches high. Don't remove the dried leaves from last summer. They offer a small amount of winter protection.

One of the best features daylilies have to offer is their freedom from insect and disease problems. It's not unusual to grow them for a decade or more without an infestation of any kind—at least, not one that adversely affects the plants. Disease is rare, too.

Divide to Multiply

Daylilies don't need to be divided as often as many other perennials. They will grow happily for years before they crowd each other. But if you're eager to increase your stock of a favorite cultivar, divide the plants more often. A well-established four-year-old daylily plant can be divided into four new plants. The best time to divide daylilies is immediately after flowering. Late-flowering cultivars can be divided in early spring when the shoots are 5 to 6 inches high. Here's how to separate a clump of daylilies into multiple starter plants.

1. Cut back the leaves to about 6 inches. This eliminates a confusing tangle of foliage and reduces the stress on the uprooted plants.
2. Use a digging fork to pry up the clump.
3. Divide the clump: Tease it apart as much as you can with your hands. Chop through solid masses of roots with a hatchet. Use two garden forks, wielded back-to-back, to separate roots. If poor visibility hampers your efforts, hose the dirt from the roots so you can see what you're doing.
4. Replant the divisions immediately. If there are more than you can handle in a single day, "heel in" the leftovers for a week or so by planting them close together temporarily in a shallow trench located in a shady spot until you can plant them properly.

You can also increase your supply of daylilies by plucking off the small plantlets, called proliferations, that sometimes appear on the stem. Root them in vermiculite. They're a nice bonus from some already more-than-obliging plants.

CHAPTER TWENTY-ONE

Plant Some Fun for Your Children

Despite a childhood spent largely in cities, gardens loom large in my memory. My mother's victory garden, a patch of beets and beans with a clump of sweet spicy pinks marking the corner; my grandfather's yard, lushly overgrown behind the old house, with hollyhocks by the shed and always a raspberry thicket; the field I passed on my way home from school, where I gathered cornflowers and blew milkweed silk and made doll furniture from burdock burrs.

Making Memories with Plant Games

We plan so many experiences for our children—lessons, museums, vacations—yet it often seems to me that children remember best and cherish most the odd little happenings that aren't part of a formal program. As our children were growing up, I often wondered what *they* would remember. Now, as I plan my garden, I keep my small grandchildren in mind and include some special delights just for those random moments.

The plant games I learned as a child began to come back to me when I had children of my own, and I collected more from friends. These tricks are a treasure lode of childhood lore that could so easily be lost if it's not passed along. For many of those earlier long-ago children, plant games and secrets *were* their toys—easily broken but readily replaced, always there in season, ready to be interpreted and manipulated in new ways.

Velvet Slippers in a Flower

Bleeding-heart (*Dicentra spectabilis*) blossoms are an age-old favorite. Our son's kindergarten teacher showed him how to find the fox, rabbit, locket, and Cinderella's slipper hidden in each of the heart-shaped flowers. Would you like to find them, too? The first step is to gently pull off the rabbits on either side of the blossom. See their folded ears? Carefully disengage the slippers that form the arch on either side of the upper part of the locket. Turn the remaining narrow fragment of the flower to face you, and split it to form the fox's head.

No doubt there are a good many other stories woven around the bleeding-heart parts. In another version, the two rounded halves of the heart that are removed first are pink swans, not rabbits. The parts that form the arch are velvet slippers. And the part of the flower left after the slippers are pulled off is a wine bottle. In another way of seeing the flower, reported by a Swedish woman, the whole blossom is called the lieutenant's heart. Removing the two rabbits reveals a ballerina—who, upon relinquishing her upheld arms (the slippers), becomes a champagne bottle.

Columbine (*Aquilegia* spp.) blossoms also reveal an interesting formation when taken apart. Tear off the outer petals to see doves feeding from the same dish in the center of the flower. Try it for yourself. What do *you* see?

From humble beginnings comes a fanciful tea party: Burdock burrs form a table, and poppy seedpods make the cups. The smartly dressed guests are fashioned from hollyhocks and poppy flowers.

Flower Dolls at a Tea Party

A grandmother I know has made countless small friends through her openhandedness with hollyhock blossoms. They do make charming dolls. Remember? Just fasten an unopened bud with a straight pin to the stem end of a blossom to form a head on a silky skirt. Quick remedy for boredom on a hot summer day: a hollyhock doll party, complete with lemonade. It's fun to make flower hats for them, too.

Hollyhock seeds can be found in any garden center or seed catalog. I prefer the enduring charm of the old-fashioned single form in luscious colors, ranging from deep maroon through peach to ivory. Seeds that we gathered along railroad tracks and received in a seed trade have produced all the colors of old silk, in petal form.

Red-orange trumpet vine (*Campsis radicans*) grows as well in town as in the country, and trumpet-flower ladies are easy to make. Simply cut a slit in two petals and pull the stamens out to form arms.

In a slightly more delicate maneuver, you can make dolls out of poppy blossoms. Cut off a fresh flower, leaving a 3-inch stem. Holding the flower upright, carefully smooth the petals down, leaving the crownlike center of the flower for the head. Then tie a piece of thin grass, a green vine tendril, or other natural "ribbon" around the doll's waist (or leave the petals loose for a smocklike effect). The fringe of

133

stamens forms a ruff or collar around the doll's head. You can add arms by poking twigs or stem pieces into the shoulder area, but these graceful ladies are quite satisfactory even without such realistic touches.

An elderly woman who responded to my interest in plant games wrote that she would hollow out the large seedpods of Oriental poppies, cutting off the tops for lids and fastening small twigs or sturdy pieces of grass to the side for a handle, to make cups and pitchers for doll tea parties.

Plant Contests and Blossom Jewelry

Violets grow nearly everywhere. They are eaten, candied, made into nosegays. But did you ever have a violet tug-of-war? Hook the flowers together, linking their hooked necks. Then pull on the stem of your flower while your opponent pulls on his. Winner gets his wish!

Seed heads of plantain, a common broadleaf weed, are props for another plant contest. Players hold the stem of a club-shaped seed head and take turns bashing the other person's seed head. The player who knocks off the other's seed head is the winner.

It's easy to stage a watermelon seed-spitting contest. Just stretch a string for the starting line, toe up to it, slurp up slices of cool, juicy melon, and take turns seeing how far you can propel the seeds. Inelegant, but refreshing!

Larkspur chains are an old country whimsy. Pick the blossoms and fit them together, inserting the spur of one into the tubular throat of another. Larkspur is poisonous if eaten, so restrict this flower game to children old enough to refrain from tasting the blossoms. An obliging plant, larkspur grows best in full sun but will also bloom in light shade. It isn't particular as to soil, either. It reseeds itself liberally and will appear in surprising and charming places the next year. (Buttercups also contain toxic compounds. No one is about to call a halt to that time-honored ritual of holding buttercups under little chins, but the game should end there. Never taste the blossoms or leaves.)

You can string a chain of florets from a lilac or a phlox blossom head into a necklace, too. Just insert the tubular base of each flower into the center of another. Games have evolved around the occasional five-lobed lilac floret mixed in with the four-lobed majority (eating a five-lobed blossom while thinking of a dear one may bring you luck in love). While you're getting all decked out with your flower jewelry, try some instant red fingernails: Moisten individual petals from geraniums and stick them on your nails.

The true value of the games, crafts, and toys we weave around garden finds is even more than momentary entertainment. It's being willing to try, taking time to see details, being eager and free to play. If you missed out on this as a child, indulge now in some simple plant amusements and discoveries. Perhaps you'll invent a new plant game to add to our informal body of lore!

CHAPTER TWENTY-TWO

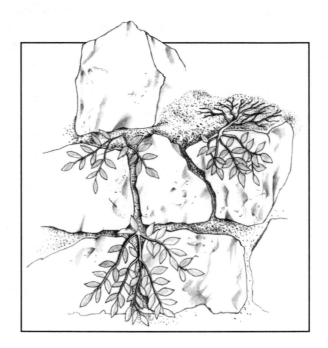

Build a Rock Wall Herb Garden

Vertical herb plantings can have a glorious effect. The first herb-studded rock wall we ever saw was on the grounds of the Sandy Mush Herb Nursery in the mountains of North Carolina. We had, in fact, traveled all the way from Pennsylvania to see the herb wall—and we were not disappointed.

Fairman Jayne already had several hundred different kinds of herbs growing in raised beds and borders and in the greenhouse at his Sandy

Mush Herb Nursery. But when he needed a retaining wall to flank the rebuilt greenhouse, he couldn't resist trying a new kind of herb patch: he planted perennial herbs in his 6-foot-high, 20-foot-long rock wall. And what seemed like a whimsical idea proved to have a number of practical advantages.

"Really and truly," said Fairman, "it started as just a pleasure. Wall gardens like this are ideal for a small place because you can add planting space within a limited area. So far, I have between 60 and 70 varieties of herbs growing in two rock walls. And in a shady yard, a wall planting will sometimes raise the plants into a patch of sunlight where they will thrive as they could not in deeper shade." Still another advantage of growing culinary herbs in a rock wall is their leaves stay clean.

In building the unmortared retaining walls, Jayne took special pleasure in using native rock, rather than bricks or railroad ties. In this handsome arrangement, the rocks and the herbs complement one another. The plants—bushy, mounded, creeping, or airily cascading from crevices in the wall—soften the harshness of the stones. The plant roots stabilize loose soil in the bank. And the plants thrive in this setting because it provides superb drainage, reflected sunlight, rock-held warmth, excellent air circulation, and a cool, root-sheltering soil.

Plants that suffer from competition thrive in the environment a rock wall provides. "Some herbs," Jayne notes, "have done better in the rock wall than in our traditional planting bed." Among these are Corsican mint, compact oregano, nutmeg thyme, golden lemon creeping thyme, and artemisia 'Silver Mound'.

An unmortared rock wall can stand for a century if it is well constructed. A sound wall is held together by the weight of the stones and by the interlocking pattern in which they are placed. Because a dry wall is loose-jointed enough to shift gently when frost heaves the soil, no concrete foundation is needed. Nor is it necessary to dig below the frostline to start the wall. There are no mortared seams to crack.

137

Building Basics

Rocks that are naturally flat make the most stable construction. Stratified stones like limestone, shale, and sandstone split readily, because they tend to absorb moisture and then crack when frozen, but there are many long-standing walls built of these materials. Granites and basalts are the most durable stones, but they are difficult to "dress" or chip into a desired shape.

A wall is stronger and more interesting if there is some variation in the shape and size of the stones used, but avoid using rocks of widely varying size, or the wall will look patchy and lack stability. The rocks in a wall should be all of the same kind; don't mix granite and shale, for example, in one wall. Here's how to get started.

- Collect plenty of rocks before you begin, so you have a good selection to fit into a variety of spaces. Collect small rocks, too, for use as shims between uneven large rocks.
- One ton of undressed stone will be enough for 25 to 40 square feet of wall with an average thickness of 1 foot.
- Have plenty of square-ended rocks for the ends of the wall.
- Put the largest rocks—the two-person kind—on the bottom. They'll look better there—and your back will feel better.
- Save some flat rocks to top off the wall.

Constructing the Wall

Dig a trench as wide as your bottom rocks. Make the trench deep enough to set the bottom layer, or course, of rocks about 6 inches below soil level in relatively mild climates, up to 12 inches below soil level where winter freezes are severe. Some experts advise putting several inches of tamped rubble or crushed rock in the bottom of the trench to ensure good drainage.

Before you begin, think about drainage of excess water that might freeze and expand in winter, pushing the wall outward. You can bury one or two drain tiles behind the wall—at the base and about halfway to the top—to carry off water. Or leave weep holes—narrow channels extending through the wall to the outside surface—to direct water runoff. When backfilling, pack the soil just behind the top course of rock to form a small depression, or swale, to direct runoff away from the face of the wall.

Placement of the rocks is important. Tilt the stones so that their inner edges are lower than the exposed edges. The slight slant provides good channels for moisture to reach the plant roots and produces a wall better able to resist the outward pressure of the earth behind it. The wall should recede inward, toward the bank, as it rises. In a wet climate, the wall should slant a good foot for every 5 feet of wall height. Where rain is less frequent, 8 to 10 inches will do.

Now for the nitty-gritty on building your wall.

Slant the rocks as you lay them to channel moisture toward the roots. Make sure the surface of the wall recedes as it rises for structural stability.

1. In the trench, use your largest stones and those that have one flat side and one irregular side. Dig out the subsoil to make room for the rock's irregularities and place the rock with its flat side up.
2. As you build up the rock courses, place the stones flat—the way you'd find them on the ground—not upright or at odd angles.
3. Place your plants as you build the wall. Fit the plants in the spaces between the rocks. It's important for the stability of the wall to have the stones supported by other stones, rather than by a soft bed of soil and plant roots.
4. To make a good bond, always top a joint between rocks with an overlapping rock, to tie the two together. The joint need not always fall in the exact center of the stone above it; a random effect is more pleasing. Just remember the old formula: "One over two, two over one."
5. Place long, large tie or header stones about every third course, setting them back into the bank for structural support. Use one header for every 10 square feet of completed wall.
6. Top the wall with large, flat rocks.

Settling In the Plants

To give them a secure foothold, add your plants as you build the wall. To balance the planting, you can add others after the wall is completed.

1. Spread a ½-inch layer of soil on two rocks.
2. Position your plant with its crown at the edge of the wall face, and spread its roots out on the soil.
3. Sift more soil over the roots and tamp firmly around the plant.
4. Anchor the plant with the next course of rock.

Use a slim trowel or a knife to slide plants into rocky crevices. Fairman Jayne suggests, "There's nothing better than a piece of cardboard. Insert it in the rock cranny, slide the plant into place, and funnel soil in around the roots. I learned the hard way to start planting at the top of the wall, not the bottom. Otherwise, as you pack the soil in, a lot of it falls on the plants below. Don't be too timid in handling the plants—really squeeze them in there. The roots need soil around them." Pack sphagnum moss around the planting to help hold the soil.

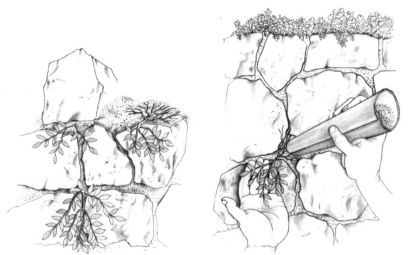

Left: During wall construction, settle plants in spaces between rocks, cover plant roots with soil, and then continue to add the next course of rocks, which helps anchor the plants below them. *Right*: Refine the planting by adding more plants after the wall is built. Wedge each plant into a cranny between rocks and funnel in soil, packing as firmly as possible.

Herbs for Rock Walls

Plants with a neat or graceful growth habit—compact, prostrate, trailing, or softly mounded—are the best candidates for rock wall planting. Stiff, shrubby herbs or those that, like lemon verbena, tend to get leggy fare better in a more conventional planting bed. Santolina, artemisia, and lavender add silvery and gray-green accents. Artemisia 'Silver Mound' (8 inches tall, with compact and soft foliage) would be a better choice for a rock wall than the 18-inch-tall, rampant-growing artemisia 'Silver King' (*Artemisia ludoviciana* var. *albula*).

A rock wall herb garden is the perfect place to show off dwarf and creeping herbs. Any of the dozens of thymes would be perfectly at home. For flowering plants, sweet alyssum (*Lobularia maritima*), candytufts (*Iberis* spp.), coralbells (*Heuchera sanguinea*), catnip (*Nepeta cataria*), and dwarf lavenders are excellent choices.

The plants Fairman Jayne introduces into his rock wall are fairly small but well rooted. A just-stuck cutting with new, skimpy roots wouldn't survive, nor would a bushy, mature specimen whose roots would be crowded and—initially—unable to support its mass of foliage. Roots will eventually find their way, but need time to develop.

Maintaining the Wall Garden

Maintenance of a rock wall planting is a pleasant chore. Usually you don't need garden boots, except when watering—and watering is essential. Using a fine spray, give the herbs a good dousing immediately after planting. If a week goes by without rain, water again. Spray in sweeps, first downward from the top and then upward from below—a good way to knock off insects, too.

Weeding is simple, but it is important to yank out weeds while they're still small. If a strong-rooted weed like amaranth becomes well entrenched, it's best to snip it rather than yank it.

Trim the plants at least once a season to encourage bushier growth. Some herbs can develop unkempt woody sections. To make the plant more attractive, clip these off, or tuck them back into the rock space if they have some green leaves. Replace any plants that fail.

Winterkill threatens any perennial planting, but is often preventable. Rock walls absorb heat, which helps protect plants. In severe climates or with half-hardy plantings, mulch the wall surface with evergreen boughs. In a dry winter with no snow and little rain, water several times.

CHAPTER TWENTY-THREE

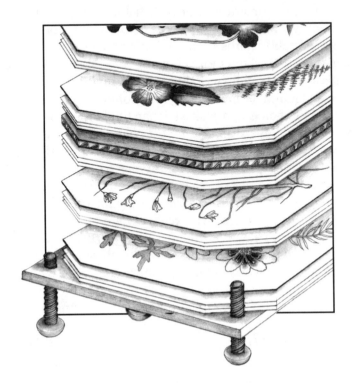

Make a Flower Press

Pressed flowers are a delightful ingredient in many crafts, from decorated notepaper and candles to framed collages. Botanists find the technique indispensable for identifying and studying plants. You don't need to be a professional scientist; amateur botanists can have a lot of fun collecting, pressing, and identifying plants. Many people find their pleasure in the natural world is heightened by learning more about individual plants.

Many of us have found a pretty flower or leaf on a hike, brought it home, and tucked it into a book to keep it. This is the simplest way to press plant materials, and it often works just fine for a few small plants. The average book page is not absorbent enough to do the best possible job of drying a pressed flower, though, and plant materials can stain pages. I've pressed ferns in old telephone books with good results. Space plant material at least eight pages apart in a phone book—otherwise the pages will stay damp too long.

The faster you can dry your flowers, the brighter their colors will be. Applying more pressure helps squeeze out moisture. For better results than book drying, you might try a screw-down flower press.

Flower Press Production

Here are the nuts and bolts for making and using your own flower press. You'll need:

½-inch plywood
sandpaper
blotting paper or newspaper
4 bolts, each at least 3 inches long
4 wing nuts to fit the bolts
paper towels
corrugated cardboard

Got everything? Now you can begin.

1. Cut a piece of ½-inch plywood to any convenient size. A 12-inch square would be large enough for most garden flowers. For ferns, cut a larger, rectangular piece—say, 12 by 16 inches.
2. Cut a second piece of ½-inch plywood to the same dimensions. These will be the covers of your flower press.
3. Smooth the rough edges of the plywood lightly with sandpaper.
4. Drill a hole, at least 1 inch from the edge, in each corner of both plywood covers.
5. Cut several sheets of blotting paper or newspaper to just shy of the dimensions of your covers. (For covers 12 inches square, for example, cut the paper to about 11¾ inches square.) Clip the corners of all sheets at an angle, to clear the bolts that will be inserted later.

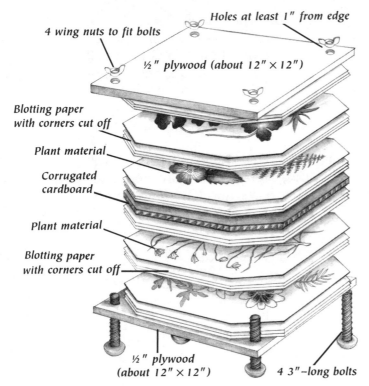

Holes at least 1″ from edge

4 wing nuts to fit bolts

½″ plywood (about 12″ × 12″)

Blotting paper
with corners cut off

Plant material

Corrugated
cardboard

Plant material

Blotting paper
with corners cut off

½″ plywood
(about 12″ × 12″)

4 3″-long bolts

A homemade plant press is a satisfying project, and much better for pressing flowers than an old telephone book. A sheet of corrugated cardboard every few layers improves air circulation and speeds up drying.

6. When you have gathered your plant materials and are ready to press, insert a bolt in each corner of the bottom cover, beginning from the bottom. Place the bottom cover, with bolts sticking upwards, on your work surface.

7. Place a layer of newspaper several sheets thick, or a sheet of blotting paper, on the bottom cover. Carefully arrange several pieces of plant material on the paper. For fastest drying, put a layer of paper towels above and below your plant material. Cover with another layer of newspaper or blotting paper.

8. Build up alternating layers of plant material and absorbent paper. To increase air circulation through the stack and hasten drying, insert a piece of corrugated cardboard about every third layer. End with a layer of absorbent paper.

9. Top the stack with the second piece of plywood, fitting the bolts into the corner holes.

10. Screw the wing nuts partway down on opposite corners, then partly tighten the other two corners. Continue to tighten the wing nuts until they are as tight as you can make them.

11. Keep the flower press in a warm, dry place with good air cir-

144

FOR BEST RESULTS

Dry fast for best color. Follow these tips for the best pressed flowers.

- Pick plant material on a bright sunny day after the dew has dried.
- Newly opened flowers will have better quality when dried.
- Press as soon as possible after picking.
- Arrange plant materials so they're flat and not touching each other. Spread the leaves so they're not wrinkled.
- Keep the plant material in each drying layer approximately the same thickness to ensure good contact between the absorbent paper and all parts of the plant. Otherwise thinner parts may wrinkle and discolor in drying.
- Remove the petals of large flowers such as hydrangeas and peonies and press them individually.
- When drying a layer of bulky flowers, equalize the amount of pressure on them by making collars of blotting paper. Place the collars around each flower before pressing.
- For fastest drying and best preservation, change the sections of absorbent paper every day for the first three days. Then change every other day for about two weeks.
- When you change papers, lift off the drying flowers carefully, without disturbing their positions.
- Dry and reuse blotting paper and paper towels. Replace newspaper with a fresh edition; it tends to crinkle slightly when dampened and dried.

culation—for example, near a heat register or a radiator.

12. Flowers will dry in about two to three weeks. Keep them well covered in a dry place until ready to use.

CHAPTER TWENTY-FOUR

Renew Your Garden with Midsummer Plantings

146

I f you planted a spring vegetable garden, you're probably feasting on beans and lettuce and watching for the first ripe tomato. Enjoy all that fresh produce while you have it, because some of those spring-planted vegetables will soon sputter out. The long, hot days of midsummer send spinach to seed and make lettuce bitter. What then? When spring plantings run their course, you can abandon the rows to weeds—or plan and plant a fall garden.

A few hours spent renewing those gone-to-seed garden rows can earn you a whole new season of good eating. And once you've feasted on your own September corn, October romaine, November escarole, or December spinach, my guess is that you'll want to make time each summer to replant for fall.

A Tasty Bonus—Instead of Weeds

The fall garden is, in many ways, the best half of the vegetable patch's productive year. True, the days are shorter and vegetables don't grow as fast—but they stay crisp and tender longer. Cooler nights help discourage insects. Except in the far North, the fall picking season can last well into December.

Some vegetables, like Chinese cabbage and brussels sprouts, are at their best once nipped by frost. And the whole range of special salad ingredients—from Bibb lettuce to endive to mustard—come into their prime in the sunny days and cool nights of fall. I might spend more time in my vegetable garden in spring, but I harvest more in the fall, thanks to plantings in July and August.

Preparing for Planting

Start by taking inventory. The rows where lettuce and spinach have sent up seed stalks or where weeds are filling in after a harvested radish crop are the ones to replant. Think in terms of individual plants, too: Replace a zucchini that succumbed to the bugs with a neat square of baby beets.

Pull all the spent plants, and toss them on the compost pile. Then dig or till up the ground so it's nice and loose for new plant roots to penetrate. If the soil was well fertilized in spring, you might not need to add plant food now. But for a second sowing of heavy-feeding leafy vegetables, it's a good idea to dig in some compost or water seedlings with diluted fertilizer.

Rotate crops to discourage insect pests and to make use of the soil's mineral resources, since each kind of vegetable removes a different assortment of nutrients from the soil. You probably grow four different types of vegetables: leafy ones (lettuce and cabbage), legumes (peas, beans, and their cousins), root vegetables (beets and carrots), and fruiting plants (tomatoes, eggplants, peppers). Try to keep these different groups hopscotching around the garden.

Seeds and Seedlings Need Special Care

In summer, when the sun's heat is quick to form a surface crust on the soil, water the bottom of each planting furrow before you sow seeds. After you've dropped in the seeds, spread fine, light soil over them to a depth of about three times the diameter of the seed. To further discourage crusting, especially for delicate carrot shoots, sprinkle a scattering of *dry* grass clippings over the row. (Green clippings will mat and suffocate seedlings.) Keep the bed moist until seedlings sprout, then mulch to conserve moisture.

Lettuce and spinach seeds are sometimes reluctant to sprout in hot weather. Outwit their natural dormancy by prechilling the seed packets in the freezer or refrigerator. Then plant as usual. Leave the seeds uncovered; light promotes germination of lettuce seeds in hot weather.

For many summer plantings, I raise seedlings in shallow trays kept on the east side of the house. I especially like to raise transplants of lettuce, broccoli, kale, brussels sprouts, escarole, and cabbage. I plant beans, corn, dill, carrots, and other less easily transplanted crops directly in the garden.

The best weather for transplanting is the kind of day you wouldn't want to go to the beach—damp, drizzly, overcast. If skies are cloudless, do your transplanting in the evening so

148

A July planting of brussels sprouts gives the plants plenty of time to produce a good crop of tender little heads, at their best after a nip of frost.

the plants can recover somewhat from transplant shock before bright sun hits them. Cover the seedlings with berry baskets or other temporary sun shades for a few days until they recover. Water immediately after you transplant, then mulch to conserve moisture and keep the soil cool.

Vegetables for Summer Plantings

When choosing vegetables to grow, remember that plants grow more slowly after Labor Day, when days gradually shorten and nights turn cool. There's plenty of time for most loose-leaf greens and lettuces to develop when planted in July or even August, and spinach can be planted as late as September for late-fall picking. But choose an early cultivar of corn, so the ears have time to develop.

Tips for Success

To make the most of your late-season garden, follow the tips below to help extend the harvest. The dates for latest seed sowing are based on an average first fall frost around mid-October. If the first frost in your area generally strikes earlier or later than this, adjust your planting dates accordingly (your local agricultural extension agent can give you average frost dates for your locality). Days to maturity given in catalogs are averages, based on long summer days; add up to a week to those estimates for fall planting. If you have the space and time, don't be afraid to take a chance on a borderline maturity date. If your crop beats the frost, you've won; if not, you've lost a bit of seed but gained some experience.

Beans. Summer-planted snap or bush beans are usually in production by late September. A nice bonus is the absence of Mexican bean beetles late in the season. Make last planting by mid-July.

Beets. For tiny salad beets to nestle on a bed of your home-grown lettuce, try 'Little Mini Ball', 'Little Egypt', or 'Pacemaker II'. Make last planting by early August.

Broccoli. Broccoli's flavor is improved by cool weather. Plant 'Bonanza', 'Cleopatra', 'Green Comet', 'Packman', or 'Bravo'. Withstands heavy frost. Transplant started seedlings by mid-July.

Brussels sprouts. These tasty little heads perform especially well as a fall crop; a nip of frost improves their flavor. 'Green Marvel' matures fast. Transplant started seedlings by early July.

149

Cabbage. Cabbage loves cool weather and withstands heavy frosts. Try fast-growing 'Golden Cross'. Transplant seedlings by mid-August.

Carrots. Keep the rows moist until sprouts appear, and weed them religiously until the ferny carrot tops grow large. Good general purpose fall cultivars include 'Kuroda Chantenay', 'Little Finger', and 'Short 'n Sweet'. Make last planting by late July.

Cauliflower. Transplant cauliflower carefully so it doesn't wilt—it's more sensitive to insult than most other vegetables. Try 'Snow-mound', 'Snow Crown', or 'Snow King'. Transplant started seedlings by late July.

Chinese cabbage. Spring plantings tend to go to seed by fall; summer-sown plants last and last, and taste better after frost. Plant no earlier than July 15. Choose either the solid, blocky wong bok or the loose-leaf, celery-stalked bok choy type. 'China Pride' is ready in 68 days. Make last planting by August 15.

Corn. For fall eating from summer planting, you'll want a quick-maturing corn like 'Silver Sweet', 'Early Sunglo', 'Earlivee', or 'Seneca', because cool nights in early September slow down the growth of this heat-loving plant. Make last planting by mid-July.

Cucumbers. Cukes grow rapidly in warm summer weather; try 'Patio Pic' and 'Straight Eight'. Make last planting by early July.

Escarole/endive. These cold-hardy greens make fine salads. Tie up the heads as they reach maturity to blanch the hearts. Be sure they're dry, though; if the inner leaves are wet when they're tied, they'll rot. Make last planting by early August.

Kale. Kale has a milder-than-cabbage flavor after frost. You can pick it all winter. 'Vates' is a standard; 'Russian' has red leaves and fine flavor; 'Winterbor' is tall, very productive, and extra hardy. I plant this nutritious green at the edge of the garden so it won't be disturbed if we plow the rest of the patch in the fall. Make last planting by late July.

Lettuce. Sow seeds of leaf and butterhead lettuce every few weeks all summer. Sow fall crops of head lettuce no earlier than late June. Try butterhead cultivars 'Bibb', 'Buttercrunch', 'Red Montpelier'; for overwintering, try 'Winter Density' or 'Kwiek'. Among leaf lettuces, 'Green Ice' is wonderful; or try 'Black-seeded Simpson', 'Oak Leaf', and 'Deer-Tongue'. For color, add 'Ruby' or 'Red Sails'. 'Ithaca' is an excellent head lettuce. Make last planting of head lettuce by August 1; leaf lettuce, September 1.

Mustard greens. 'Tendergreen', 'Green Wave', and Burpee's 'Fordhook Fancy' add zip to the salad bowl. Make last planting by mid-August.

Onions. You'll get plenty of green scallions from onion seed planted in summer. Make last planting by mid-June.

Peas. Some gardeners find that peas planted in midsummer do well once nights turn cool. Peas survive light frost but must be planted in time for pods to develop before weather turns very cold. Try 'Wando', which tolerates both heat and cold. Even if the plants don't produce, they'll make good green manure to turn under as a soil-building crop. Make last planting by mid-July.

Radicchio. Red Italian chicory takes a bit of care to grow but makes a smashing salad. Pick the plants lightly in the fall, toss some mulch over them in December, and watch for the deep red sprouts early in the spring—just when you need them most. Make last planting by early August.

Radishes. Even though they will produce in less than a month from seed, radishes are seldom remembered in fall. I especially like 'French Breakfast', 'Icicle', and 'Cherry Belle'. Make last planting by mid- to late August; for cooking/storing radishes like 'Black Spanish' or 'China Rose', by August 1.

Spinach. Spinach is a garden staple for fall and winter. 'Indian Summer', 'Tyee', and 'Melody' are fine choices. For overwintering spinach you can pick in late fall and again in early spring, try 'Savoy' or 'Winter Bloomsdale'. Make last planting by mid-August.

Tomatoes. Root a sideshoot from an established tomato plant to carry on the harvest until late fall, when earlier plantings are past their prime. Or set out started plants by July 10. At least they'll give you green tomatoes to ripen in the attic.

Turnip. Yes, I know, turnips lack glamour. I thought so, too, until I tried 'Des Vertus Marteau'. It has a sweet flavor and a buttery texture; it's truly a whole different vegetable. According to an old tradition, July 25 is *the* day to plant fall turnips. Later plantings will yield good greens, even if they don't have time to form roots. Make last planting by August 1.

151

Zucchini. I make a second planting of zucchini in mid-July to take over when squash-bug damage cancels out the early crop. These late plants bear by early September and sometimes continue until frost. Make last planting by mid-July.

CHAPTER TWENTY-FIVE

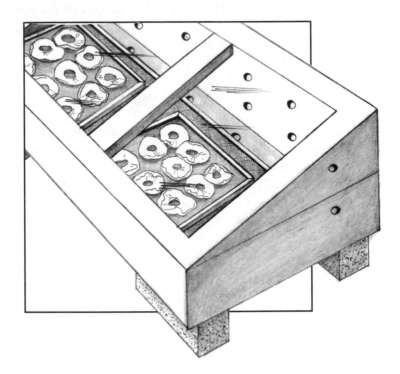

Dry It Now, Enjoy It Later

152

Several years ago, our sheep pasture produced an unusually large crop of meadow mushrooms (*Agaricus campestris*). We picked into 2-quart buckets and filled them day after day, a constant supply of fresh, firm, button mushrooms that lasted for several weeks. We feasted on mushroom omelets, soups, and casseroles, and we gave some away, but still we had a surplus.

So we began to preserve them. First I pickled some mushrooms, then I froze a few batches, and finally I dried all I could manage to slice each day. The pickled mushrooms were delicious, but they lasted only a few days in the refrigerator. The frozen ones got rubbery, and I eventually tossed them out. The dried mushrooms retained their flavor best of all. They're still good four years later!

Slow and Simple

Drying is the oldest method of food preservation, and the simplest. With 80 to 90 percent of its moisture gone, dried food is no longer very attractive to the organisms that cause spoilage. Most molds can't grow at moisture levels below 13 to 16 percent. Bacteria need more than 18 percent, and yeasts more than 20 percent. But unlike canning, which destroys microorganisms, drying only arrests their growth. When moisture levels rise, the spoilers become active again.

You can dry all kinds of garden fruits and vegetables, from beans to squash and apricots to plums. You can even dry strawberries, chard, spinach, and zucchini—that's one way to shrink a glut of prolific summer squash! I can't imagine bothering to dry lettuce, but dried leaves of dark green leafy vegetables like amaranth and beet greens—

153

There's no need to labor over a hot stove in summer. Put the heat of the sun or your attic to work drying foods like mushrooms, apple rings, and hot peppers.

or even nutritious weeds like lamb's quarters—add nutrition and flavor to soup.

Some foods, such as mushrooms, hot peppers, herbs, and dates, seem to be best preserved by drying. Others that you might already can or freeze, like dried corn, apples, and grapes, are tasty alternatives with enjoyable flavors and textures. Carrots and onions are best kept for home use in simple root-cellar or other cold storage. For camping, though, a few bags of these or other home-dried vegetables make a nourishing treat on the trail.

Preparing Foods for Drying

There's no need to amass bushels of produce as you do for canning. Gradually, handfuls of dried produce add up to quarts. Once you get in the habit and have a convenient setup worked out, you can simply chop up that extra cabbage or slice that spare hunk of squash and dry it for the soup jar. Those dried apple slices can be habit-forming, too.

Many foods require pretreatments to preserve quality and flavor. Blanching is one common pretreatment, required for many vegetables. In the sections below, you'll find a crop-by-crop guide to pretreating common fruits and vegetables.

Blanching Methods

Steam blanching is a good way to conserve nutrients. Here's how.

1. Heat 2 inches of water to boiling in a covered kettle.
2. When the water boils, set a basket or colander of cut vegetables in the kettle. Keep the vegetables *above* the water level.
3. Cover the kettle and steam the fruits and vegetables for the amount of time recommended in the following guide.
4. Rinse to cool, drain, and spread out to dry.

Water blanching takes less time than steam, but nutrients are lost in the process. Follow these steps.

1. Bring a kettle of water to boiling.
2. Put cut-up vegetables in a cheesecloth bag or wire basket for easy retrieval. Cover completely with water.
3. Drain and rinse to cool. Spread the vegetables out to dry.

Preparing Fruits for Drying

Most fruits don't need blanching before drying because the acids they contain help to prevent loss of quality from enzyme action in storage. To decrease darkening of fruits like apples that tend to turn brown when cut, dip the slices in an ascorbic-acid solution (available in canning-supply sections of food markets). Sulfur is sometimes used to treat fruits to preserve their color and their content of vitamins A and C. Sulfur destroys thiamine, though, and the treatment takes time and trouble. I prefer to dry without it.

Apples. Cut pieces about ⅛ inch thick, either crosswise or lengthwise. It's not necessary to peel them, but you may wish to if you intend to use the slices for pies. Steam blanch for 5 minutes or treat with ascorbic-acid dip.

Apricots. Cut in half and remove pits. Do not peel. Slice, if desired. Steam blanch for 5 minutes. Ascorbic-acid treatment may be used to help preserve color, although it is not a substitute for blanching.

Bananas. Slice; dip in lemon juice or ascorbic-acid solution.

Dates. Wipe off fruits, but do not wash. Pit and slice or dice. (When dried, warm in 150°F oven for 30 minutes to kill insects.)

Figs. Dry only ripe fruit. Small figs may be dried whole; cut larger ones in half. Blanch whole figs in boiling water for 15 to 45 seconds to crack skins.

Grapes. Wash and pick over to cull imperfect fruit. Leave on stem. Blanch in boiling water for 15 to 30 seconds to crack skins, or dry without pretreatment.

Nectarines, peaches. Peel; slice or halve. Pit. Dip in ascorbic-acid solution.

Pears. Peel; halve or slice, and core.

Persimmons. Peel large persimmons. Small varieties may be dried without peeling. Halve and pit.

Plums. Halve, pit, and blanch larger plums for 1 to 2 minutes in boiling water. Leave small fruits whole. Use ascorbic-acid treatment for cut fruit.

Preparing Vegetables for Drying

Vegetables require a bit more preparation before drying than fruits, because enzymes they contain tend to cause changes in color, flavor, and vitamin content.

Food-processing authorities recommend blanching vegetables that will be stored for more than half a year to inactivate enzymes that cause deterioration in storage. But blanching can be a nuisance, and many gardeners skip this recommendation and settle for an easier-to-produce, if less highly flavored and nutritious, product.

155

Beans, green. Wash, cut in lengthwise or crosswise pieces. Blanch for 2 minutes in water, 2½ minutes in steam.

Beets. Wash, cook, peel, and slice roots. Cut into ⅛-inch-thick slices.

Broccoli. Wash, slice stalks. Blanch 2 minutes in water, 3½ minutes in steam.

Brussels sprouts. Wash, halve; blanch 5 minutes in water, 6 to 7 minutes in steam.

Cabbage. Remove wrapper leaves. Shred coarsely. Blanch 3 minutes in steam, 2 minutes in water.

Carrots. Wash, peel, slice ⅛ inch thick. Blanch in water 3 minutes, in steam for 4 minutes.

Corn. Blanch ears 4 minutes in water. Cut off kernels.

Eggplant. Wash, peel, slice ⅛ to ¼ inch thick. Blanch 3 minutes in water, 3½ minutes in steam.

Greens (spinach, kale, chard). Wash; blanch 1½ minutes in water, 2 minutes in steam.

Herbs. Wash; shake off excess moisture.

Mushrooms. Wipe clean with damp cloth. Stalks tend to be tough when dried; caps are the choicest part. Slice caps ⅛ to ¼ inch thick. Peel large caps.

Onions. Remove dry outer skin. Slice crosswise ⅛ to ¼ inch thick. Cut off root ends.

Peas. Shell peas and blanch 2 minutes in water, 3 minutes in steam.

Peppers, bell. Wash and remove stems and seeds. Cut into ¼-inch thick rings or slices.

Peppers, hot. Wash; thread small chili peppers, whole, on string.

Potatoes, sweet. Wash. Steam blanch whole about 30 minutes. Peel and slice ⅛ to ¼ thick.

Potatoes, white. Wash, remove skins. Slice ⅛ to ¼ inch thick. Steam blanch slices for 4 minutes; water blanch for 3 minutes.

Squash, summer. Wash, peel if skin is tough, slice ⅛ to ¼ inch thick. Experts recommend steam blanching for 3 minutes, but many gardeners skip this step.

Squash, winter. Cut squash open and divide into sections sized for ease of handling. Peel and remove seeds and pulp. Cut flesh in slices ⅛ to ¼ inch thick, or shred for drying.

Tomatoes. Remove skins by steaming or dipping in boiling water. Slice. Experts recommend blanching slices 3 minutes in steam, 1 minute in boiling water, but many gardeners dry tomatoes without blanching.

EASY VEGETABLE TREATS— WITHOUT BLANCHING

- Dip tomato slices into a solution of 1 quart water, the juice of one lemon, and 1 tablespoon of honey. They'll keep their color and lots of flavor.
- Frozen zucchini usually tastes bland, but drying concentrates the flesh for a nutty flavor and crunch. Dried cucumbers are good, too, although they're too small for dips. They have a somewhat saltier flavor.
- My favorite dried-vegetable product is tomato leather. I whir fresh tomatoes in the blender, and cook them in a roasting pan set on my wood cookstove until they are as thick as ketchup. Then I spread the resulting tomato pulp ¼-inch thick on a cookie tin lined with plastic food wrap. I return the tomato-pasted tin to the warm regions above the huffing-hot stove until the leather peels easily from the clear food wrap and looks and feels, well, leathery. It is good eaten plain or torn into bits and stirred into your favorite campfire hot dish.

Drying Methods and Equipment

The most basic way to dry food is exposure to the sun, but direct drying in sunlight is practical only in areas where the air is relatively dry and the daytime temperature is hot. Use wire racks, screens, or wire-mesh trays, and protect drying food from contamination by insects and animals with cheesecloth or screening. Under ideal conditions, fruits and vegetables dry in two to three days outdoors. Slow sun drying—for a week or so—fades food color and destroys vitamins. In most cases, sun-dried foods are started in the sun but finished under partial shade.

In most eastern states, the air is too humid to permit effective sun drying, but if you're determined to try it, try spreading your produce on a flat roof where it will receive reflected heat. Bring the food inside if night temperatures drop more than 20°F, or if it rains.

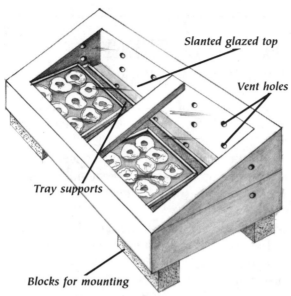

Slanted glazed top

Vent holes

Tray supports

Blocks for mounting

At first glance, a solar food drier looks something like a cold frame. The glazed top keeps things clean and insect-free inside. Trays in the frame support drying apple slices or other goodies.

Solar Food Driers

A solar food drier is another, more effective, way to use the sun's energy. Mount a box with a slanted, glazed top—like a cold frame—on blocks. Cut vent holes in the bottom, sides, and back of the box to admit air, and provide supports for trays inside the box so that air can circulate around them.

The state-of-the-art solar food drier is probably the barrel dehydrator designed by Leandre Poisson, who offers plans by mail. (See Resources beginning on page 337.) Most foods dry in two to three days in his Solar Survival Dehydrator. The drier consists of a steel barrel painted black on the outside and silver on the inside, surrounded by an arch of Kalwall Sunlite glazing, and mounted on a plywood base. Natural convection draws heated air over food-filled trays inside the barrel. Drier temperatures average 115°F on a sunny day. The design provides for a three-lightbulb back-up system for use in cloudy weather.

Dry with Heat

I've dried hot peppers and plenty of herbs by spreading them on screened trays in a hot attic. Herbs also may be hung in loose bunches. Attic drying takes one to two weeks.

Most of my drying has been done on, in, or over a woodstove. I happen to have a wood cookstove, the only source of heat that our small solar house needs during the cool months, but a heating stove works just as well. We spread apples and mushrooms on racks made

TIPS FOR SUCCESSFUL DRYING

No matter what method you choose for drying your produce, keep in mind the following general guidelines, which apply to any drying techniques you might use.

- Dry only *good* produce. Discard any fruits or vegetables that are overripe, bruised, or moldy.
- For quicker drying, cut food into pieces as small as you can conveniently manage.
- Make the pieces as uniform as possible so they'll dry at the same rate.
- Use screens or racks made of untreated nonresinous wood, nylon, cotton, or stainless steel. Avoid galvanized metal, aluminum, copper, or used refrigerator shelves, which may react with food acids to produce unwholesome compounds. Beware of vinyl screening; not all vinyls are food-safe.
- Spread the pieces on the drying screen or tray, separating them so that they don't touch. As the pieces shrink, you can move them closer together.
- Keep the drying temperature high enough to discourage spoilage organisms, but don't let the food cook or scorch. Leave the door ajar if you are drying foods in an oven.
- Keep the air moving through the drying food to carry off moisture. Good air circulation is as important as heat in the drying process.
- If you have several trays on a rack, rotate their positions for more uniform drying.
- Don't interrupt the drying process. Rapid, steady loss of moisture is the key to good dried food. If the food is removed from the drying chamber before drying is complete, it may still retain enough moisture to encourage the growth of molds and may spoil even if later returned to the dehydrator for a second drying period. Discard any moldy foods, because molds can produce harmful toxins.

159

of stainless-steel mesh, suspended from the ceiling above the stove. A friend of mine dries food *under* her woodstove. Be careful not to leave any wood, string, or other flammable material within scorching distance of the stove.

In the summer, when it's too hot to light the cookstove, I have used stainless steel wire-mesh racks in my convection oven, an effective food drier because it has a fan to circulate air. Use the lowest temperature setting, and keep the oven door cracked open about an inch the first couple of hours so moisture can escape.

A metal drying tray mounted over a water reservoir, like the old-fashioned Bumble Bee drier, makes good use of a woodstove surface and dries vegetables in a few hours. An opening in the reservoir permits filling with water and escape of steam. Such a drier may also be heated on a gas or electric range. Unfortunately, the sensible Bumble Bee is no longer manufactured. Look for one at country auctions, or persuade a local welder to make one for you (using stainless-steel joint solder for extra-strong joints). Or improvise with a cookie sheet set over a steel lasagna pan. Be sure to keep water in the reservoir, or the food may burn.

Electric Driers

Commercially produced electric driers range from small counter-top models to large cabinets. Check to be sure that the drier's heating element is well enclosed to prevent fire. Electric driers should have thermostats. Insulation, easy-to-clean cabinets, and strong food racks are other qualities to look for. Depending on the kind of food, and the amount and size of pieces, drying will take 5 to 20 hours in an electric dehydrator.

When Is Dried Food Dry?

It's impossible to predict exact drying times for fruits and vegetables because humidity, moisture, and air circulation vary considerably, and all of those factors determine drying speed. The size and moisture content of food pieces influences drying time, too. In general, fruits take the longest time to dry. Tomato slices dry more slowly than most other vegetables. Zucchini, cucumbers, and other sliced vegetables dry fairly fast.

Properly dried fruits have a somewhat pliable, leathery texture, but we've dried delicious batches of thin-sliced apples that were almost as crisp as potato chips. They lost their crispness after several months

160

in storage. Vegetables should be brittle; herb leaves and leafy greens should crumble readily.

Storage and Use

Food-science experts recommend conditioning dried food before you store it, to distribute moisture more evenly. Conditioning is a simple process: Keep the dried food in a clean, open container, in a dry place where it will be safe from animals and insects, for a period of several days (up to a week for large batches). Stir daily so unequally dried pieces will be well mixed with the others. Heat sun-dried food in a 150°F oven for 30 minutes to kill insect eggs before putting it in storage.

Dried foods are easy to store. Scoop them into clean jars or cans with tight-fitting lids, and keep in a cool, dry, dark place. Food-grade plastic bags with a locking seal work well for small quantities of foods and for herbs. Dried food is spacesaving, too. A bushel of bell peppers fills 16 to 18 quarts if canned, and 12 quarts frozen, but only 1 quart dried.

To rehydrate dried vegetables, pour boiling water over them and cook until tender. Presoak dried root vegetables, beans, and peas for an hour or more before cooking. Soak fruits in water to cover for several hours and then gently steam. If you intend to sweeten the food before serving it, wait to add the sweetener until after cooking is complete. Sweetening dried fruit before cooking can toughen it.

CHAPTER TWENTY-SIX

Brew Your Own Teas

There's nothing like a steaming mug of hot herb tea after a chilling session of raking leaves, planting bulbs, or hiking in a raw November wind. Blending the tea yourself makes it taste even better, and growing the plants doubles your satisfaction in drinking and serving. Dozens of wild and cultivated plants are used to brew tea—some for medicinal uses, some purely for pleasure. I'm sure tea contributes some nutrients to our meals, but we drink it

MAKING A PERFECT CUP OF TEA

For tasty tea, follow these tips.

- Start with a glass, ceramic, or enameled teapot. Acids in plant material may react with aluminum or other metals.
- Use freshly drawn water; stale water has less oxygen and experts insist it makes a flat tea.
- Figure on ¼ cup of chopped, fresh leaves to each cup of water. Dried tea is more potent; 1 tablespoon of dried, crumbled leaves per cup of water is a good proportion. Dried berries such as elderberries pack even more flavor: Use only a teaspoon or 2 per cup of water. Tea making is not an exact science. Teas will vary in strength depending when, where, and how they were picked, dried, and stored.
- Brewing tea by the potful? Add an extra tablespoon of dried tea (or 2 tablespoons of fresh) "for the pot."
- For iced tea, make a double-strength batch.
- Steep coarse leaves like borage directly in the pot. We use a tea ball for finer teas.
- For the most delicate flavor, pour boiling water over the tea and let steep for 5 minutes. Boiling the tea can cause bitterness, especially in chamomile tea.
- Perk up mild-flavored teas like rose hip or comfrey with lemon and honey.
- Use woven-grass tea strainers, available in kitchen specialty shops, to filter out stray leaves and flowers when pouring the tea into the cups.
- Here's where the wood cookstove shines: While the tea steeps gently, we keep it warm on a trivet. Heat from the woods, tea from the garden. The shivering gardener is grateful for blessings such as these.

mainly because we enjoy it, and because we like being able to turn to the garden to put tea on our table, too.

The suggestions in this chapter are just the beginning of all the good teas that you can make. Herb teas taste good. They are an inclusive beverage: Children can drink them along with their parents. Most herb teas we make cost us nothing, other than the initial investment in plants or seeds. We have a wide choice of flavors to suit our individual tastes and the whim of the moment.

Pick Your Favorite

A tea made with a single herb is simple and satisfying, and it's a good way to learn the subtle fragrances and flavors that make one tea different from another. But when you're ready to get creative, try your hand at blending your own tea mixtures. Start small, with a pinch of this and a snip of that. When you hit on a tasty combination, write down the ingredients immediately.

Choose from these edible plants, both wild and cultivated, for concocting your teas and tea blends. There are no rules. Experiment with whatever combinations appeal to you.

Leaves. Basil, bee balm, blackberry, borage, costmary, horehound, lemon balm, lemon grass, lemon verbena, marjoram, mints, mullein, nettle, New Jersey tea (*Ceanothus americanus*), parsley, raspberry, rose geranium, rosemary, sage, strawberry, sweet goldenrod (*Solidago odora*), thyme, wintergreen.

Homemade teas taste extra special. Hang bunches of bee balm, mint, chamomile, and other herbs from a wooden rack to dry leaves and flowers. Dry elderberries and rose hips on a screen tray.

PICKING AND DRYING HERB TEAS

Stock up on dried herbs for your tea recipes by following these steps.

1. Harvest on a dry, sunny day, in late morning, when aromatic oils are at their highest concentration.
2. Pick leaves before the flower buds open; flowers when fully developed, but before they begin to fade.
3. Dry all tea materials in a hot, shady spot with good air circulation. Keep them in the dark; sunlight robs herbs of color and flavor.
4. Spread berries, large quantities of leaves, and fleshy-stemmed leaves on a large, flat surface. Stainless-steel or fiberglass screens are ideal because they allow excellent air circulation. Avoid galvanized surfaces, which could release toxic substances when in contact with plant acids. We use clean pieces of corrugated cardboard, cut from extra-large cartons, to dry elderberries and bushy herbs.
5. Hang herbs and other tea plants to dry in bundles of about one to two dozen stems, fastened together with a rubber band. (Stems shrink as they dry; string would need retying, but a rubber band will stay snug.) Keep bunches small. Hang them where the air can reach them.
6. Leaves and flowers are ready for packaging when they're dry enough to crumble when rubbed between the fingers. Package berries when they are shriveled and hard enough to resist thumbnail denting. To package, lightly press the dried material into jars or cans, then label them and seal tightly.
7. Store containers of tea in a cool, dry place.

Flowers. Borage, calendula, feverfew, hibiscus, jasmine, red clover, rose.
Seeds. Anise, caraway, fennel, star anise.
Fruit. Elderberry, rose hips.
Roots. Comfrey, ginseng.

Tasteful Blends

Try these tea blends—our family's favorites—or use the recipes as inspiration for your own creations. For all recipes, steep the ingredients for 5 minutes in 1½ cups of boiling water. Yields enough tea for one good-sized mug or two teacups.

Lemon Delight
1 tablespoon dried or 2 tablespoons fresh chopped lemon grass
1 star anise
Fragrant Refresher
1 teaspoon dried or 1 tablespoon fresh chamomile flowers
3 to 4 sprigs lemon balm
Pinch of fennel seed
Anytime Tea
1 tablespoon dried rose hips
1 tablespoon dried spearmint leaves
Hot Fruity Punch
1 tablespoon dried elderberries
1 tablespoon dried rose hips
1 tablespoon dried lemon verbena leaves
Breath of Summer
2 borage leaves
3 to 4 lemon verbena leaves
8 to 10 rose petals

Tea Plants for Your Garden

Many of the best tea plants can be homegrown right in your garden. And, even better news, the selections here are enthusiastic growers. They'll thrive with an occasional shearing to give you plenty of material for tea making.

166

Bee Balms (*Monarda* spp.)
The leaves of bee balm make a pungent, refreshing tea. *M. didyma*, the red-flowered species, has a finer flavor than wild bergamot (*M. fistulosa*), the coarser, lavender-flowered species. Hummingbirds love the flowers. Both spread rapidly.
Growth habit: Perennial; 2 to 3 feet tall.

Where to grow:	Full sun to part shade. Tolerates a wide range of soils and growing conditions. Hardy to Zone 4.
How to start:	Beg a division from a friend, or buy plants from a nursery. Stem cuttings will root easily, or start from seed.
Spacing:	Space plants 18 inches apart. Start seeds in nursery bed and transplant 18 inches apart.
Growing tips:	Pinch shoot tips to encourage bushy growth. Occasionally affected by mildew, a fungal disease that causes gray, shriveled leaves. Don't use diseased leaves for tea. To help prevent fungus, be sure plants have good air circulation.
Harvest:	Collect a few leaves from each plant before the flower buds open. Or, cut plant to the ground once or twice a year for a large harvest of leaves.

Chamomile (*Chamaemelum nobile; Matricaria recutita*)

Picking chamomile blossoms requires some patience, but it can be a restful task. Just sit next to the plants with a picking basket and snap off the little white daisies with yellow centers using your thumb. Its mild flavor goes with all kinds of foods. However, if you are sensitive to ragweed, chrysanthemums, or other daisy-family members, be cautious about drinking chamomile tea. Chamomile flowers, and hence the tea, contain pollen that may cause allergic reactions.

Growth habit:	*Matricaria recutita:* annual; 12 inches tall. *Chamaemelum nobile:* perennial; 6 inches tall.
Where to grow:	Full sun; well-drained, ordinary to poor soil. *C. nobile* is hardy to Zone 3.
How to start:	Start seeds for *M. recutita* in spring, indoors or in a cold frame, for bloom the same year. Start seeds of *C. nobile* for bloom the following year, or buy plants. Seedlings are fine and feathery; keep them well weeded. Once established, *M. recutita* self-sows readily.
Spacing:	Space plants 10 to 12 inches apart.
Growing tips:	Pick flowers regularly to encourage more blooms.
Harvest:	Before flowers begin to fade.

167

Elderberries (*Sambucus* spp.)

Elderberry tea, sweetened with honey, tastes like a hot fruit punch. The unsweetened brew is dark and rich enough to substitute for coffee. Although raw berries aren't what you'd call delicious, cooked and sweetened, or dried and brewed as tea, they are as rich and flavorful as they are nourishing. According to the USDA's *Composition of Foods, Handbook No. 8* (1975), 1 pound of elderberries contains 2,560 international units of vitamin A, 154 milligrams of vitamin C, 0.30 milligrams of thiamine, 0.27 milligrams of riboflavin, and 2.3 milligrams of niacin.

Forage for wild elderberries in damp places—along culverts, along bordering swamps and rivers, along railroad tracks. Early summer is a good time to spot them, when the creamy white, flat umbels of flowers (a bit like oversized Queen-Anne's-lace) are in bloom. The berries are ready to pick by late August in our area. Break off the whole cluster of berries and leave on the stem until they're dry.

Cultivated forms are larger than the wild ones, but have less flavor. 'Adams' and 'Johns' are two reliable cultivars. When elderberry bushes are happy where they are, in a moist spot with generous applications of fertilizer, they grow very fast.

Growth habit: Tall shrub; 6 to 10 feet.
Where to grow: Full sun to shade; moist or wet soil. Hardy to Zone 4.
How to start: Buy nursery stock. Or sow seeds from wild plants.
Spacing: Space bushes 6 feet apart.
Growing tips: Keep your eye on ripening berries or use netting to protect them from birds.
Harvest: Pick in clusters when berries are purple-black.

Lemon Balm (*Melissa officinalis*)

Lemon balm is a most obliging plant that is less invasive than mint, but milder in flavor and less aromatic when dried. Pick leafy sprigs and use them to brew a fresh pot of tea. I don't usually dry lemon balm leaves because other lemon-flavored herbs (especially lemon verbena) retain more aroma when dried. Honeybees like lemon balm blossoms.

Growth habit: Perennial; 2 feet tall.
Where to grow: Full sun; well-drained, ordinary to poor soil. Hardy to Zone 4.

How to start:	Start from seed, cuttings, or by division. Or purchase plants.
Spacing:	Space plants 2 to 3 feet apart.
Growing tips:	Lemon balm thrives with regular shearing.
Harvest:	Anytime.

Lemon Verbena (*Aloysia triphylla*)

Lemon verbena really has a marvelous aroma of lemons, and makes a delicious brew by itself or mixed with another less interesting tea. The plant is a perennial in its native Chile, but it is frost-tender, and must be overwintered indoors. It doesn't need a warm room—just protection from freezing. We usually keep ours in the cool green-house, but a cool porch or spare room also make good wintering spots. Plants brought indoors have an alarming habit of shedding their leaves, but with weekly watering and plenty of light, plants will send out fragrant, tender shoots in several weeks. Most people who grow lemon verbena enjoy its aromatic leaves so much that they don't mind taking the trouble to keep it over winter, even though it isn't the most handsome houseplant. Just brushing a leaf with your fingers releases that clean, refreshing lemon fragrance.

Growth habit:	Tender perennial; shrubby; can be trained as standard. Reaches 10 to 15 feet in warm climates.
Where to grow:	Full sun; well-drained, light soil, not too acid. Hardy to Zone 9.
How to start:	Buy plants or root cuttings from new growth. Start cuttings in fall, and overwinter indoors for next year's planting.
Spacing:	If you plan to keep the verbena well cut back, space plants about 10 to 12 inches apart.
Growing tips:	Cut back overwintered plants by about one-half when you set them out again after the weather warms.
Harvest:	Summer.

Linden (*Tilia* spp.)

Linden tea is a haunting, perfumy beverage that most people enjoy at first sip. In Europe, especially in France, the gathering of linden blossoms for a spring beverage called tisane is a yearly ritual carried out with the kind of overtones that only long dependence on the land can impart. Brew up a pot of fresh tea and dry the remaining blossoms. The flowers contain vitamin C and carotene.

American linden (*T. americana*) grows wild by the roadsides in some eastern and midwestern states. It is also grown as a street or shade tree. Once you've encountered the linden in bloom, you'll know it from a good distance the next time. It bears clusters of pale, white to yellow, waxy flowers and will most likely be humming with bees. The flowers of European lindens (*T. cordata, T. × europaea,* and *T. platyphyllos*) are more fragrant and flavorful than those of the American species.

Growth habit:	Tall trees, to 100 feet.
Where to grow:	Moist or well-drained, fertile soil. *T. americana* is hardy to Zone 3; European species to Zone 4.
How to start:	Buy nursery stock. Or forage from wild trees.
Spacing:	Give it plenty of room.
Growing tips:	Mulch the tree well; it does not stand drought. It will take a few years to bear the first blossoms.
Harvest:	Pick just-opened or full-blown flowers on a clear, dry day.

Mints (*Mentha* spp.)

Mint is an old dooryard favorite that grows almost everywhere. A square stem is the characteristic sign of the aromatic mint family. Mint has the virture of blending well with other teas and giving flavor to leafy brews like comfrey that don't have much flavor of their own. Three of the most common mints are apple mint (*M. × rotundifolia*), with woolly, rounded leaves; spearmint (*M. spicata*), with pointed, almost hairless leaves; and peppermint (*M. × piperita*), with its familiar, pungent scent. We also like orange mint (*M. × piperita* var. *citrata*), a rather sprawling plant with a delightful orangey aroma. Mint leaves make an excellent, full-flavored tea either fresh or dried.

Having assumed mints were practically indestructible, I was puzzled when a thick clump of apple mint by our back doorstep petered out. Enlightenment came when I read mint will die out if given a heavy dose of wood ashes, which is just what I'd given it, in a misguided burst of generosity. It's taken several seasons, transplanting of the bed, and begging new starts from friends, to build up my mint patch again. In some areas, mints are susceptible to rust, a fungal disease that speckles leaves with orange spots. It can't be cured. If it strikes your mint, start a new bed in a different area, using clean plants.

170

Growth habit:	Perennial; 1 to 2 feet tall.
Where to grow:	Full sun to light shade; tolerates a wide range of growing conditions. Hardy to Zone 5.
How to start:	Beg a division from a friend, root cuttings, or buy plants. Plants started from seed may not come true to flavor.
Spacing:	Space plants and cuttings 1 foot apart. They will soon spread and fill in.
Growing tips:	Keep mints confined by planting in a sunken, bottomless, metal bucket with the rim extending an inch or two above ground. Mints benefit from frequent shearing.
Harvest:	Anytime. Cut plants back to 2 to 3 inches when they're 10 to 12 inches tall, just before the blossoms open. Expect three to four cuttings each summer.

Roses (*Rosa* spp.)

Rose hip tea is winter vitamin insurance. Hips of any rose are good to use for tea, as long as the plant has not been subjected to noxious sprays. Dry the vitamin C-rich hips on screens for use as a nourishing cold weather tea. I've read that rose hips taste like apples, but to me, plain rose hip tea doesn't have much flavor. It is mild and blends well with a stronger-flavored tea like mint or elderberry.

Look for rose hips—the red, ripe seedpod of the rosebush—in your flower garden, hedgerow, or in the wild. Single-flowered roses are likely to produce more hips, because they're easier for bees to pollinate than double blossoms. Vitamin C content varies somewhat with variety, but all are worth using. If you want to plant roses especially for the harvest of hips, choose *R. rugosa*, a hardy bush with somewhat wrinkled leaves and single white or rose flowers. Some old farms have hedge plantings of *R. multiflora*. These have smaller hips, but when they are plentiful you can gather many in a short time.

Growth habit:	Shrubs.
Where to grow:	Sun; well-drained, fertile soil. *R. rugosa* is hardy to Zone 2.
How to start:	Purchase nursery stock. Or forage from wild plants.
Spacing:	Depends on cultivar.
Growing tips:	Increase *R. rugosa* by dividing an established clump or planting seeds from the rose hips.
Harvest:	When hips are ripe, in late summer to autumn.

PART THREE

*S*ing a song of seasons!
Something bright in all:
Flowers in the Summer,
Fires in the Fall.

—*Robert Louis Stevenson*
(1850–1894)

AUTUMN

CHAPTER TWENTY-SEVEN

Discover Goldenrod

In the fullness of midsummer, the golden plumes of goldenrod announce that fall is on its way. I usually notice goldenrod in August, about the time the barn swallows leave. As summer cycles into September and October, the fields are colored by great sweeps of these feathery golden blooms. They evoke all our various feelings about fall—a delight in ripeness and in sunny, cool days, a tinge of regret that another summer is passing, and a touch of resolve as we prepare for a winter now only hinted at, but certain to come.

175

Goldenrods of All Descriptions

Any schoolchild can identify a roadside goldenrod, but even the best botanist sometimes has trouble distinguishing among the approximately 130 species of the genus *Solidago* native to North America. The individual florets are small, and their subtle differences are not apparent without magnification. In addition, many species are highly variable. To compound the confusion, many goldenrod species hybridize naturally, giving rise to intermediate forms that defy classification. But while individual differences are often subtle, the range within the genus is wide, from the Northeast's alpine goldenrod, *Solidago cutleri*, which is scarcely a foot tall, to *S. fistulosa*, found from New Jersey to Florida, which can top 6 feet.

Goldenrods belong to the daisy family Compositae. The tiny, daisylike flower heads consist of ray florets, which resemble petals, surrounding tiny disk florets, which make up the center of the bloom. Except for the white-flowered silverrod, all species of goldenrod have gold or yellow blossoms, and, except for a few with biennial tendencies, all are hardy perennials. They bloom from midsummer until frost. Most golden-

176

Even experts have trouble sorting out some goldenrods, but these are easy to find. Gray goldenrod (*Solidago nemoralis*), *top left,* common in fields, has dense golden tufts. Seaside goldenrod (*S. sempervirens*), *top right,* has showy flowers and succulent leaves. Grass-leaved goldenrod (*S. graminifolia*), *bottom left,* is bushy, with flat-topped flowers. Silverrod (*S. bicolor*), *bottom right,* is the only white-flowered goldenrod.

rods are sun lovers, but a few prefer open shade, and there are dry-land, moist-land, and even seaside species.

Underappreciated and Wrongly Maligned

If goldenrods were rare plants, we would surely be more appreciative of their rich color and graceful shape. In Europe, where only a species or two is native, breeders have developed a whole range of goldenrod hybrids that are sold as cut flowers and displayed in bouquets. Several cultivars of both European and American species are available from nurseries.

A clump of goldenrod in an informal perennial bed complements groups of asters and chrysanthemums. When grown in good soil, with less competition, even the coarser species tend to produce stronger stems and larger flower heads. Goldenrods are also an easy-to-grow choice to naturalize a meadow or a strip of ground by an old stone wall. Seaside goldenrod can serve two purposes on a beach property: It softens the landscape, and it prevents dune erosion by holding the sand with its roots.

Because goldenrod blooms during hay fever season, its pollen has been blamed for this allergic response. But goldenrod is pollinated by insects. The pollen is too heavy to become airborne and almost certainly not responsible for hay fever. Rather, it is the light, wind-borne pollen of the inconspicuous green flowers of the ragweeds that is so irritating to hay-fever sufferers.

Dried goldenrod flower heads make a useful addition to "everlasting" wreaths and bouquets. Leaves of the sweet goldenrod, *Solidago odora*, may be used to brew tea. The botanical name *Solidago* is derived from Latin words meaning "to make whole," a reference to its use as a healing plant. According to Maud Grieve's *Modern Herbal* (1931), infusions of the leaves were used to treat urinary ailments, including kidney stones, and as a diuretic, an astringent, and a treatment for hemorrhage.

Growing Tips

Goldenrods do best in poor soil and full sun. Most are hardy to Zone 4. The plants are easy to grow from seed, which is offered by wildflower specialists and general mail-order seed companies. Nurseries carry named cultivars of goldenrod, including some dwarf selections.

Some goldenrod species have rhizomatous roots, with swollen protuberances on the fibrous roots, much like those of a daylily. Others arise from crowns of fibrous roots. For fibrous-rooted species, place the crown level with the soil surface and prune off any extra-long roots. Allow 2 feet between plants; they will fill in. Keep well watered until new growth begins. Rhizomatous species can have invasive tendencies when roots spread into surrounding soil. To prevent plants from running wild, plant in a bottomless gallon can or bucket buried in the ground to its rim.

Goldenrods for the Wild Garden

You could spend a lifetime learning all our native species of goldenrod. The following are common native species, relatively easy to distinguish, and good candidates for garden cultivation. Time of flowering varies; you may find a species in bloom anytime during the suggested period.

Canada goldenrod (*Solidago canadensis*). This is one of the species you're most likely to see by the wayside. Blooms are true gold, in terminal plumes; leaves are quite narrow and sharply toothed. The 3- to 5-foot stem tends to be smooth toward the base and rather downy toward the tip. A highly variable species, found in fields, often on dry soil. Blooms August to October.

Grass-leaved goldenrod (*S. graminifolia*). A rather bushy, 1- to 5-foot-tall plant, much branched toward the top, with flat-topped flower clusters at the stem tips. Leaves are very narrow, lance-shaped, and often ribbed. This plant is found in rich, damp ground, often in thickets. Blooms August to early October.

Gray goldenrod (*S. nemoralis*). Densely tufted panicles of yellow flower heads on the upper sides of the branches arching from gray-green, 1- to 3-foot stems make this an attractive species. Lower leaves are wider than the narrow, pointed upper leaves. Found in fallow fields and other open places, usually on dry soil. Blooms August to October.

Hard-leaved goldenrod (*S. rigida*). Sturdy, 3- to 4-foot stems, covered with fine hairs, support large flat-topped clusters of golden yellow flower heads. Most leaves are in the basal clump; those on the upper stalk clasp the stem and are usually toothless. Rough, thick leaves have finely branching veins. Also called stiff or prairie goldenrod, it grows in dry, sandy places. Blooms August to October.

Seaside goldenrod (*S. sempervirens*). This attractive, 1- to 8-foot-tall species is highly variable in size and shape, but appreciated for its color and ability to stabilize windswept sand dunes. Leaves somewhat succulent. Found in salt marshes and near ocean beaches. Blooms September to October.

Silverrod (*S. bicolor*). Our only white goldenrod; 1 to 4 feet tall. Three to 12 white rays surround pale yellow disk florets, thus the white or cream appearance. Leaves are rather hairy with finely branched veins. The stem is often covered with fine white hairs. Blooms appear at the leaf axils and the tip of the stalk. Silverrod grows on dry ground, in meadows, or in open woods. Sometimes biennial. Blooms July to October.

Tall goldenrod (*S. altissima*). A common species, 3 to 6½ feet tall. Pyramids of golden yellow flowers, the individual flower heads lining up on the upper side of the arched branches. Stems have a downy, gray surface. A dry-soil plant of roadsides and open fields. Blooms August to November.

Wreath goldenrod (*S. caesia*). Sometimes called blue-stemmed goldenrod; flexible, bluish purple, 1- to 3- foot-tall stem tends to bend over, often arching into a partial wreath shape. The light golden yellow flowers appear in clusters at leaf axils along the whole length of the stem, not just at the top. Leaves taper to sharp points and often have sharply toothed edges. Found in woods. Blooms August to October.

CHAPTER TWENTY-EIGHT

Save Your Own Vegetable Seeds

On the National Public Radio program "All Things Considered," commentator Susan Stamberg once asked for nominations of things that function admirably, things that work. Listeners had a lot of fun with that one, contributing such diverse suggestions as pipe cleaners, Timex watches, and congressional investigations. I nominated the garden seed.

Seeds *work*. They work so reliably that we tend to forget how amazing they are, how varied, how complex, how practical.

Saving garden seeds is an adventure that can continue for years, lead to a study of botany, lure you into plant breeding and hybridizing, and engender new friendships with other gardeners. Careful seed saving combined with periodic replanting to renew the seed stock is also the only way to perpetuate local favorites or heirloom cultivars no longer offered by commercial seed houses. There's even the possibility, remote but nonetheless real, of discovering a new or different plant after years of observation and seed selection. At the very least, you'll have fresh, free seed for next year's planting.

Just Waiting to Grow

Remember the garden seeds you've planted in the past? They came in more different sizes and shapes than you could have imagined: little flecks of lettuce seed, flakes of peppers, tiny pellets of cabbage, black specks of chives, and wrinkled dry peas. No matter how tiny, wispy, wizened, or flat they may appear, all seeds have one thing in common: Each contains an embryonic plant capable of producing a plant, another generation of seed, then more plants, and more seeds in turn.

The seed you hold in your hand is not waiting for a chance to live. It *is* alive. Seeds may appear dry and lifeless, but the spark of continuity between generations lives in a compact embryo, folded in plant "fetal position" and enclosed in an often tiny case. While in storage, in fact, these deceptively passive-looking seeds carry on respiration: They take in oxygen and give off carbon dioxide.

Inside each seed lives a minuscule potential plant—complete with a rudimentary root tip, leaf bud, leaves, and a tiny stem, all protected by a seed coat designed to keep it alive through cold and drought. Stored inside the embryonic plant is the vital genetic information that will direct its growth and development, plus the color, taste, and appearance of the mature plant.

181

What Seeds to Save

Gardeners often begin saving seed solely as a matter of economy. Many soon progress to improving their homegrown strains of vegetables by selection, saving seeds each year from the most outstanding plants. Selection can help you develop a strain of vegetable particularly well suited to your climate and soil. By carefully selecting

for qualities that are important to you, you can gradually improve the size, flavor, earliness, keeping quality, yield, disease resistance, or insect resistance of the crop.

For your first efforts in seed saving, stick to the annual and perennial vegetables. Annuals, such as lettuce and tomatoes, are plants that form seeds the same season they're planted. Perennials, such as asparagus, bear seeds yearly once they reach maturity. Save the biennial

Heirloom cultivars or nonhybrid family favorites can be perpetuated by the simple act of saving seeds. Scoop melon seeds from the ripe fruit, then wash and drain on paper towels.

vegetables, which must overwinter to bear seed the year after planting, until you've had a year's experience collecting seeds from the easier kinds.

Don't bother saving seed from hybrids unless you're just curious to see what happens. Hybrid plants are highly inbred, and their seed, when it isn't sterile, produces plants that are almost always inferior to the parent plants. (When you buy seed, you can recognize hybrids because the package will say "hybrid" or "F1.")

Pollination Patterns

The flowers and fruits *we* consider primary crops are, for the plant, only a means to an end. Flowers exist to perpetuate the plant. Fruits grow from pollinated flowers to bear seed. In order for a plant to produce seed, the plant's flower must be fertilized, or pollinated.

Self-pollinated plants—those plants whose flowers can fertilize themselves with their own pollen—are your best bet for your early seed-saving trials. Self-pollinated plants almost always produce seed

SAVING BIENNIAL SEEDS

Biennial vegetables bear flowers and seeds the second year of growth. Biennial crops include most of the root crops, such as parsnips, turnips, beets, carrots, and rutabagas, and the cabbage family crops, including kale, broccoli, cabbage, brussels sprouts, and collards. In order to save seed from these crops, plants must be dug up, stored in sand or sawdust over the winter, and replanted in the garden in the spring. (Parsnips and salsify will overwinter in the ground with protective mulch in most areas of the United States; in gardens where temperatures seldom drop below 0°F, carrots may also live over winter.)

Here are the details on how to collect seed from biennial crops.

1. Dig several well-developed, table-ready roots—the kind you'd want to serve for dinner. Avoid the immature, half-grown ones and the old, woody specimens. Clip the leafy tops off, leaving a 1-inch stub.
2. Place the roots in a suitably deep container, such as a plastic dishpan. Cover them completely with sawdust or sand.
3. Store the roots over winter in a cool basement or shed. A temperature of 33° to 40°F is ideal. (They may not all make it through the winter.)
4. In early spring, select the roots in best condition and plant them out as soon as the soil can be worked. Space them at least twice as far apart as they would be planted for vegetable production.
5. The flowering stalk grows as spring advances. Stake if necessary to keep it upright. Seed of most biennials is ripe for harvesting in early to midsummer.

183

that will come true, meaning plants grown from this seed will resemble the parents. (I say almost always because there is a small margin of error in which random crossing by insects may occur.) Here are some good self-pollinating garden crops to start with: beans (all kinds—dry, lima, snap, or soy), endive, escarole, lettuce, peas, peppers (these may be pollinated by insects if different pepper cultivars are closer than 50 feet), and tomatoes.

Traveling Bee Feet

Seeds from insect-pollinated plants may come true if the insects haven't visited other plants of different cultivars or closely related species. For example, if you've planted only one cultivar of pumpkin, and there are no others growing in a nearby yard, it's unlikely insects would transfer pollen of a different cultivar to your plants. Seed saved from your pumpkins would most likely come true.

But crossings between cultivars of related, insect-pollinated plants frequently take place, especially if the plants are less than 200 feet apart. Melons cross readily with melons, squash with squash, and cucumbers with cucumbers. If your pickling cucumbers grow in the bed beside your slicing cukes, honeybees can easily transfer pollen between them. Seed saved from that cross will yield a combination of the qualities of both parents: sometimes a welcome surprise, sometimes an unremarkable crop.

For best seed-saving results, keep cultivars of insect-pollinated crops far apart in the garden. The results may not be as predictable as saving seeds from self-pollinated plants, but they're still worth a try. Insect-pollinated crops include asparagus, broccoli, brussels sprouts, cabbage, carrot, collards, cucumber, eggplant, kale, melons, onion, parsley, parsnip, pumpkin, radish, rutabaga, squash, and turnip.

Blown on the Wind

Wind-pollinated plants like spinach, beets, and Swiss chard can cross-pollinate over distances of up to a mile! (Corn is also wind-pollinated, but since the pollen is heavy, it doesn't travel as far. For most home garden purposes, 200 feet between different cultivars of corn will assure acceptable purity. To avoid even a small percentage of crossing, make that 1,000 feet or plant early and late cultivars, which usually don't shed pollen at the same time.) Beets can cross-pollinate with chard, sugar beets, and other garden beets. Since there's no way of knowing where the pollen came from, the results of seeds saved from spinach and beets might not be what you expect.

Be Selective

To obtain seed from the very best plants, observe the plants throughout the season, and make notes to help you remember. Consider the whole plant—its vigor, yield, and disease resistance. Don't make the mistake of saving seed from a single huge tomato growing on a weak or sickly plant. Your seed selection program is more likely to be furthered by choosing a fruit that is one of many fine ones—even if they're slightly smaller—on an outstandingly healthy vine.

Early bearing, particularly in corn, tomatoes, and peppers, is often a desirable trait to encourage. However, the first fruit to develop must be left on the plant to form ripe seed—so you have to forgo eating that first red tomato if you want to collect seeds selected for early bearing. Choose parent plants that are slow to go to seed for leafy crops, such as lettuce, escarole, spinach, and corn salad.

Collecting and Storing Seed

When you've decided which plant or fruit you want to save, tie a tag or strip of colored cloth to it, or drive in a stake, to designate the plant as one that should not be harvested. This is especially important if more than one family member routinely picks vegetables. If you've had problems with raccoons eating your corn, choose a corn plant in the center of the patch, rather than at the edge, to save for seed.

Allow the fruit to remain on the plant until the seed is fully mature. Here are some hints to help you judge readiness: Collect seeds of squash, pumpkins, cantaloupes and other melons when the fruit is ripe. Save seed from red, ripe bell peppers, not green ones. Allow tomatoes, cucumbers, and eggplants to turn overripe. Pick them when they're just "over the hill"—too ripe for ideal eating, but not rotten. (Seed I've saved from tomatoes sliced when they were just right to eat has germinated well, too.) Harvest zucchini and other summer squash after they've formed a hard shell, with coarse, tough flesh and well-developed seeds. Seeds of lettuce, carrot, cabbage, onion, and other vegetables fall soon after they are ripe and dry. Gather the seeds promptly before they scatter. Lettuce seed is ready soon after the yellow flower changes to a ball of fluffy down.

Air-dry your seeds—even those that seem dry when you pluck them from the plant—on trays or several layers of newspapers for a week or two in a shaded, well-ventilated place. Seeds that don't separate readily from the plant may need a little extra preparation before air-drying. Try these tricks: Open seedpods or rub seed heads to free seeds. Separate pepper seed from the pith. Scoop squash, pumpkin, and melon seeds from the fruit; wash, and drain on paper towels. Remove small amounts of bean seed from the pods by hand. Thresh larger harvests by beating the beans with a stick or plastic baseball

TOMATO-SEED BREW

Fermenting your tomatoes for a few days kills the organisms that cause bacterial canker, a seed-borne disease. Squash the tomato in a glass. Add ¼ cup of water and set the brew where you will see and remember to check on it. Stir the tomato/water mixture once a day for three to four days. It will begin to bubble on the second or third day, depending on the room temperature. On the fourth or fifth day, spoon or pour off the pulp and lifeless floating seeds that have risen to the top. Strain, rinse, and air-dry the heavier, viable seeds that have settled to the bottom.

bat. Winnow them by pouring from one container to another in a stiff breeze that will blow away the chaff.

Moisture and heat are the two enemies of seed viability. Keep the seeds dry until you're ready to put them away. Seal the dried seeds in small bottles, cans, or film containers, or in sealed envelopes kept inside a large can with a lid. Label each container as you fill it. Then keep the packaged seeds in a cool, dry place, ideally between 32° and 41°F. At planting time, don't put seed packets on wet ground or leave them out in the hot sun. If leftover seeds exhaust their stored resources before they're planted, they might not have enough energy left to sprout.

The various species of plants differ in the longevity of their seeds. Parsnip and onion seeds are notoriously short-lived. Pumpkin seed, on the other hand, will often sprout after spending many years in storage. If storage conditions are favorable, seeds of any species or cultivar are more likely to retain their full genetic viability, and in some cases exceed that expectation.

CHAPTER TWENTY-NINE

Harvest Flowers for Drying

187

We all know that fragrances help us recall memories, whole scenes from our past. I think plants can do that, too. When I see Chinese lanterns, I'm four years old again, in the living room of my grandmother's Philadephia house, the sun streaming through the bevelled, oval door glass, making rainbows on the rug, my grandmother whistling a nameless tune under her breath as she stirs the gravy, essence of roast beef wafting from the kitchen, and a bunch of papery, deep orange, dried lanterns glowing there in a vase on the sideboard, as always.

Even a few dried flowers in a simple vase will keep living color in the house over winter. More elaborate arrangements can set the tone and color scheme for a whole room, and they make elegant gifts. Dried flowers look lovely when woven into wreaths, too. A friend of mine who makes garlic braids tucks strawflowers and other everlastings in as she plaits the tops, and sells all she can make. Some everlastings are tough enough for childrens' crafts. My three-year-old grandson was delighted with the gift of an oatmeal box full

What could be simpler? Arrange stems of orange Chinese lanterns (*Physalis alkekengi*) in an empty container; your bouquet will dry in place and last for years.

of strawflower heads for his collages. (Everlasting is a relative term, of course. Some dried flowers and pods will stay in good condition for many years. Others are best renewed every year or two; often, their colors fade.)

Simple Air-Drying

The easiest flowers to dry are the papery-stiff ones we call everlastings, and the simplest way to prepare them is air-drying. Several other flowers, such as larkspur, salvia, goldenrod, and others, while not as naturally dry as everlastings, also air-dry well. Air-drying is as simple as it sounds: Pick, bunch, and hang to dry. Most flowers and foliage air-dry in three to five weeks. How can you tell whether they're dry enough? Just bend a stem—it will break when well dried.

Collecting and Preparing Flowers

A little forethought can make your flower drying easier and give you better results. Choose a dry, sunny day—late morning if possible—just after the dew has evaporated. In most cases, it's best to pick before the flowers are fully open. They'll usually open more as they dry. Don't collect flowers that are diseased, damaged by insects, or past their prime. Strip the leaves from the stems as you gather, so they don't interfere with air circulation during drying. Flowers retain their color and shape better if the drying process is started as soon as possible after picking. They're less likely to rot if dried quickly.

Which End Is Up?

Choose a dark, warm, dry place with good ventilation for air-drying flowers. An attic, utility closet, or closed shed will do. People who dry flowers for sale sometimes use a small fan to improve air circulation, but for most of us that's not necessary. It *is* important to keep the drying flowers in a dark place. They lose more color if dried in the light.

Hang drying—head down—works well for most flowers. As you bundle stems for hang drying, keep the bunches small—ideally only six to eight flowers, certainly no more than a dozen in each bunch. Arrange them so that the heads don't crowd each other. Rubber bands work well to keep bundles of flower stems together because their elasticity allows them to contract as the stems shrink. String-tied bunches will probably need retying as the stems dry. Hang the bunches about 1 foot apart. If you have many bunches to dry, string clothesline or wires across the drying room, or suspend wire fencing from ceiling hooks. Use a short piece of string or a wire hook to hang each bundle of flowers.

In some cases, it's preferable to dry material head up. Chinese lanterns, for instance, must be dried right side up so that the pods hang naturally from the stems. Grasses also look best when dried head up. To do this, fit a cap of chicken wire over the open end of a large can or other container, and poke the flower stems through the wire mesh. A few kinds of dried material, such as hydrangea and bells-of-Ireland, dry best when started head up in a jar containing about 1 inch of water. Don't replace the water when it evaporates; leave the flowers, a few in each can, to dry right there.

Wiring

Flowers that have weak stems, such as strawflowers, must be wired with floral wire *before* drying. Wire gauge #22 or #23 is a good all-purpose size. Heavier gauge #20 or #21 may be needed for heavier flowers. For sturdy stems, follow these steps.

1. Cut off the stems, leaving a ¼- to ½-inch stub extending from the flower head.
2. Insert a 6- to 8-inch-long piece of wire in the stem, up to but not through the flower. As the stem dries, it will shrink and grip the wire.
3. Stick the wires into a block of Styrofoam, or put them in a large empty can topped with wire mesh for support.
4. Later, for arrangements, wrap green or brown floral tape around the wire. Or dry stems separately, and insert the wire from the flower into the stem.

Flowers for Air-Drying

Here are some good flowers to start your drying experiments. All will air-dry well and can be bundled and hung to dry unless otherwise noted. If you pick a selection from this group, you'll have plenty of color and texture for a good bouquet or wreath. But remember, half the fun of drying flowers is experimenting. If your favorite's not on this list, give it a try anyway.

Annuals

Bells-of-Ireland (*Moluccella laevis*). Stand stems upright in an inch of water; hang upside down after the water evaporates.

Celosia or cockscomb (*Celosia cristata*). Pick flower heads just short of full bloom; don't remove the leaves. Stand stems upright in an empty container, leaving plenty of space between stalks, until the juicy stems dry. Then hang to dry.

Globe amaranth (*Gomphrena globosa*). Gather for drying when the flower heads are plump. If heads have elongated slightly, they'll fall apart when dried.

Helipterum (*Helipterum roseum*). Pick the flowers while still in bud, otherwise they'll go seedy in the center.

Larkspurs (*Consolida* spp.). Pick when flowers are half-open and half-in-bud.

Love-in-a-mist (*Nigella damascena*). Grown for its interesting seedpods. Pick pods when they start to open at the top.

Queen-Anne's-lace (*Daucus carota* var. *carota*). Cut the flowers when just fully open; dry face-up, with stems poking through a screen suspended between shelves, blooms resting on screen.

Statice (*Limonium sinuatum*). Cut statice when the majority of the florets are open or nearly open.

Strawflower (*Helichrysum bracteatum*). Pick when only two or three rows of outer petals have spread open, otherwise when dried they'll have a fuzzy center, less color, and a blowsy appearance.

Perennials

Artemisias (*Artemisia* spp.). Dried for the silvery or gray-green foliage, which can be picked anytime.

Baby's-breath (*Gypsophila paniculata*). Cut stems while flowers are still in bud. Stems are brittle when dried; rehydrate them slightly in a damp room so they won't snap when you arrange them.

Chinese lantern (*Physalis alkekengi*). Cut stalks when lanterns color up; remove the leaves. Dry upright.

Onions (*Allium* spp.). Pick chive or onion blossoms before all the individual florets have opened. Dry stems upright to retain their globular shape by standing them in a container with an inch of water until the water evaporates and the blossoms are dry.

Delphiniums (*Delphinium* spp.). Pick when flowers are half-open and half-in-bud.

Goldenrods (*Solidago* spp.). Cut when about one-third of the flowers are open and two-thirds still in bud.

Honesty (*Lunaria annua*). When the flat, round, satiny pods start to dry, cut stalks and hang in small bunches. When well dried, peel off the outer membrane on either side of the satiny white "silver dollar."

Lamb's-ears (*Stachys byzantina*). Both flower stalks and fuzzy, silver leaves are used. Spread leaves flat on newspaper or on racks to dry; hang flower stems in loose bunches.

Pearly everlasting (*Anaphalis margaritacea*). Pick stems before the flowers are fully open.

ARRANGING DRIED FLOWERS

Arranging dried flowers takes more thought than putting together a bouquet of fresh-cut blooms. Since the dried blossoms are often fragile or brittle, think about the arrangement before you put it together—you can't push or pull dried flowers into place. The creative part is up to you. These tips will make it easier.

- If your material is too stiff and brittle to work with, put the flowers in a damp room for a few hours, or leave them outdoors overnight to make more pliable.
- Use wire to extend stems that are too short. Wind it around the existing stem; tape with floral tape.
- To help position flowers in an arrangement, fill the container with sand or dry floral foam cut to fit the container opening. Or use crumpled chicken wire in the bottom of the container as a "frog" to keep the flowers in position.

For an unusual wall arrangement, try a weaving made with dried herbs and dried flowers. Wrap an empty picture frame vertically with twine (natural-colored jute is a good choice). Then weave plant stems in horizontally. (Or make it the other way around, if you prefer.) Add flowers as you go, if their stems are long or wired, or dot the finished weaving with blossoms attached by floral picks or glue.

Tansy (*Tanacetum vulgare*). Pick stalks of flowers when they're all gold; if they've begin turning brown, it's too late.

Yarrows (*Achillea* spp.). Gather stalks with open flowers, and leave the foliage on. If picked before the flowers are fully open, they'll shrink too much in drying. Hang to dry, or stand in 1 inch of water for a week or so after the water evaporates.

Microwave Drying

You can process only a few flowers at a time in the microwave, and you must watch the time closely, but your dried flowers will be ready almost instantly and the colors keep well. Since microwave ovens vary in power, microwave drying requires some experimenting. If your plant material looks beige and cooked, it is. Try a new batch.

To dry flat, thin-petaled blossoms, ferns, or other foliage, simply fold a paper towel in half and place your material inside without overlapping. Place in the oven. (Don't wire your flowers—metals are unsafe in the oven.) If you want your material to dry flat, set a flat-bottomed, microwave-safe dish on top. For thicker flowers, or those with more petals, use a microwave-safe dish, such as a glass casserole dish. Place a paper towel in the container, arrange the blossoms on the towel so they are close but not touching, and carefully place a second paper towel over the flowers. Don't cover the container. Use a layer of borax or sand in the container, if you wish, to prop and support flowers so the petals don't droop.

Set a cup of water in the back of the oven, so the flowers won't dry out too much. Use a high setting on the microwave oven. Try 1 to 2 minutes for most small blossoms. After microwaving, let the flowers cool before you handle them. A cooling period of 10 minutes is adequate for thin-petaled single blossoms, like pansies and violets. Thick flowers, such as peonies, need up to 36 minutes of cooling.

Drying with Desiccants

Desiccants are substances capable of absorbing relatively large amounts of water. Silica gel, a common desiccant in dry, granular form, works fastest—it will dry most flowers in five to ten days. Much depends on variables such as humidity, temperature, and volume of flowers in relation to the amount of packing material in the container. Widely available under such brand names as Flower-Dri, silica gel is expensive but effective. Soft-petaled flowers dried in silica gel retain more color and better shape than those hung to air-dry. And, with silica gel, you can dry flowers like roses, daffodils, and tulips that don't air-dry well. Silica gel can be reused repeatedly. Just heat it in a 250°F oven or dry it in a microwave. Colored granules in the gel are a moisture-indicating feature that will help you know when it's ready. Pink gel is full of moisture; blue gel is dry and ready to use.

It *is* possible to overdry flowers in silica gel, so you'll need to check on them as they dry. In damp air, flowers that have been dried in silica gel may rehydrate to some extent and become limp more readily than air-dried flowers. Still, the process is worth trying if you want a supply of highly colored, dried flowers in great variety.

Use an airtight container for silica gel drying. Cookie or fruitcake tins, or covered plastic boxes, are ideal. Cover the bottom of the container with ½ to 1 inch of silica gel. Arrange the flowers for drying. Blossoms should not touch each other or the sides of the container. Cover flowers with another ½- to 1-inch layer of silica gel. Add more layers of flowers and gel if your container is deep enough. Cover the container with a tight-fitting lid (or tape the edges of a less snugly fitting cover). Check small flowers or those with a single layer of petals in a couple of days; check larger blossoms with more petals in about a week. Properly dried flowers are crisp, like paper, but not so brittle that they shatter easily. Test one flower before removing the rest.

Now comes the fun! Carefully pour off the desiccant to expose the dried flowers. Never pull them out; they're too delicate for that, and they're likely to break apart. Use a small paintbrush to gently brush off any desiccant that sticks to the flowers, or blow on them with a rubber infant aspirator.

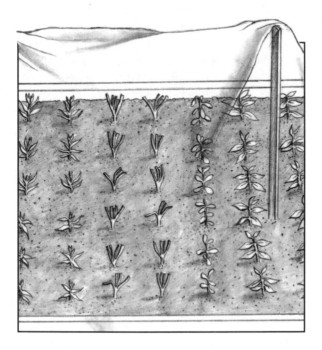

Root Some Cuttings

A single forsythia bush can foster a whole row of bright golden spring bloom—from simple stem cuttings. Plant stems have such an awesome eagerness to grow that many of them quickly form roots and grow into new plants when cut from the parent plant. Most of us have at least a few plants around our home places that can be increased by rooting cuttings. Many shrubs, vines, herbs, perennials, and annuals can be increased by rooting cuttings. Some plants, however, like mountain ash, can be virtually impossible to root from cuttings, and others, including aza-leas and blueberries, are difficult. I've started grapevines, pussy wil-lows, rosemary, lemon verbena, bee balm, mints, elderberries, and other plants from cuttings. In some cases, I've wanted extra plants to give to friends; often, I just want to add to my own stock.

You might also root cuttings to increase stock of a rare plant, obtain a start of a favorite shrub when moving a long distance, or propagate a plant that doesn't produce viable seed. Another very practical use for this skill is to root cuttings of favorite flowering annual plants, like petunias, dahlias, snapdragons, marigolds, portulaca, and others, either to carry over winter or to increase plantings in the current season. Or perhaps you need a lot of little herb plants for the next Friends of the Library plant sale.

Casual Cuttings

My aunt was able to bring a start of an heirloom rosebush to her suburban backyard by rooting a cutting from the old rose. She would simply poke the cutting (usually a branch pulled from the main stem with a bit of "heel"—a shred of the main stalk—attached) into the soft soil under a shrub in her backyard flower bed, pop a quart jar over it, and come back a month or two later to pot up her new, rooted rose plant.

Even easier is the homey old method of putting a few cuttings into a handy jar by the kitchen sink. Impatiens, philodendrons, gerani-ums, mints, and softwood forsythia cuttings, among others, will often root this way. In one test, cuttings kept in brown or green glass con-tainers rooted more quickly than those in clear glass. Pot up the cut-tings as soon as you see roots have formed.

Some agreeable plants sprout roots if you simply stick a stem cut-ting directly in the ground. Bury at least one of the leaf nodes along the stem. Such casual treatment will work for easy-to-root plants such as roses, willows, poplars, chrysanthemums, tomatoes, and petunias.

Taking Cuttings

Let's consider some general directions for sticking cuttings, as the process is called by those who do a lot of it. A careful approach to taking cuttings from the parent plant will help to increase your chances of success.

ROOTING IN AN OASIS

Oasis, that green floral arranger's foam, works especially well with stiffer-stemmed cuttings, which can easily be inserted into the block of foam. Just poke the cuttings in about 2 inches deep. Then put the piece of Oasis in a pan with ½ to 1 inch of water. Keep a small reservoir of water in the pan so that the Oasis can absorb it and stay constantly moist. When roots form on the cuttings, break up the Oasis, separate the cuttings, and plant them, leaving fragments of foam attached to the new roots. Thicker-rooted plants like forsythia will often pull free of the Oasis if you remove them before the roots get tangled.

Sharpen your knife before taking cuttings; a keen blade does less damage to plant tissues. Keep all your cutting and rooting equipment as clean as possible to reduce the possibility of fungal infestation. Early morning is a good time to take cuttings. In dry weather, water the parent plant a few hours before taking cuttings so the tissues will be well supplied with water.

Cuttings taken from the lower parts of the plant, closer to the roots, tend to root more easily than those from stem tips. Young shoots root more readily than old ones. To obtain a lot of young shoots for rooting next year, prune the plant heavily so that it will produce an abundance of new growth.

Use only healthy branches from disease-free plants. Choose slender branches about ¼ inch in diameter. Make cuttings on the short side. Most experts recommend a length of 3 to 4 inches for cuttings you plan to stick immediately. Flowering stems won't root as readily as those that haven't bloomed. It's all right to use a branch with a flower bud on it, but remove the bud so it doesn't sap energy that could go into making roots. When taking cuttings from the center of a branch, use a diagonal cut for the lower part and a straight cut for the upper part so you won't try to root the wrong end. The plant knows the difference.

Keep the cuttings from wilting. Protect them from sun and heat. Put cuttings into the rooting medium as soon as possible.

Softwood or Hardwood?

The cuttings you take in fall are treated differently than those you may do next spring. Here's how to handle the different kinds of cuttings you might make.

Softwood Cuttings

Softwood cuttings are taken from new green growth in late spring and early summer. With a few exceptions, they are the easiest of all to root. Root 3- to 4-inch cuttings directly in your choice of rooting medium. Some softwood cuttings, like forsythia, rambling roses, and willows, will even root in water. Keep the water at a temperature of about 70°F. Stir it every few days to incorporate some air (remove the cuttings briefly from the water so they won't be bruised), but don't change the water.

Cuttings from geraniums, impatiens and other houseplants are soft and exude sap when cut. To reduce chances of stem rot, set these cuttings aside in a dry, shady place for a few hours so the cuts can seal over before you put them in the rooting medium.

Semi-Hardwood Cuttings

These cuttings are taken in mid- to late summer, when the new growth is partly mature. Plants that root well when cuttings are stuck at this time include flowering currant, deutzia, weigela, forsythia, broadleaf evergreens, and some dogwoods. Most plants are just not as interested in rooting in midsummer as they are in spring. An application of rooting hormone powder can speed things along.

Hardwood Cuttings

Hardwood cuttings are taken from mature, woody stems. As the plant starts to enter its dormant period, a month or so before frost, its energies are focused on living over winter, not on making new growth. Make your hardwood cuttings in late fall or even early winter, taking dormant stems from the previous season's new growth—the youngest woody material on the plant. Store hardwood cuttings in a cold place over winter. In storage, they'll develop callus tissue on the cut end from which roots will emerge when the cuttings are "stuck" in spring.

Cut hardwood stems 7 to 10 inches long. Make the bottom cut just below a leaf node and the top cut just above a node. Cover the cuttings with a damp cloth or newspaper as you make them, to keep them from drying out. For easy identification, cut all twigs from a certain kind of plant the same length. Tie cuttings of each kind of plant together in separate bundles. Since hardwood cuttings are often leafless, it's especially important to keep track of which end is up; cut the lower stem diagonally and use a straight-across cut to the top. Bundle the cuttings with the tops pointing all in the same direction.

Cover the bundles of cuttings with a loose, sterile packing medium; a half-and-half mix of perlite and sand, or vermiculite and peat moss, works well. Keep the packing material moist, but not sopping wet. Store the dormant cuttings over winter in a spot that's cold but not freezing—a root cellar, cold porch, or old refrigerator. Then plant in spring.

The list of plants that will root well from stored hardwood cuttings is long. Try your hand at some of these: abelia, bittersweet, boxwood, cotoneaster, crape myrtle, currants, forsythia, grapes, hibiscus, honey locust, honeysuckle, hydrangea, mock orange, pear, plum, poplars, privet, roses, spirea, viburnums, wisteria; many narrow-leaved evergreens such as arborvitae and hemlocks; and many vines.

Sticking the Cuttings

Cleanliness and moisture are the keys to success, regardless of the type of cutting you've taken. Sterilize the soil mix to kill disease organisms that can attack your cuttings. And remember to keep the cuttings moist—not sopping—at all times.

Use a fairly deep container—at least 3 inches—so that moisture can wick up from the bottom. In shallow containers, the rooting medium tends to be either too dry or too soggy. A 3- to 4-inch-diameter pot is big enough to hold several cuttings. You can also root cuttings in an old aquarium or dishpan.

No matter when you made your cuttings, or from which stage of growth, the basic procedures for planting and care are the same. Increase your chances of success with semi-hardwood or hardwood cuttings by applying rooting hormone. Dip the bottom 2 inches of the cutting in water, then dip the end of the cutting into the powder. Rooting compounds such as Rootone, Hormex, and Jiffy Grow are available from garden centers and mail-order catalogs. *199*

These steps will get your nursery off to a good start.

1. Prepare the rooting mix of your choice. I prefer a mix of equal parts perlite and vermiculite. Moisten until it is well soaked but not soggy.

2. Strip off all the leaves that will be below soil level and remove any flower buds.
3. Use an old pencil or a dowel rod to make a hole in the rooting medium for soft-stemmed cuttings and for those to which you've applied rooting hormone powder (so the powder won't be brushed off on its way in).
4. Insert the cutting into the rooting medium to a depth of 1½ to 2 inches.

Caring for the Cuttings

Cuttings take best when you keep the root end warm and the leaf end cool. Root zone temperatures between 75° and 85°F encourage rooting. A heating cable or mat will warm the root zone. Cool air reduces the rate of metabolism in the leaves, so keep your cuttings at an air temperature of about 70°F.

To keep the top part of the cutting from drying out, pull a clear plastic bag over the cutting. Poke a couple of sticks into the pot to support the plastic bag so it doesn't drape directly on the plant and cut off all air circulation. Remove the bag from time to time to allow

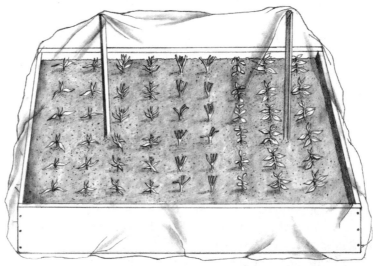

Start your own nursery in a container of moist sand. Insert softwood cuttings of forsythia, lemon verbena, weigela, willow, or other easy-to-root plants. Cover with plastic to provide humidity. Move to individual pots when new growth shows that the cuttings have rooted.

air to enter and help prevent fungal diseases. People who go into rooting cuttings in a big way—either as a hobby or a business—often invest in a special misting apparatus, available from greenhouse supply catalogs, to provide vital moisture without cutting off air circulation. You can improvise a mister using a discarded humidifier (*not* a hot-water vaporizer) on a timer.

Keep the newly planted cuttings where they will receive some light, to stimulate the production of rooting hormones. Indirect light is fine. You can also enhance rooting by applying water in which willow cuttings have been soaked. The willow contains compounds that promote rooting. And some hard-to-root houseplant cuttings have, reportedly, rooted more readily in water when cuttings of episcias (*Episcia* spp.) or wandering Jews (*Tradescantia* spp.) were inserted in the container with them.

Regardless of where your cuttings are put to root—in water, special rooting medium, or open ground—remove any that die, to prevent diseases from spreading among the remaining cuttings.

Signs of Success

It is easy to see the roots on cuttings kept in water, and well-developed roots will be visible on cuttings stuck in floral foam, too. Often you'll notice new leaf buds, another sign that the cutting has taken hold. To check for roots on cuttings in soil mix, pull gently on the cutting. It will slip out of the rooting medium easily if it lacks roots, but will resist, at least a bit, if roots have anchored it in place.

Pot up the rooted cuttings individually in potting soil. Water well. Gradually expose them to drier air and increasingly direct sun (unless they are shade lovers). Feed them regularly, weekly for the first few weeks, then monthly. Withhold fertilizer after July for plants that will remain outdoors. You don't want to encourage sappy new growth that would be likely to winter-kill.

Then, in a year or two, step back and enjoy the sight of a whole garden (or windowsill) full of plants that wouldn't be there if you hadn't taken cuttings and helped them on their way. Before long, you can even take cuttings from some of these plants—a doubly satisfying project!

CHAPTER THIRTY-ONE

Brush Up on Broom Corn

202

Take another look at your kitchen broom. The corn broom is an elegantly simple tool. No plastic imitation-straw or sponge broom can match it for springiness or versatility. "Like cork," wrote the editors of *The American Agriculturist* in 1908, "broom corn is one of those natural products that are so perfectly adapted for the uses to which they are put that no substitute has been, or is likely to be, found for it."

Equally appropriate for sweeping kitchen floors and patios, barns and marble steps, the broom is also a particularly effective cleaner for braided rugs. The broom as we know it has, in most western countries, largely superseded the more ancient besom made of twigs lashed to a stick. Early brooms were round like the besom, though, with the broom straw tied on in a circular arrangement around a central stick. The first known flat brooms, like those we use today, were made by the Shakers.

Broom corn (*Sorghum bicolor*, Technicum group) is a highly specialized member of the large and varied sorghum genus, not a true corn at all. (Sweet corn is a member of the genus *Zea*.) It is grown for the whisk or brush, the stem that branches into a panicle of long, stiff straws, which bear flowers and then seeds on their finely branching tips.

IDENTIFYING GOOD BRUSH

High-quality brush is long, green, springy, straight, and free from kinks. Good fibers appear almost round when seen in cross-section. Brush with fine fibers near the tips is valuable because it will sweep even fine material thoroughly. Stemmy brush, in which the brush fibers branch off from the stem at several places rather than at a single joint, is considered poor quality because much of the head must be wasted and it takes considerable labor to make it useful. If you're raising broom material on a small scale, especially if you intend to make your own brooms, such commercial considerations are less important. You can use some stemmy brush for the inside layers of your broom.

Green brush is desirable because such fibers are flexible and resilient. I grew broom corn for a number of years, though, before I found out that green-colored brush was supposed to be the ideal, and I've been quite well satisfied with all the brooms I've had that were made of the more mature tan brush. It is true, though, that the drier, mature brush is somewhat more brittle and probably less durable.

Grow Your Own Broom

Like sweet corn, broom corn should be planted when soil temperature has warmed to about 60°F. Germination is slow and less complete in cooler soil, and seed may rot before sprouting if soil is very cool and damp. Broom-corn planting time runs from mid-May to mid-June, except in California and the South, where it may be planted as much as a month earlier.

Hoe a shallow furrow and drop a seed every 2 inches. Cover the seeds with no more than an inch of fine soil. Broom-corn seedlings are delicate, almost grasslike—not nearly as robust as new corn shoots—so don't plant too deeply and be sure to break up clods in the soil covering the seeds. Germination takes one to two weeks, depending on soil temperature.

Broom corn will grow on drier, leaner soil than corn. If the ground is decidedly poor or dry, allow the plants a bit more room than on rich, well-watered land. Adequate soil fertility and moisture produces a high-quality brush.

Thinning is important to encourage strong-stemmed plants. It's easy to oversow broom corn seeds, because they are finer than corn seed. When very small, the seedlings look just like grassy weeds and are difficult to identify, so be sure you know what you're pulling. Thin seedlings to stand 3 to 4 inches apart.

The old farmers' manuals warn against planting broom-corn seed on weedy land, because the young plants aren't strong enough to compete with weeds, so be sure to remove weeds before they encroach on your crop. When plants are crowded, the seed head often forms a spike, with branches radiating off the central stem for some distance rather than originating at a single joint to form a whisk, or brush. If too much room is left between plants, the whisk may be coarse and the heads may flop over before the fibers have grown straight, forming "crooks."

Care during the growing season is simple. After thinning, I hand-weed the rows three times before they grow waist-high. After that, they're on their own. To control weeds between rows, I rototill, usually twice, until the plants grow large enough to shade out much of their weedy competition.

Disease Concerns

Neither insects nor disease have threatened my south-central Pennsylvania broom-corn plot. Here in the Western Hemisphere, we are free of many pests native to this sorghum's African place of origin. Broom corn is, however, susceptible to leaf anthracnose, a fungal disease found in warm, moist climates. In a severe infestation, small circular lesions appear on the leaves and eventually defoliate the plant. Spores overwinter on dead stalks, leaves, and larger weeds in the patch. Practice good housekeeping in your patch, cleaning up debris after harvest. Take care not to work when the leaves are wet to avoid spreading disease spores. Destroy any infected plants, preferably by burning.

In an extremely rainy season, the brush will sometimes be coated with mildew, especially if air circulation is poor. This once happened to me at the end of one of the rainiest growing seasons I can remember. There's not much you can do about mildew except to harvest the brush as early as possible and expose it to the sun for a day to kill the fungus. Dwarf broom corn is more likely to be affected by mildew than tall, or standard, broom corn. In most dwarf types, the brush is closely wrapped by the upper leaf and slower to dry after repeated rain. In taller varieties, the brush originates well above the highest leaf axil, and is therefore better ventilated.

Bend for Straight Bristles

When broom-corn whisks are allowed to develop in an upright position, the straws will often, by force of gravity, splay over into a whorl or cascade of bristles. Nice for dried plant arrangements, perhaps, but not very functional for a broom. It's customary to bend over the whisks as soon as they are fully formed, so that they will hang straight. I've talked to broom-corn growers who do not bend down their whisks before harvesting, but they're experienced growers and know what they're doing. For your first crops, I'd recommend bending. Work your way backward down the row, bending over the tops of two rows toward each other. Bend the stem at a point 12 inches below the brush for dwarf broom corn, about 18 inches for tall broom corn.

205

Cutting and Curing

About a week or two after the stalks have been bent over, the whisks are ready to harvest. Experts agree that broom-corn brush should be harvested before the seeds ripen. Older directions specify that the finest whisk, or brush, is obtained when the panicle is cut while the plant is still in flower, or when seeds have just begun to develop.

Whisks that are harvested too early are weak and lack elasticity. It's better to cut them while the seeds are still milky or, at the latest, in the soft-dough stage when the milky interior of the seed has turned to a doughy-soft solid. (To be sure of having viable seed to plant for next year, many broom-corn growers allow plants in a small corner of the patch to develop fully mature seed.)

Lop off the whisk with a knife, leaving a stem at least 8 inches long. Cut whisks must be cured before being used to make brooms. Dry them in a shady spot where air circulation is good. (If the fibers are mildewy, dry in the sun for a day.) They will turn brittle if left outdoors to cure completely. For a small patch, spread the cut heads on a bed of stalks to dry for several days, and then tie them into bundles and hang under cover for about two weeks.

Thresh broom-corn whisks right after harvest to remove seeds, because the process causes less damage to green fibers than to those that have been cured. Traditionally, small growers usually used a simple device—a curry comb or homemade wood sawtooth comb nailed to a bench, through which the seed heads are drawn. Or they would hold a carpenter's saw flat on the whisk while pulling the fibers through; the seeds get caught in the saw teeth.

Make a Simple Broom

Try your hand at making a simple round broom. Soak the stalk end of the whisks in lukewarm water for an hour or 2 before working with them, to make them more flexible. See the illustration on the opposite page to help with the following steps.

1. Tack one end of a 4-foot-long piece of strong cord or twine to a broom handle, 3 inches from the lower end. Tie the other end of the cord to a stick.
2. Step on the stick to hold the cord taut. Then add the brush, a piece at a time, as you rotate the broom handle, so that each succeeding whisk of straw is bound on by contact with the cord. Continue to turn the handle and add more stalks, constantly pulling the cord taut, until you've built up three layers of whisks.
3. Tie off the cord after the third layer has been added.
4. Wind on two more tiers of three layers each, wrapping the cord immediately above the preceding tier. Save your longest and best-looking brush for the final layer.

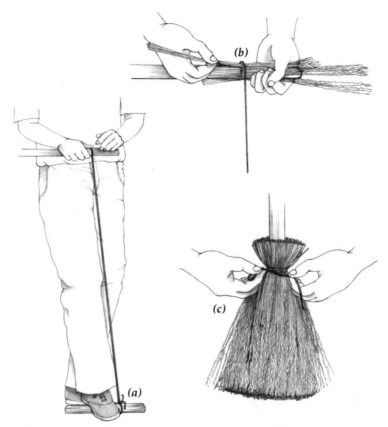

(a) Tack a strong cord to broom handle. Tie the other end to a stick; step on the stick to hold the cord taut.

(b) Add pieces of broom corn one at a time, rotating the handle to wrap cord.

(c) Knot cord when broom corn is three layers thick. For a fuller broom, add two more tiers one above the other.

Flat brooms are more complicated and best left to experts. A standard flat broom requires about 100 stalks, 12 feet of wire, 20 feet of string and five nails or staples. The stem ends of the stalks are sewn with strong thin cord to keep them in place. A broom press is necessary to keep the broom flat while it's being sewn. Old-timers often improvised broom presses by putting two short boards in a vise, or by fastening two boards together at the ends with a piece of strong leather.

The old craft of broom making is alive and well in many small towns and rural areas. Because these craftsmen seldom advertise, tracking them down can be an interesting adventure. If you hope to find a broom maker to bind your crop into useful form, start by calling your local agricultural extension office. Ask at area livestock feed stores and hardware stores, too, especially in smaller communities, and inquire of older farmers. These people usually know what is going on. One excellent way to find a broom maker is to visit craft fairs, especially those devoted to pioneer or Early American arts.

CHAPTER THIRTY-TWO

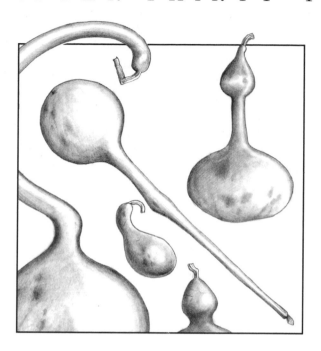

Learn Gourdsmanship

Sometimes I wonder if there are memories in our bones that harken back to the early days of the human race. When I discovered hard-shelled gourds, I was captivated by their shapes, their smooth surfaces, their mottling, their many uses. As I read about gourds, I found that, long before people learned how to make clay pots, they used gourds to store foods. Later, gourds were made into a wide variety of useful objects—among them, musical instruments, masks, floats for fish nets, and even hanging baby cradles.

Gourds from 7000 B.C. have been found in Mexico, making the gourd one of the oldest cultivated plants of the Americas. Scholars tell us, though, that it is even older than that. Gourds originated in Africa. Historians theorize that they arrived on our shores by floating across the ocean. Eventually, gourds of many kinds reached every continent, and they are still used today by native peoples around the world for both utility and ceremony.

Gourds have long been put to peaceful domestic uses, and that old, rich human association—unknown to me until I tried to fathom why I found the gourd so fascinating—somehow adds a special patina to every gourd I grow.

Meet the Hard-Shelled Gourds

I've grown two kinds of gourds: The white-flowered gourd, *Lagenaria siceraria,* produces tan hard-shelled fruits that keep for many years. The yellow-flowered gourd, *Cucurbita pepo* var. *ovifera,* is the decorative gourd often used in autumn displays. Its gourds come in many forms and colors—yellow, white, green, and orange; solids and stripes; smooth, warty, round, crooknecked. These small, thin-shelled fruits of the cucurbit vines don't last as long as those of the hard-shelled *Lagenaria* species. Cucurbits are fun, but I find myself especially drawn to the hard-shelled gourds. They have more uses and they last longer.

Hard-shelled gourds come in a wonderful variety of shapes, some of them named for the objects commonly made from them. There are bowl gourds, dipper gourds, birdhouse gourds, and club, bottle, dumbbell, spoon, bushel, and other named shapes. Each category may have its own special gourds—African wine kettle gourd, Brazilian bottle gourd, black pear gourd, and giant dipper gourd to name a few.

My first gourd seeds came from a friend who grows dipper gourds and sells them at craft fairs along with her handwoven rugs. Later, I started planting other types after visiting a country shop where I saw a wonderful display of beautifully crafted gourd objects. There was a shallow serving piece, made of the flat bottom of a large gourd, with two leather thongs for handles. There was a salt holder on display, too, the kind used in colonial days—a small dipper gourd with a hole cut in the upper half of one side—filled with salt and hung near

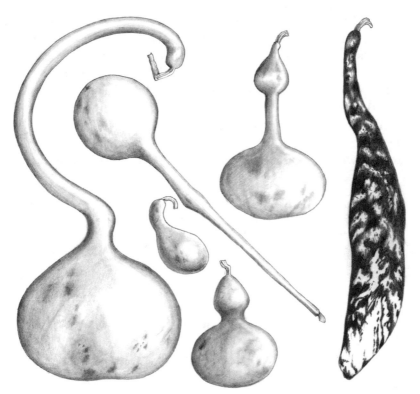

Hard-shelled gourds (*Lagenaria siceraria*) come in all sorts of shapes, and keep for years. They can be made into scoops, birdhouses, or even musical instruments.

the stove. The absorbent inner surface of the gourd helps soak up dampness from the air and keeps the salt from caking, and it's handy to have hanging on the wall, especially near a wood cookstove like mine. At the shop were other amazing examples of artistry: a puzzle gourd, cut into pieces that could be taken apart and reassembled; gourds with basket-woven handles or inserts; gourds with perfectly fitted scalloped lids; gourds painted with beautiful wildflower designs—gourds no one else could duplicate.

Although a great many gourd growers live in states with warmer weather than ours here in Pennsylvania, there are plenty of successful growers in other states north of the Mason-Dixon line: Michigan, Nebraska, Illinois, Montana. There are even gourd growers in Canada. The world's largest gourd show is held annually in Ohio.

Growing Gourds with Success

The year my friend gave me my first hard-shelled gourd seeds, I had already laid out my garden. The only place I could fit another planting was next to the compost pile. So I filled the bottomless half of a 30-gallon plastic barrel with finished compost, planted the seeds, and let the vines climb on the compost pile. This arrangement worked so well that I've planted gourds by the compost pile ever since.

Hard-shelled gourds like warmth and can't be planted outdoors until settled warm weather arrives. Use these tips to get a jump on a successful season.

- Presprout the seeds. Roll them up in damp paper towels, place in a plastic bag, and keep in a warm place (I put mine atop the water heater). Check every day for signs of growth.
- Start seeds early in pots. Keep graduating them to successively larger pots until weather is warm enough to set them out. Try not to disturb the roots when transplanting; just tip the plant out and resettle it in its larger container, adding more soil around the roots. I never plant gourd seeds in flats, because they don't do well if their roots are disturbed.
- If all else fails, plant a small-fruited gourd in a 5-gallon container and bring it into a greenhouse or sun porch to ripen the fruits if frost threatens.
- Keep your vines cozy by mulching the ground around the vines with black plastic to keep soil warm.
- If you live in one of the colder states, plant one of the smaller gourds, such as bowl or spoon gourds. These mature somewhat earlier than huge specimens like the kettle gourds.

Around the end of May or the beginning of June—about two weeks after the last frost—I set the plants out, in their bottomless tub of compost. In the garden, space hills of three or four gourd plants 8 feet apart. After a week or so of settling in, the vines will start to grow.

Gourd vines are rampant—long vined and large leafed, and they're good climbers. Last year my gourd plants rambled from the compost pile over to the nearby grape arbor and even draped over a peach tree. Although the gourd fruits were large, they hung on until harvest time, suspended from branches and arbor.

PLAIN AND FANCY SUPPORT SYSTEMS

My gourds don't rot during the growing season because they're either suspended from a climbing vine or resting on straw. If you don't mulch your gourds, slip a shingle, board, or handful of straw under each gourd to fend off the rot-encouraging effect of damp soil.

Gourd vines will spread across an arbor or lattice of wood or wire, providing temporary shade. The gourds that dangle under an overhead planting make an interesting arrangement—relaxing to contemplate from your favorite lounge chair in the shade. Trellised gourds are often longer and usually more symmetrical than those that loll on the ground.

Speeding Up Production

Gourds, I've learned, are late starters. It's early August before I see any fruits on my gourd vines. When I joined the American Gourd Society (see Resources beginning on page 337), I learned there are steps expert growers take to get earlier fruit. Pruning the vines, hand pollinating the blossoms, and a little extra care can bring you earlier gourds and a better crop.

Pruning

The long leader vine is the first shoot to grow. It produces only male blossoms, which are necessary for pollination but incapable of producing fruit.

Female blossoms are born on the sideshoots, or laterals, that eventually branch off from the main stem. On an unpruned vine, female blossoms appear later and there may be only a few bearing side branches on the vine.

Pruning encourages laterals to develop earlier and more abundantly, giving you both more and earlier fruit. To prune, wait until the vine has grown 10 to 12 feet long and then cut off the growing tip. Snip off the growing tip of each lateral when it has developed four leaves. Don't prune the shoots that arise from the laterals.

213

Hand Pollinating

Hard-shelled gourds bloom at night, because night-flying insects are their natural pollinators. The blossoms last only a single night, though, and if it rains all night or the evening air is very cool, the moths and other pollinating insects won't get there and that night's blossoms will be duds. Sometimes these insects may be scarce, too, because of weather, climate, spraying on neighboring land, or other factors beyond your control. If the female blossoms don't get pollinated, the tiny fruits at the base of the flower fall off. Hand pollinating gives you a more abundant fruit set, and possibly an earlier one.

To distinguish the pollen-bearing male blossoms from the pollen-receptive female blossoms, look for the small swelling at the base of the female flowers. This tiny potential gourd is not present on the male flower. To hand pollinate, pick the male flower, remove its petals, and brush it against the female flower, making sure that the pollen-bearing anthers of the male contact the stigma of the female. Or you can use your finger or a small fine-bristled brush to do the job. Some veteran gourd growers have found they seem to get a better fruit set when they pollinate female flowers with a male flower from the same vine.

Tender, Loving Care

To coax more fruit from a vine, you need to be sure the vine is planted in rich soil and that it receives enough water. End-of-season care is also essential to a successful harvest.

I give my vines one or two extra feedings of fish emulsion or manure tea during the first two months. Gourd vines need at least 1 inch of water a week. I turn the sprinkler on them for a good soaking in prolonged dry weather. Hard-shelled gourds have shallow roots that tend to run parallel to the soil surface, so don't cultivate close to the main stem of the plant. It's better to control weeds by mulching.

As the end of summer draws near, it's time to direct the plant's energy toward ripening the fruits. Don't fertilize gourds late in the season: There's no point in stimulating a lot of tender new growth that doesn't have time to develop fruits before frost. In early September, stop watering so the fruits start to harden. If you grow only a few vines, remove the blossoms after mid-September so the plant's energy can go to already-developing fruits that have a chance of ripening. (In a large, tangled plantation of gourd vines, though, this would be a big job!)

Harvest How-To

A fully mature gourd has a dry tendril growing out of the stem next to it, and the stem is dry, too. In our area, hard-shelled gourds are mature but still green when we get our first frosts. Frost won't damage the mature gourds—but it will kill the vines, and the gourds will stop growing.

Some people leave their gourds outside until they dry and lose weight. Because we often have lots of rain in the fall, which can cause mildew and other fungal problems, I usually pick mine in November and dry them under cover. For perfect gourds, follow these tips.

- Harvest your gourds before wet weather gets to them.
- Pick only gourds with a hard surface; soft ones will rot.
- Cut gourds from the vine when harvesting—don't pull them off. To make it easy to hang them later, leave several inches of vine on either side of the stem when you harvest small gourds.
- Uncured gourds are heavy. Don't pick them up by the stem, which might break from all that weight.

Many people wipe their newly picked gourds with a disinfectant of ½ cup vinegar or Clorox bleach to 2 quarts water, to reduce the chances of surface spoilage. I've had a problem with the large late-maturing bushel gourds rotting before they dried out, but my percentage of "keepers" is improving.

Drying, Curing, and Crafting

Gourds dry slowly, and large gourds, like the bushel gourd, can take several months to dry. As they cure, gourds tend to develop a mottled surface. This is caused by a fungus and, if confined to the surface, does no harm. I happen to think that it gives the gourd skin an interesting antiqued, almost leathery, look. If you prefer a smooth, unmottled, plain tan skin, harvest your gourds before the weather gets to them and wipe them regularly with vinegar-water disinfectant to kill surface molds.

To cure gourds thoroughly so they'll dry, not rot, keep them in a well-ventilated place. Slatted shelves, net hammocks, old hardware-cloth screens and other air-admitting supports work well. Turn the gourds at least once a week so that all surfaces can air-dry. Or, suspend gourds individually in discarded stockings or mesh onion bags. Hang small gourds by their stems to cure. A dry gourd is light in weight for its size. The seeds may rattle when you shake it.

If you want to embellish your gourd in any way, you'll need to prepare it first. Here's how.

1. Soften the thin outer skin of a well-dried gourd by soaking the gourd in water for an hour or two, wrapping a damp towel around it for 24 hours, or enclosing several gourds in a large plastic bag, adding 1 quart of water, and hanging the bag in the sun for a few hours.
2. When the skin has softened, remove the thin outer layer. Scrape it off with steel wool or a dull knife.
3. Smooth the surface with fine sandpaper or 0000 steel wool.
4. To clean pulp from the inside of a cut-open gourd, pull off all you can of the loose seeds and dried fiber, then put some water in the gourd to soften the pulp that clings to the walls. Scrape this out with a spoon. My favorite tool for cleaning out gourd insides is an old wood-handled scraper, shaped like a fat teardrop, that I found at a yard sale.

What can you do with a gourd? Well, I use mine as containers for fruit, nuts, magazines, dried arrangements, and for scoops and serving bowls. More ambitious gourd growers carve or burn or paint designs on the gourd. Some people enjoy crafting gourd animals—penguins, dinosaurs, frogs. Gourds can make good houses for purple martins, wrens, and other birds. (If you aim to attract martins, group at least a dozen gourd houses on crossed poles for these colony nesters.) Gourds with thick shells will last three to four years without treatment, longer if you paint, varnish, or oil them. To prolong their life, take them down at the end of the summer, clean, and store them in a dry place.

CHAPTER THIRTY-THREE

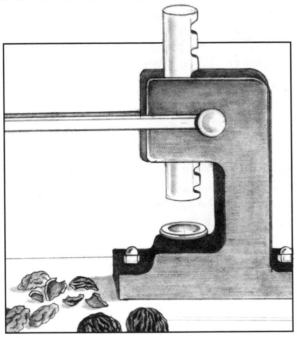

Plant a Nut Tree

We had a head start on nuts here on our farm. Our great hedgerow trees—hickories and black walnuts—had been left to themselves over the years and even enriched by washes of topsoil from the open fields. At the edges of the back pastures, small thickets of hazelnuts bloomed and bore in secret, known only to the squirrels. We even have a mystery—a single butternut we found on a rock along the mountain clearing. We hope the parent tree is on our land; finding it has become a cause, and the object of many pleasant hikes over the fields and woods.

Consider what a nut tree could do for you: beautify your home grounds, add value to your property, shade your house in summer, and produce a rich harvest of nuts. Nut trees have been sadly overlooked by homeowners, perhaps because most of them begin to bear six to eight years after planting, a somewhat longer waiting period than for fruit trees. Unlike most fruit crops, though, nuts need no processing in order to keep them for winter use; simply store the unshelled nuts in a cool place. On a small property, nut trees may be planted as shade trees, just as maples and oaks would be used, and as curbside plantings. The smaller almonds and filberts lend themselves to backyard plantings.

A Bushel of Nut Trees to Pick From

Because they do take time to mature, I always recommend planting nut trees the very first thing after moving to a new location or starting on a landscaping plan. The trees will grow while you're busy with other concerns. The first year we moved to our farm, we made time for planting nut trees, even when other garden chores were waiting to be done. Now we're glad we did. The young trees are branching out, developing sturdy trunks, and we're planting a second batch of them. We've enjoyed quite a few crops of filberts and have begun to pick from our black walnuts. Here are some nut trees to consider for your home grounds.

Almond

Although commonly considered tender exotics, there are hardy strains of almonds (*Prunus dulcis* var. *dulcis*) that will grow wherever peaches do well. Almonds are, in fact, closely related to peaches, and resemble them closely. The nearly ripe fruit of the almond tree looks like a runty peach. It has a thick skin, a thin layer of pulp, and a large hard-shelled kernel.

Almond trees are delicate in appearance, seldom topping 15 feet, and bear masses of pink flowers in early spring. Although the trees are hardy (Zone 6), they can get into trouble in far northern climates because they tend to bloom early, usually earlier than peaches. If spring frosts threaten the blossoms, it's easy to cover almond trees

PLANTING TIPS

Most nut trees have a deep taproot with only a few small roots along the side. They suffer more from transplanting than fruit trees, which usually have an abundance of fine roots. When you plant, clip ½ inch from the bottom of the taproot to encourage growth of feeder roots. Be sure not to bend the taproot when planting.

Spring is the best time to plant nut trees; fall-planted trees sometimes die when their small, scanty feeder roots die out over winter. When you can, plant nut trees, particularly the early bloomers, on a north slope to delay blooming and thus lessen the chance of frost damage.

That saying about the wisdom of putting a $1 plant in a $5 hole, rather than a $5 plant in a $1 hole, is especially true when planting nut trees. Dig a generous hole, at least as wide as a bushel basket, and no less than 6 inches deeper than the depth of the roots. The roots of the tree should fit into the hole easily without crowding or bending.

Plant grafted trees with the graft union above the soil level or the tree may send up suckers from the less desirable root-stock. Set stakes to support the tree at the time of planting; they will not injure newly formed feeder roots as they might if you added them later. Nut trees are susceptible to sunscald. Protect the trunks by wrapping them with burlap or commercial tree-wrapping paper or by whitewashing them.

with a sheet for protection. Almonds are good choices for lawn plantings. Even if you don't reap a crop every year, you'll get more good food from a hardy almond than you would from most other widely planted lawn trees.

Black Walnut

The wild black walnut (*Juglans nigra*) is valued for both its nuts and its beautifully grained wood. Black walnuts are native to every state east of the Rockies, and trees can reach 150 feet. Extremely late to leaf out, and usually the first of trees to lose their leaves in fall, black walnuts are hardy to Zone 5.

The nuts retain their rich flavor in cooking better than many other nuts. Try black walnut cookies or—our favorite—black walnut waffles (just stud your favorite waffle recipe with a fistful of black walnut meats and pass the maple syrup).

Grafted walnuts, available by mail from nurseries, often bear early, at a height of about 7 feet. The cultivar most often found in catalogs, and the one we've planted, is 'Thomas'. Other grafted cultivars include 'Stambaugh', 'Ohio', and 'Sparrow'. 'Thomas' grafted trees commonly bear as early as five to six years. Most named grafted trees bear nuts with larger meats and thinner shells than the average wild tree. Some of them even shell out in perfect halves. A 15- to 20-year-old 'Thomas' black walnut produces about 2 bushels of nuts, from which you can crack a good 20 pounds of nutmeats.

We've found the easiest way to husk the nuts is to spread them in the driveway where the car can run over them and split open the husks. If you're in a hurry, you can crack off the green, aromatic husks with a well-aimed hammer blow. Wear your best cellar-cleaning outfit to do this job, though, for the brown-staining juice spatters. The dye in the husks will stain your hands, too, unless you wear gloves.

Leaving the nuts unhusked for too long, or letting unhusked nuts remain too long on damp ground, can cause blackened or moldy nuts. A fungal disease, walnut anthracnose, causes blackened or shriveled kernels. It shows up as round spots on the leaves in early summer and causes early leaf drop. Defend your trees against this fungus by raking and burning affected leaves and nuts to destroy the spores that would otherwise live over winter.

Butternut

The butternut (*Juglans cinerea*), sometimes called the white walnut, is the hardiest nut tree. Its range extends well northward to Zone 3, above that of the black walnut. Attaining a mature height of up to 100 feet, the trees are broad with a short, thick trunk and many low, heavy branches. Like black walnuts, butternuts grow in a thick husk often used to dye fabric brown. The nuts are elongated and roughly ridged, pointed on the end. Their meats, though well hidden, are delicious, with a milder flavor than black walnuts. They are somewhat prone to turning rancid if not kept cool.

The life expectancy of butternuts is shorter than that of the long-lived black walnut or hickory. But if your tree lives only 40 years, it will still bear a good many nuts in that time.

Chinese Chestnut

The Chinese chestnut (*Castanea mollissima*) is an imported replacement for the doomed American chestnut (*C. dentata*). Hardy to Zone 5, it bears satin-surfaced, sweet-tasting nuts in husks that bristle with sharp spines. The nuts usually fall free from the husk when they drop and should be gathered promptly. The young trees are shallow rooted and thus quite vulnerable to drought, but they also need good drainage and should never be planted in a spot where water puddles. Mulch the soil surface to retain moisture. Be sure to keep mulch away from the trunk so mice won't set up housekeeping there and gnaw on the bark.

A single tree will sometimes bear nuts, but not nearly as many as you'll get if you plant two for better pollination. Space them 35 feet apart. A mature tree will be up to 60 feet tall with a spreading habit. A fully grown tree may produce as much as 150 pounds of nuts. Chinese chestnuts usually begin bearing three years after planting. By the sixth year, you should have plenty of nuts for chestnut stuffing and chestnut roasts to boot.

I'm indebted to our friends Dick and Betty Parsons for the roasting method that seems to work best. Nick a slit in the shell of each nut. Rinse the nuts in water. Then roast them in a shallow pan in a 350° oven for 30 to 40 minutes. Perfect! Far superior to my former methods of boiling or steaming them, which tended to make them watery. Chestnuts, by the way, are 50 percent water, about 42 percent starch, 5 percent oil, and the rest protein. They do not keep as well as other nuts. Plastic-bag storage often encourages mold. Keep them in a paper bag and they'll last several weeks in a cool place.

English Walnut

The English walnut (*Juglans regia*) has been improved tremendously over the centuries, by simple selection and replanting of superior nuts.

Most regular strains survive winters as cold as − 10°F. Some winter chilling is necessary in order to promote nut production, but severe chilling will kill the buds. A relatively recent introduction, the Carpathian walnut strain, is hardy to −30°F. Late spring frosts may also damage blossoms and affect yield. One year, in fact, a severe late frost made our English walnut tree shed all its leaves suddenly in one day. They grew back, and some late-blooming flowers did form nuts, but the harvest was small that year. Since English walnuts do sometimes bloom early, you might consider planting them on a site with a northern exposure where cool temperatures will foster later blooming. Ours (not a Carpathian) is on a slight southern slope—fine when there is no late freeze, but risky when there is.

A five-year-old English walnut tree will begin to bear female blossoms, but the pollen-contributing male blossoms will not show up until the seventh year. This is why young trees may puzzle you by flowering but bearing no nuts. After the seventh year, the tree will be self-pollinating.

Filbert

The European filbert (*Corylus avellana*) is the cultivated European counterpart of the native American hazelnut (*C. americana*). Although slightly less hardy than hazelnuts, filberts bear larger nuts.

Filberts do well wherever peaches thrive, as long as temperatures don't fall below −15°F. The bushes can stand lower temperatures, but dormant buds will be killed. Most filberts begin producing nuts three years after planting.

European filberts are large, shrubby bushes, and may be grown as a cluster or in a hedge. If you want a filbert tree rather than a bush, prune off all extra shoots, leaving a single main stem, when planting the young tree.

In the fall, when loss of leaves bares the bush, you'll notice tassels hanging from the branches. These are the catkins—bearers of next year's flowers. Both male and female flowers appear on a single plant, but you'll need at least two bushes of different cultivars because filberts do not accept their own pollen. 'Royal', 'DuChilly', and 'Barcelona' are some of the most widely sold cultivars. If you order three bushes, for instance, get two 'Barcelona' and one 'DuChilly' for pollination.

Our filberts have never been troubled by insects or disease. Their one weakness is the tendency of the catkins to be very responsive to the kind of deceptively mild day that can occur in early March. This early exuberance of bloom is sometimes laid low by a hard April frost.

Our first planting of filberts, in a sunny sheltered spot, has more than once bloomed early, only to be hit when a hard frost slid down the mountain and froze out the blossoms. Our second planting, on a western slope that receives some winter shade, has fared much better and started bearing in its second year—only a few nuts, but they were marvelous.

The nuts are handsome, with smooth, rusty brown shells, and are borne in attractive fringed husks which are themselves worth saving for wreaths and dried arrangements. The nuts are delicious raw. If you must toast them, toast lightly and toss them in a little oil—the perfect continental dessert, with some choice fruit and a wedge of room-temperature cheese.

Hickory

Both shagbark hickory (*Carya ovata*) and shellbark hickory (*C. laciniosa*) are handsome shade trees, achieving a height of 120 feet, although they grow rather slowly. Both have bark that resembles a loose, shaggy coat of semi-detached strips (the characteristic is most pronounced in shagbark). Shagbarks are hardy up to Zone 5; shellbarks are slightly more tender, to Zone 6.

The trees are self-fertile, needing no extra pollinating trees. Unless you have access to wild seedlings, you'll most likely begin your hickory-growing venture by buying a young tree from a nursery. Be prepared to give it your very best care; hickories can be difficult to establish.

Hickories are long-lived trees, and once you've had a taste of the nuts, I'm sure you'll consider the effort worthwhile. Hickory flavor is more subtle and versatile than black walnut, and at least as good as pecan, if not better. Just a few hickory nuts added to a bowl of granola make it a very special dish.

Japanese Walnut or Heartnut

Relatively new in our country, heartnut (*Juglans ailantifolia* var. *cordiformis*) seems well prepared to thrive in the humid summers of eastern North America. Well worth planting as a lawn or specimen tree, heartnut trees reach a mature height of up to 60 feet. They grow well in climates from Georgia to Nova Scotia and even in sandy or heavy soil.

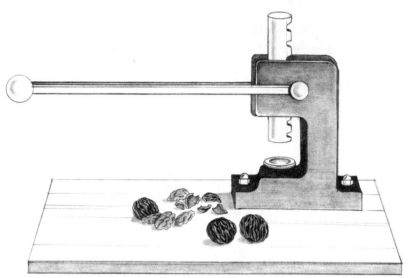

This gear-action nutcracker cracks nuts with precision, without crushing them. Nutmeats of even hard-to-crack hickories and black walnuts are released in large pieces.

Heartnuts are similar in flavor to butternuts, and borne in clusters. The shells are smooth and easy to crack. Frost damage is seldom a problem.

Pecan

One of my husband's colleagues, a native of South Carolina, has the enviable skill of cracking pecans so that the nutmeats come out whole. Apparently he grew up knowing how. Anyone who can do that should have his own pecan tree. When the pecan trees (*Carya illinoinensis*) we've planted here begin to bear, we hope to become adept at this art, too.

Pecans in Pennsylvania? Yes, there are cultivars selected especially for northern regions. These include cultivars like 'Major', 'Indiana', and 'Colby', which often ripen nuts by October, given 180 to 200 frost-free days. Southern pecans like 'Schley', 'Burkett', and 'Stuart', need 220 to 270 good, warm—not just frost-free—days. The hardy northern trees bear smaller nuts with thicker shells than their southern cousins. Pecan blossoms open fairly late; still, even northern cultivars are not always safe from frost. Very sudden, severe freezes may damage not only the blossoms but also the tree. The upper limit of the northern range for hardy pecans, Zone 6, runs along a line from Pennsylvania through Iowa and Oklahoma.

Although annual crops of pecans are not by any means a sure thing for midwestern and mid-Atlantic gardeners, the tree is a handsome ornamental and entirely worth its keep as a shade tree.

NUT LORE

Here are some tips to help you enjoy your nut trees year-round.

- Let the nuts dry for a week or two after husking, before you crack them. Then try a few to see whether they've lost their "green" taste.
- How can you tell which nuts are empty? Dump them in a pail of water. Those that float are duds.
- Black walnuts, hickories, and butternuts can be tough nuts to crack. Strike the pointed end with a hammer or crush the nut in a vise. Or use one of the new gear-action nutcrackers—a marvelous invention that cracks the nut without crushing it, and releases complete halves in hickory nuts and quarters in black walnuts.
- The roots of black walnuts and English walnuts exude juglone, a toxic substance that may retard the growth of many plants, including soybeans, beets, tomatoes, and azaleas. If possible, plant your walnuts a good 60 feet from your garden. But if you don't have that much space, don't despair. An English walnut tree planted at the corner of my kitchen garden did not seem to have any ill effect on flowers, peas, lettuce, cauliflower, parsley, and onions planted near it.
- For more on nut trees, and access to unusual cultivars, write the Northern Nut Growers' Association (see Resources beginning on page 337). Some states have nut growers' associations, too; call your local extension agent for information.

225

CHAPTER THIRTY-FOUR

Try Your Hand at Seed and Plant Trading

226

Some plants can't be found in any seed or nursery catalog. Here in my garden, I've grown an extra-solid, almost seedless Italian tomato, an heirloom butterhead lettuce, German multiplier onions, and dwarf broom corn, none of which I could have purchased through any seed catalog with which I am familiar. Seed for each of these plants came from other gardeners who have kept these strains alive by replanting them and saving seeds. Seed trading,

I've found, is a double adventure, involving the challenge of raising new kinds of crops from seed (and saving that seed again myself to assure another harvest) and the warmth and stimulation of contact with other gardeners in all sections of the country.

I've seen seed trading ads in barter columns in magazines and in local newspapers, but my primary source for seeds of heirloom or hard-to-find cultivars is the Seed Savers Exchange. Perhaps you've been trying to find seeds of a vegetable you remember from childhood. Or maybe you want to enlist the help of other gardeners in maintaining a special heirloom strain of beans you've been saving. If you share the concern for preservation, try the Seed Savers Exchange.

The spirit and intent of the exchange is to foster sharing and cooperation among gardeners in the absorbing venture of preserving old and unusual vegetable cultivars that, for one reason or another, are not propagated commercially and are therefore in danger of dying out.

Founder Kent Whealy started the exchange as a newsletter, prompted by the death of his wife's grandfather, who had given him tomato, bean, and morning glory seeds that had been kept alive by four generations of his family. Whealy realized that it was now up to him to keep those seeds alive, and he wondered how many other good old vegetable cultivars had already died out with the elderly gardeners who had been keeping them.

The grassroots exchange that numbered 29 members in 1975 has now grown to a seed preservation effort that is international in scope, with over 900 members who offer seed, and many more supporters. Its publications retain the homey flavor of the early back-fence exchanges. The Winter Yearbook lists members' names and addresses and the vegetable seeds offered and wanted by each member.

Recent offerings include a full range of vegetables—12,000 listings (some are duplicates, of course)—more than any seed catalog. There are 'Scotch Bonnet' peppers, 'Powderpuff Breadseed' poppies, Hmong buckwheat, 'Moon and Stars' watermelon, 'Pole Cat' peas, corn for flour and popping as well as for fresh eating, Cherokee beans and more cultivars of endive, rutabagas and other lesser-grown vegetables than you knew existed. Membership forms and information are available from the Seed Savers Exchange, Rural Rt. 3, Box 239, Decorah, IA 52101. Please enclose $1 with your request.

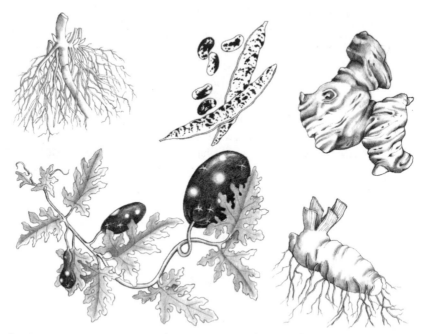

Sharing your extras is a good way to meet other gardeners. You can swap stories while you trade treasured bean seeds for a handful of peony roots.

One Man's Trash . . .

Giveaways are another gardening tradition. You know how we gardeners hate to toss out perfectly good plants, even when it's evident that ruthless thinning is needed. Some of us, in fact, develop a reputation for pressing extra plants on everyone who opens the front gate. The solution to this dilemma, pioneered by imaginative suburban gardeners, is to put out a carton of extra plants with a large sign on it: "Free Plants, Help Yourself."

Plant societies and gardening clubs are good places for gardeners to exchange their extras, too. A women's club in a town not far from us sponsors an annual plant-trading day. Town residents as well as club members arrive with boxes of iris rhizomes, peony clumps, rhubarb roots, tree seedlings, houseplants, and other garden treasures, and leave with the same cartons jammed with a completely different assortment. Our neighborhood food co-op does the same thing each spring, on a smaller scale. Special-interest plant societies also often

228

have plant exchanges among members, usually by mail but some-times in regional gatherings. Some organizations charge an entry fee to defray club expenses or even to add to the group's treasury. There's an old saying among gardeners that the plant for which you thank the giver will not prosper. Perhaps the plant exchange has the answer for that old taboo. Certainly the mutual satisfaction that fills the air at a good plant-trading event makes formal thank-yous irrelevant.

Ask and You Shall Receive

There's another, even simpler, way to obtain plants for which you may be searching. Post signs on food market bulletin boards offering to trade your surplus plants for varieties you need. I've had good luck in locating strawberry, rhubarb, and Jerusalem artichoke plants, as well as trees and shrubs, by tacking up these informal offers on com-munity bulletin boards. An extra dividend is the delightful opportu-nity to meet other gardeners and admire their plantings. Instead of waiting for a special catalog or event to bring you what you want or need, see what will turn up when you take matters into your own hands.

CHAPTER THIRTY-FIVE

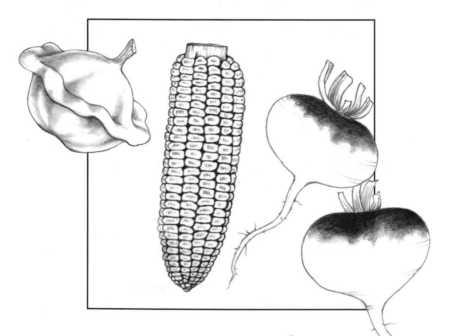

Serve Heirloom Vegetables for Thanksgiving

T ry as we might, we can never duplicate that first Thanksgiving feast. According to one estimate, at least 70 percent of the vegetable varieties that existed in the Americas when Columbus landed have become extinct. The gradual improvement of vegetable strains has given way to intensive breeding programs and rapid introduction of new cultivars. Many tough, stringy vegetables have been improved, but a lot of special, tasty cultivars have been lost, simply because seed companies needed catalog (and growing) space for new introductions.

I have no wish to return to those early days and subsist on pumpkins, corn, and cider. I'm glad to live here and now—to be able to grow tomatoes and other foods the early settlers hadn't yet discovered (and to be able to wear jeans, enjoy running water, and take vacations, too). But I celebrate the garden's abundance by serving some of the foods that have sustained generations of gardeners. Perhaps you will want to consider planning your Thanksgiving meal around some of these nourishing foods. It seems fitting to celebrate our freedom, abundance, and family ties by savoring some of the best of our heirloom vegetables.

A Sampler of Abundance

While there's no way to recapture the very same kinds of vegetables that fed the Puritans and Indians at that first groaning board, we can come close, thanks to the efforts of some enlightened seed companies, individual seed savers, and seed-saving groups. When the first colonists arrived, the native people of North America were cultivating corn, beans, squash, gourds, and pumpkins. Some tribes grew sweet potatoes, and many ate sunflower seeds and Jerusalem artichoke roots. Picture it all on the table: With bowls of corn, beans, and squash crowding the turkey platter, you've got quite a meal.

Corn was a new food for the early settlers. Although it had been introduced in Mediterranean countries by the seventeenth century, it hadn't yet been grown in northern Europe. The people who arrived on the *Mayflower* were fortunate to have landed near an easily cultivated, cleared field formerly worked by a group of Indians who had died in a recent epidemic. They were also indebted to the Indians for corn seed (of the long-keeping dent or flint type) and advice on growing it.

Corn became a staple food of the early colonists. It was prepared in various ways: hulled and ground as hominy grits; ground and mixed with water to make corn pone, a flat, unleavened bread; or stewed and mixed with beans for succotash. Blue corn is traditional in the American Southwest as well as Mexico. We sampled tortillas made from the traditional blue cornmeal, and the flavor was superb. Try an early flint or flour corn, such as 'Longfellow', 'Vermont Yellow', or 'Texas Shoepeg', for Thanksgiving corn bread.

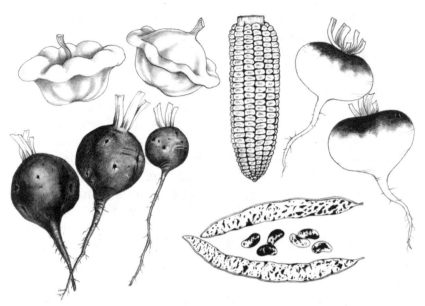

You won't find them in most catalogs, but heirloom vegetables are worth seeking out for a taste of long-ago America. 'White Patty Pan' squash was grown by Native Americans a hundred years ago; you can serve it on your own Thanksgiving table along with other old-timers like dent corn, 'Purple-Top Strap Leaf' turnips, 'Jacob's Cattle' beans, and 'Winter Keeper' beets.

Sweet corn was sometimes grown by the Indians but was not widely adopted by European immigrants until after 1850. 'Stowell's Evergreen' and 'Black Mexican' are among the earliest sweet corn cultivars for which seed is still available.

Pumpkins, or "pompions," as the settlers called them, grew abundantly. Squanto, an English-speaking Indian, taught the settlers to plant pumpkins among the corn to shade out weeds. Pumpkins would later be used for livestock feed, but in the early years they often appeared at every meal, according to an anonymous colonial poet:

If fresh meat be wanting to fill up our dish,
We have carrots and pumpkins and turnips and fish.
We have pumpkins at morning and pumpkins at noon,
And if it were not for pumpkins, we should be undone.

The 'Connecticut Field Pumpkin' is a contemporary cultivar similar to the type of pumpkin the colonists would have grown.

Some old squash cultivars survive to this day. 'White Patty Pan', or 'Bush Scallop', was grown by North American Indians. 'Boston Marrow', 'Hubbard', and 'Summer Crookneck' squashes have all been around for more than a century. Take a moment to reflect that, until manufactured stoves appeared around 1850, most cooking was done in an open fireplace, in a kettle hung on a pothook. Boiling, or stewing, was the most popular cooking method and produced a dish of watery, mushy squash. Let's be glad we can bake or sauté ours.

Fortunately, beans have survived in glorious profusion. Could the wide variations in seed colors and markings have something to do with that? The seeds themselves have become an item of interest, rather like a collection of marbles. Bean enthusiast John Withee accumulated about a thousand cultivars. His collection is now maintained by the Seed Savers Exchange (see Resources beginning on page 337). Seed catalogs carry a good many of the old cultivars 'Jacob's Cattle', 'Wren's Egg', 'Cranberry', 'Caseknife', 'Scarlet Runner', and 'Black Valentine'. Or you might want to try a less common bean like 'Wild Goose', said to have been found in the crops of wild geese bagged by hunters. For Thanksgiving, you could serve green beans, or perhaps a soup made of 'Black Turtle' beans, or a cassoulet of dried beans with sausage, herbs, and wine.

More Old-Fashioned Crops

Turnips were frequently included in soups and stews, and often cooked separately and mashed. Seeds of this European crop were brought to the New World by the early settlers. 'Purple-Top Strap-Leaf' was a common early cultivar. 'White Egg' is also still available. My vote for a fine-flavored heirloom turnip goes to 'Gilfeather', an old Vermont cultivar that has only recently become commercially available.

Beets were important to the colonists, too, both for their leaves and their long-keeping roots. You'll still find 'Egyptian' and 'Detroit', both introduced in the last century, in contemporary catalogs. My favorite beet, 'Long Season' (also called 'Winter Keeper'), is probably virtually the same as that grown in many nineteenth-century gardens. Unlike many good keepers, it is fine-grained and sweet.

Carrots have been greatly improved since those early days. Two seventeenth-century cultivars were 'Horn' and 'Long Orange'. In the seventh century A.D., carrots were purple; the Romans had a white

233

form. By the fourteenth century, a yellow mutation had appeared, followed by an orange mutation in the seventeenth century. Nineteenth-century catalogs offered 'Danvers', 'Oxheart', 'Nantes'—three types that are still popular.

Lettuce was not likely to have been included in that first Thanksgiving menu, but if you use Reemay or plastic tunnels to coax along a late crop, you can have the best of both worlds: fresh lettuce, old variety. 'Parris White Cos', grown here by 1800, is still a super lettuce, and one of our family favorites. We might also raise a late crop of 'Mescher', an heirloom butterhead that I plant from home-saved seed.

Old cabbage cultivars include 'Early Jersey Wakefield', late 'Flat Dutch', and 'Drumhead Savoy'. 'Jersey Wakefield', a fairly loose-leafed, cone-shaped cabbage, is usually grown as an early crop, but any of the Dutch or solid savoy types would be in good condition in the fall—perfect for a dish of country coleslaw (tossed with apple slices) or homemade sauerkraut.

As you use this Thanksgiving to revel in our rich vegetable heritage, remember that the choices we make now will help determine what kinds of seed are available to future gardeners. If we choose to save these good vintage vegetables, we can pass them on to the young hands that follow us.

CHAPTER THIRTY-SIX

Craft Cornhusk Dolls

C rackly cornhusks left behind after the harvest to rustle in the crisp breezes are one of the signs of autumn. With a little know-how, and a bit of string, these reminders of the season just past can be transformed into small dolls that seem to have a life of their own. Cornhusk dolls are easy to make, and creating them is an absorbing pastime right from the start. The raw materials are fun to gather and a pleasure to work with (wet cornhusks drape just like fabric). And, since most of the makings cost nothing, you can use them in all kinds of experiments.

We've found doll making a good way to create gifts, but we've kept some of the masterpieces we've made, too. In fact, our doll population grows as one or another of us creates a character we simply *must* make room for. If only we could put them all to work sweeping out the kitchen!

Would you like to try your hand at a doll or two? I'll gladly tell you how we make ours—not *the* way to construct them, mind, but *a* way, the one we're using now. Next year our technique may change if we discover new possibilities. In fact, who knows what new wrinkles you yourself may create, once you get started!

Make a whole family of dolls for practically nothing but a bit of string, a handful of husks, and some spare time. Add personality with accessories like a bonnet, broom, or apron.

Keep in mind that making cornhusk dolls is a good craft for children, too. There's plenty of room for improvisation because no two cornhusk dolls are alike. This project is the real thing, an age-old art that's fun to play around with today.

Collecting Materials

First, collect your husks, ideally on a bright blue and gold autumn day. We gather cornhusks from a friend's farm field. Husks that have dried on the plant seem to work better than those that are picked green and then dried. Although most farmers are happy to let you help yourself to such "waste" material, they appreciate your courtesy in asking permission. If you're not near any cornfields, I've seen cornhusks offered for sale in craft supply stores. Remove all the husks from about five ears of corn, so you have plenty of material to choose from as you construct your first doll. Use the following guidelines to choose the best materials for your work of art.

1. Collect dry, not green, husks. Wipe any that are spotted with mildew with a solution of ½ cup Clorox bleach to 1 gallon water. (This may make them a bit more brittle than unbleached husks.) Collected husks will last for years if kept free of moisture.
2. Discard the coarsest parts of the outer husk, which are likely to be discolored and wind-shredded.
3. See how the cornhusk is "gathered" around the stalk so that it flares from the stem's small diameter to the plumpness of the rounded ear? Carefully tease away the ample outer pieces of husk from the stalk (some will tear, but can still be used). Save the fullest and heaviest of these for the doll's skirts; save the cleanest for the outer skirt.
4. Select the lighter-weight, but still flared portions from the inner layers of the husk. These will come in handy as sleeves.
5. Put aside especially clean and pliable, but opaque, bits of husks. They make good faces for cornhusk people.
6. Save the silk for hair.

Findings and Notions

Next, gather the few other findings you'll need.

- Lightweight string, crochet cotton, or whatever similar cord you have on hand. Color isn't important; the string binds parts of the doll together, but will be hidden from sight.
- Tan, ivory, or other cornhusk-colored sewing thread to tie the parts of the doll that will show when finished.
- Wire or pipe cleaners for arms.
- A base for the doll's head. I use small Styrofoam balls (1 inch to 1¼ inches in diameter), but you could also use acorns, nuts, or beads from old jewelry.
- Straight pins.
- White glue, such as Elmer's.

Step-by-Step Doll Making

When you're ready to work on your first "little person," pour luke-warm water into the sink, a pan, or a shallow basin, and soak the husks for a few minutes to soften them. Any that you don't use can be left to air-dry and put away for another time.

Next, choose a comfortable, well-lit location. Place a folded bath towel on your work surface to absorb moisture from the husks during handling (unless you especially enjoy the sensation of cool water dripping down to your elbows!).

Head and Body

According to our method, cornhusk dolls are made head first.

1. Select a long, thin piece of husk, about 1½ inches by 5 or 6 inches. Form the ribbon of husk tightly around whatever base you're using. (Don't worry about the uncovered sides of the head. They'll be concealed by a bonnet.)
2. Pinch the two free ends together at the neck and tie them firmly with lightweight string. Let the excess length of husk trail below the string to help attach the head to the body later. (See the illustration on the opposite page.)
3. The doll's body, actually an underskirt, is made from the outer husk pieces that you set aside earlier. Choose 12 to 15 pieces of husk, each 2 to 3 inches wide at one end and tapering to a point at the other—a natural formation that lends itself well to this purpose. Further covering will be added later, so don't be concerned about small imperfections in the material.
4. Pick up the dozen or so chosen pieces by their narrow ends. Arrange these tips around the ribbons of husk that dangle below the head, forming a neck. (Placing the tapered ends at the neck helps to avoid bunchiness there.)
5. Tie the bundle of pointed husks together with string, as far up and close to the head as you can. Usually I wrap the string around twice to give me a good tight pull. Use a secure knot.

Arms and Sleeves

You now have a tentlike body of husks tied at the narrow end and topped by a head. Looks awful, doesn't it? Cheer up, it'll get worse before it gets better.

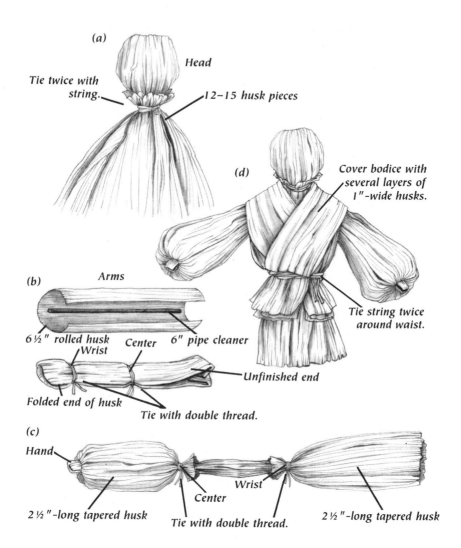

(a) Head

Tie twice with string.

12–15 husk pieces

(d)

Cover bodice with several layers of 1"-wide husks.

(b) Arms

Tie string twice around waist.

6½" rolled husk   Center   6" pipe cleaner

Wrist

Unfinished end

Folded end of husk

Tie with double thread.

(c)

Hand

2½"-long tapered husk

Center

Wrist

Tie with double thread.

2½"-long tapered husk

(a) Tie a bundle of cornhusks to the doll's head, wrapping tightly around neck.

(b) Roll a husk around a pipe cleaner. Just before completing the roll, fold in ends; then finish rolling. Tie at wrists and center to form hands and arms.

(c) Tie the sleeves to the wrists inside out. Then turn the sleeves back, exposing hands. Tie both sleeves to center of armpiece.

(d) Cross several strips of husk from front to back to form bodice, and tie at waist.

1. Cut a 6-inch piece of wire or pipe cleaner. This one continuous length will form both arms, with a hand at each end.
2. Place the wire on a piece of husk that measures about 1½ inches across by 6½ inches long. Roll the husk around the wire core. When this step is *almost* finished, fold the outer ends of the wrapper in over the tips of the wire; then complete the roll. (See the illustration on page 239.)
3. Tie the arms with tan thread, doubled, at the wrists and in the center to hold it in place. (See the illustration on page 239.)
4. To form the sleeves, take advantage of the cornhusk's natural shape at the point where it was attached to the stalk. Choose a flared piece, not too stiff, about 1½ inches wide at the narrow "gathered" end, 3½ inches wide at the opposite end, and 2½ inches long. The idea is to fasten this covering around the arm at the wrist, tie it on in the reverse of its final direction, and turn it back to form a puffed effect. (For a "rolled-up sleeves" look, attach the piece at the elbow rather than at the wrist.) This is a tricky maneuver, but accounts for much of the doll's charm.
5. Place the hand end of the wrapped wire arm on the gathered edge of the sleeve, so it extends about ½ inch onto the piece of husk.
6. Wrap the "gathers" around the arm with an overlap of no more than ½ inch. Tie the sleeve tightly at the wrist with several turns of string and a firm knot.
7. You now have a bare arm with a sleeve that is tied on at the wrist and extends out over the hand. You're ready to carefully turn the covering back—as if it were fabric—both to expose the hand and to form a nice puffy peasant-blouse look. Once it's been folded back, tie the open end of the sleeve to the arm near the center of the length of wire. (See the illustration on page 239.)
8. The other sleeve is made in the same way—and there's no need to worry if the two don't look just alike. When the arms are attached to the body, their coverings will tend to even out.

You've just completed what I consider the most difficult step in making a cornhusk doll. If you've gotten this far, you can do the rest. Your doll doesn't look like much yet, but she'll shape up fast from here on in.

Assembling the Doll

Now the doll begins to hang together.

1. Take the sleeved arm piece and thrust it firmly as far up under the head as it will go, so that half the body husks fall in back and half in front.

2. Firmly tie a length of string around the torso just under the arms to form a high waist.

3. The next step is to smooth out the bodice and you'll no doubt work out your own favorite way to do this. Meanwhile, here's mine: Choose several long, thin strips of husk, each about 1 inch wide. Hold one with your thumb at the left front of the doll's waistline, cross the band over her right shoulder, and hold its end down at the back. Wrap the next strip from the right front, up over the left shoulder, and down to the right side of the back. Continue alternating such strips until the bodice is well built up. Although stained husks can be used for the under layers, the two final pieces of shuck should be unblemished. (See the illustration on page 239.)

4. Tie a string around the waist to keep the wrappings in place. At this point there are a lot of long—usually too long—pieces of husk flapping about below the waist. Whack them off with strong scissors so that the doll will stand about 6 to 7 inches tall. (When I made my first cornhusk people I left them taller than that, and ended up with a wraithlike, El Greco quality. Now I bring them down to earth a bit more. The choice is yours.)

5. Choose two of your widest, cleanest pieces of flared husk to form the front and back of the skirt. If you're short of wide material, add an extra piece or two to cover the gap at each side. (The doll's skirt is treated in much the same way as the sleeves. Tie it on in the reverse of its final direction, and pull it down to produce a full effect, with the rough edge hidden under the bouffant gathers.)

6. Tie on the front with string first, with the gathered, narrow end at the waist and the wider part extending up over the doll's face. Then fasten the back panel in the same way, so it slightly overlaps the first, front one.

Once you've made a few cornhusk dolls, you may want to attach both sections in one operation, but you'll find it easier at the outset to proceed as I've suggested. And don't worry about all that string bunched around your little lady's waist—it helps keep her together.

7. Your doll now appears to be standing on a hot air register with her skirt flipped up over her head. Gently turn back the two parts of the garment, one at a time, so they fall as they should.

8. Find a long, thin strip of scrap husk and pin it loosely around the bottom of the skirt, without actually piercing the skirt's "fabric," to hold the pieces in position as they dry.

9. Remember that corn silk you saved? Select a small hank of silk (about as much as you'd get from one ear of corn) and tie a piece of thread around the center of the bundle.

10. Dunk the silk in water, and lift it out at once. Then drape the wet wig over your doll's head. Use a straight pin to anchor it to the husk covering until it dries. You can let the hair hang down the doll's back, form it into a bun, or make a separate braid (which you tie on around the neck before adding a cap) and tuck the rest under the bonnet.

11. A bonnet will cover the sides of the cornhusk lady's head and help keep her hair in place. Choose a good clean piece of husk about 2 inches wide by 3 inches long. Wrap it from shoulder to shoulder over the head, holding it together at the neck.

12. At this point, the cap material will be sticking straight out behind the doll. Put a pin in each side of the bonnet, if you wish, to hold it in place while you form and tie it. Hold the doll in one hand—with the headgear still pinched together under her chin—and with your other hand crease the "fabric" (as if you were wrapping a package) to fit the back of the doll's head. Tie a string or doubled thread tightly around the doll's neck, catching and holding the edges of the bonnet.

13. Make a bow for the front or back from a wisp of husk, about $\frac{1}{8}$ inch wide by 4 inches long, and attach it with a dab of glue or a straight pin.

ACCESSORIZING

It's great fun to make tools for your little people by modeling sticks, twigs, weeds, and wild findings. I'm sure you'll think of other touches to add to your dolls: various objects for them to hold, different poses for them to assume. There's plenty of scope for imagination. Here are a few ideas to start you off.

Apron. Use a piece of flared husk about 2 by 3 inches and fasten it on just as the skirt was: Position with the gathered edge at the waistline and the wider part extending up over the bodice, tie, and flip down. Try an apron made from dark red Indian cornhusks or even calico fabric.

Broom. Pampas grass seed heads make good brooms. Or, tie pine needles or thin dried grass to a small twig.

Churn. Start with the dasher—a thin stick—and roll a 2-inch-wide piece of husk around it to a thickness of about ⅝ inch. Tie the wrapping near both ends. Then cut a ribbon of husk 1¼ inches wide and continue to wrap the barrel, this time just at the lower end, until it reaches a thickness of about 1 inch. Again fasten the roll near both its top and bottom. Tie or glue the dasher to the doll's hand, or leave the churn freestanding.

Bread. Next time you bake, set aside a small lump of dough about the size of a golf ball. Bake into a miniature loaf, and pose your doll with her hands offering a loaf of homemade bread.

Knitting. Use two round toothpicks as needles, and cast on about 12 stitches of lightweight string or wool. Knit an inch or so. Then wrap a small ball of yarn and glue the last few strands around the bundle to prevent unraveling. Tie the work to the doll's hands and let the ball of wool fall to the "floor" or dangle partway down.

243

CHAPTER THIRTY - SEVEN

Create a Terrarium

244

A terrarium can provide a welcome spot of greenery all winter long—and fall is a good time to make one. There's a special satisfaction to be found in arranging this small, bounded green world to your own liking. In a woodland terrarium I once made, a tiny mushroom emerged from the clump of forest sod that I had tucked into a covered bowl. It didn't last long, but it added an extra dimension while it was in fruit.

Choose slow-growing plants with similar soil needs for your terrarium. Look for adaptable plants that are happy in low light and high humidity. For a pleasing effect, include plants with different forms and textures—some creeping, others bushy.

Many houseplants—including peperomias (*Peperomia* spp.), mosaic plant (*Fittonia verschaffeltii*), and baby's-tears (*Soleirolia soleirolii*)—are perfect candidates for a terrarium. Other adaptable terrarium plants include episcias (*Episcia* spp.), small ferns, sedums, mosses, and evergreen seedlings. If you have woodland plants such as wintergreen (*Gaultheria procumbens*), bearberry (*Arctostaphylos uva-ursi*), and pipsissewa (*Chimaphila umbellata* var. *cisatlantica*), consider digging a slip or two and add a small rock or an interesting piece of wood to make a woodland scene under glass. Most herbs, especially rosemary and thyme, and other plants requiring excellent drainage and favoring dry air, would not do well in a terrarium.

Planting the Terrarium

You can use almost any glass container that is transparent, waterproof, and easily covered—from a jelly jar to a three-gallon jug—for your glass garden. A round, covered candy jar makes a good terrarium container. Try planting and positioning a large jug on its side, but shim it so it doesn't roll. Once you've found your jar, here's how to plant your glass garden.

1. Wash and dry the jar. Make sure the sides of the jar are completely dry before putting the planting medium into it—the soil will adhere to any damp spots that remain.
2. Arrange a layer of sphagnum moss on the bottom of the container. Although the moss isn't essential, it provides air spaces, absorbs water, and even exerts a mild antibiotic effect.
3. Scatter a bed of sand or fine gravel over the moss. Use about ½ inch of sand or gravel in a 1- to 4-quart jar. Use ¾ inch in a 3-gallon jug or retired aquarium. These materials improve drainage by providing a "well" for excess water.
4. Spread ½ inch of charcoal on top of the sand. If your container is tall, such as a 3-gallon jug, spread charcoal about 1 inch deep. The porous charcoal absorbs impurities and provides a small reserve air supply. Use plain wood charcoal, not barbecue briquettes,

245

2" potting soil

½" layer of
charcoal pieces

½" layer of sand
or fine gravel

½" layer of sphagnum
moss

Fill your terrarium container by using a rolled newspaper for a funnel. It's easier to keep the sides from getting dirty than it is to clean them. Bottom layers of sphagnum moss, sand, and charcoal improve air circulation and drainage. A few inches of soil is enough for the small root systems of the plants you will add to the terrarium.

which can injure plants.

5. Top the charcoal with a base layer of potting soil. Use a sterile commercial soil mix to reduce the number of molds introduced into the system. For a tiny, ½-cup terrarium, about ½ inch of potting soil is enough. The bigger the container, the deeper the soil. Use 1 inch of soil for a 3- to 12-cup container; 2 inches or so for jars taller than 12 inches. To direct the soil into a narrow-necked container without messing up the sides, pour it through a long slender funnel made of rolled newspaper.

6. Next add the plants. If you can't reach to the bottom of the jar, use long-handled tweezers or a straightened coat hanger with a loop on one end to settle them in place. An old spoon taped to a long stick makes a good miniature trowel for a deep terrarium.

7. Once the plants are in position, fill in around them with potting soil. The soil surface should be about about one-fourth the height of the container; fill a 12-inch-tall container about 3 inches deep.

Firm the soil gently around the plants. Use a cork or spool attached to a stick as a tamper for hard-to-reach areas.

Care and Feeding

Add water *sparingly* to your newly planted terrarium, just enough to settle the plant roots in the soil. You can always add more water if it's needed, but if you flood the jar with water, you can't remove it. Excess water fosters mold and decay. It's much easier to prevent mold than to remove it once it starts. Later, if the soil appears dry and the container feels light in weight, add a couple of teaspoons of water with an eyedropper.

Cover the opening of the terrarium with a lid, a piece of glass, or a sheet of clear plastic wrap. Plants need some air, so don't make the lid completely airtight. When the terrarium is covered, it becomes a self-contained system with its own weather. Moisture that transpires from the plant leaves condenses on the cover and sides of the jar and trickles down to keep the soil moist. If you notice the glass looks misty, mold forms on the soil surface, or water pools at the bottom of the jar, the moisture level is too high. Leave the cover off for a day to ventilate the terrarium.

Once planted, terrariums seldom need watering. Because you don't want to encourage the plants to outgrow their space, don't fertilize either, at least until the terrarium is about a year old. To prevent mold from forming, trim off spent flowers and dead leaves by cutting rather than pulling, to avoid dislodging the plants, and remove any plants that die.

Most terrariums thrive in indirect light. Strong sunlight can cook the glassed-in plants. In a dark room, the terrarium will need several hours of artificial light each day. Regular incandescent lighting may be enough for many terrariums, particularly those filled with ferns, mosses, and other woodland plants. Fluorescent tubes provide an economical source of extra light.

Pinch back plants that threaten to grow too rangy to keep them short and bushy. Once in a while, a plant will outgrow the terrarium. Out-of-bounds plants can often be carefully uprooted and replanted in pots or in the ground, depending on their hardiness.

CHAPTER THIRTY-EIGHT

See How Long You Can Keep Your Garden Going

Frost sweetens things, and so it is with the harvest. Sometimes I think we appreciate most those crops that we're able to tide over, keep going, sneak by old Jack Frost so we can continue picking. With a bit of preparation, you can extend your harvest by a month or more. Having something fresh in the garden to pluck during December and even into January helps shorten the winter.

What does it take to get fresh lettuce for Thanksgiving, spinach salad for Christmas, Chinese cabbage to usher in the New Year? Mostly timely planting, sensible care, and some protection. Choice of cultivars can help, too. Extending the harvest can get to be a game—and expending a little extra care and effort can make you a winner. Most gardeners who put away the hoe with the first frost can gain at least another month of good picking by following some of these easy steps. There's still time to save some of this year's garden vegetables. Remember to jot down picking dates and the methods of protection you use. Then you'll know what you're gaining, and what works for you and your garden.

Fresh Pickings All Year Round

We live in south-central Pennsylvania, where tender plants are usually frost-killed by the second or third week in October. We often have light frost early in October and even in September. But last year, we picked broccoli and mizuna into mid-December, a good seven weeks after our tomato-killing frost. Two years ago, in a season of record cold, we harvested broccoli until mid-November. Cauliflower, fennel, radishes, and lettuces are usually good well into November. By the third week of that month, parsnips and brussels sprouts are finally worth picking, their flavor much improved after a couple of good frosts.

A little protection from frigid nights can keep hardy plants alive for several weeks longer. During the first week of January, we have picked kale, brussels sprouts, butterhead lettuce, Chinese cabbage, and parsley—from under the snow. The kale and brussels sprouts are cold-loving, but adding some insulation made the difference for the others. We had covered the other crops with a sheet of Reemay, held down by bricks and stones, bags of leaves, and—now—by snow. Spinach, nestling in a loose blanket of leaves frosted with snow, was still usable, too.

In early January, we ate the last 'Long Keeper' tomato from a mid-October picking. And later in the month (according to our kitchen calendar notations, it was January 23), we savored the first tender, pale green leaves of the new crop of Belgian endive from the roots I had dug in fall, replanted in buckets, and brought inside. Of course, there were still beets and potatoes in the root cellar and onions in a cool storeroom, so the cycles of growth and storage overlapped.

THE COOL-WEATHER CALENDAR

Our planting timetable for eating well after frost goes something like this.

May. Broccoli, brussels sprouts, cabbage, cauliflower, kale, parsnips, witloof chicory; 'Long Season' beets for storage.
June. Chinese cabbage, endive, escarole. June is a good time to make a second carrot planting, too.
July. Repeat plantings of butterhead or head lettuce, mizuna, turnips.
Mid- to late August. Leaf lettuce, radishes, spinach.
September. Dill, leaf lettuce, radishes, perhaps some more spinach.

Planning a Garden That Laughs at Cold

Few weeks go by—even in summer—that we don't plant something. Our garden is no showplace, and occasionally a planting fails to flourish, but because we make frequent and varied plantings, the cupboard is seldom bare. The idea is to plant cool-weather crops in time for them to reach near-maturity by frost time. Then the cold air will keep them on hold. Many gardeners plant Chinese cabbage, cauliflower, broccoli, and turnips as spring crops, too, but for us they grow and taste best in fall when nights are cooler.

Cold-Tolerant Cultivars

Cool-weather vegetables are hardy by nature, so even the most commonly available cultivars can usually be counted on to weather repeated frost. But a number of cultivars have been especially bred to endure low temperatures; comb the seed catalogs to find them. Here are a few extra-hardy cultivars of hardy vegetables to start your long-season garden.

Broccoli 'Christmas Purple' or 'Premium Crop'
Brussels sprouts 'Cambridge' or 'Dolmic'
Cabbage 'Green Jewel'
Kale 'Winterbor'

Pile a deep, loose blanket of leaves on the spinach row to protect it from frigid temperatures, and you'll be picking fresh greens for a Christmas salad.

Kohlrabi 'Early White Vienna'
Leek 'Gabilan'
Mustard 'Savannah'
Onion 'Sweet Winter'
Parsley 'Banquet'
Spinach 'Vienna' or 'Winter Bloomsdale'
Turnip 'Royal Crown'

Late-Season Care

Vegetables are more likely to produce well past frost if they aren't smothered by weeds. It's a good idea to water and fertilize your late-season crops generously in early fall. Then, as frost approaches, give them additional water only if the weather is very dry. Water sparingly and avoid fertilizing cold-season vegetables in mid- to late fall to keep the plants from producing new growth. Tender, sappy new growth is more vulnerable to frost.

To supply elements and trace minerals, many growers spray plant leaves with seaweed solution as frost time nears. Use a dose of diluted seaweed extract, 1 tablespoon to a gallon of water. Insects usually aren't a problem once frost hits, except for aphids on kale and brussels sprouts. Insecticidal soap will help control these pests.

Mulching fall crops can help to prolong their usefulness. Tuck leaves, straw, or pine needles around plants to keep the surrounding soil a bit warmer, or even toss it over them for extra protection. The mulch also enriches the soil for next spring's vegetable patch as it rots down over winter. One year, I carefully bent over a brussels sprouts stalk until it touched the ground and mulched it with leaves. It lived until spring and started growing again in March.

Hilling soil around bulbous-stemmed plants like leeks, fennel, and sometimes celery protects them from cold and helps these vegetables to grow more tender. Use a hoe to pull loose soil toward the plant from both sides of the row. Till the spaces between rows first, so the soil is loose and easy to work.

Pinching conserves plant energy. By removing immature buds that will not have time to develop to usable size, you give the plant a chance to channel available nutrients to existing fruits.

- If the end of the season is nearing, pinch the growing tips of cucumbers, melons, and squashes, so they can put all their efforts into vegetable production.
- Nip out the top rosette of leaves from brussels sprouts plants to encourage the development of sprouts all along the stem. Snap off the plant's bottom leaves as the sprouts start to shape up, so they'll have room to expand.
- Celeriac forms a larger knob if you prune off the straggly side roots after the ball-shaped root begins to look round. Cut off the side roots with a knife or break them by gentle hoeing around the plant.

A Blanket to Keep Away Cold

As every gardener knows, the first frost of the season is often followed by a spell of mild Indian summer weather—a good growing time for those plants that have been spared frost damage. The hardiest vegetables—kale and brussels sprouts—will stay in picking condition when the pond freezes over, even if uncovered. Bare spinach will persist through some mighty hard frosts. But, covering frost-sensitive crops like tomatoes and beans can often buy you another week or two, or even more, of continued harvest. And our Chinese cabbage, escarole, and lettuce would succumb to frost much sooner if not covered by a floating row cover.

The berry boxes and cut-open plastic jugs we use to protect small spring seedlings aren't much use in fall for big, bushy, mature plants. Until recently, when frost threatened, my late fall garden would become a crazy quilt of old sheets, curtains, and tablecloths, draped over the still-good plants I hoped to keep alive. These improvised plant blankets offered at least a few degrees of frost protection when dry. If they got wet and icy, though, they weren't much help. And they kept sunlight off the plants unless I removed them each day. Storage was a problem, too: The covers had to be hung to dry before I stored them so they wouldn't get moldy.

Row Covers: A Modern Invention That Works

I admit some initial skepticism when these products—lightweight blankets of polyester or polypropylene—were introduced. I thought they would be more trouble than they were worth. But the protection they offer has prolonged our fall vegetable picking season by about six weeks, so they've earned a place on my garden tool shelf. Floating row covers certainly look better than my hodgepodge of linen-closet leftovers, and they work better, too. Rain can pass through their pores, so they don't get waterlogged. Plants stay healthier because air circulation is good. Row covers are so lightweight they can rest directly on the plants. And you won't need to lift them off every day— enough light penetrates the fabric to keep plants growing. Row covers can ward off up to three degrees of frost (you can use a double layer for extra protection). They keep plants and soil warmer all day, so plants can absorb soil nutrients that might not be available at lower temperatures.

Floating row covers come in long sheets, so you can cover a whole 50-foot row uniformly. And they come in different widths, so you can easily secure them across a wide row. Be sure both sides of the row covers are securely held to the ground with sticks, bricks, stones, or other easily removed props. I often bank both sides of the row with black or dark green bags of leaves to break the force of the wind and to soak up and release a bit of the sun's warmth.

253

I've used the same sheets of Reemay for two to three garden seasons, longer than the generally projected lifespan of one to two seasons. Ultraviolet inhibitors added to Tufbell, Harvest Guard, Agryl 17, and several other brands keep them stable longer in sunlight and lengthen their useful life by a season or two, offsetting their higher cost.

Other Frost Blockers

The cold frame you used to start spring seedlings can keep lettuce, endive, and other cool-weather crops alive for a few more weeks of picking. Transplant young plants into the cold frame in early fall. Or use a portable frame, and move it around the garden as you need it. You can make an impromptu cold frame with hay bales: Make a barricade of bales around the plants and place a storm window over the top of the hay bale enclosure.

Some gardeners use plastic tunnels of clear polyethylene sheeting. Supported every few feet by 12- to 18-inch-high, U-shaped wire hoops, these mini-greenhouses stretch over the length of the row and are secured by piling soil over the edges. These tunnels are more cumbersome to set up than floating row covers, though, and they tend to overheat on a warm Indian summer day. Unless they are well-ventilated at both ends and along their length, they block air circulation, and they shed rain, too.

Umbrella greenhouses are handy for modest-sized gardens. These dome-shaped umbrellas of clear plastic sheeting are stabilized with strong anchor shafts that plunge 9 inches into the ground. They're easy to pop over small groups of plants, and they're easy to store—they fold up just like an umbrella. To ventilate plants, just pull the umbrella up a bit so there's an air space between the soil and the bottom edge of the plastic dome.

CHAPTER THIRTY-NINE

Coax Winter Bulbs into Indoor Bloom

I f you've ever feasted your eyes—or your nose—on a pot of bright daffodils or fragrant hyacinths while cold winter winds tossed bare tree branches outside, then you know that the planning and effort that goes into forcing bulbs is truly worthwhile.

Before they can burst into bloom, planted bulbs require a lengthy period of chilling, during which they form roots. Forcing is the official name for the process of planting and chilling flowering bulbs for early bloom indoors, but I prefer to consider it in less aggressive terms—more like coaxing. After all, it's only by understanding and cooperating with their nature that we can succeed in getting bulbs to bloom early for us.

It's All in the Timing

Sometimes it takes a bit of finagling to make the timing come out right. Most spring-blooming bulbs like crocuses, hyacinths, and daffodils need 12 to 16 weeks of cool but not freezing temperatures—45°F or lower—to stimulate the development of the strong root system that is necessary to support the plant through the blooming period. You want to plant the bulbs as early as you possibly can, but you must shield them from warm temperatures. Above 55°F, potted bulbs produce premature top growth before they have a chance to form enough roots to support it. Don't let your potted bulbs freeze for long periods, either, because root growth stops at around 32°F.

BEST BULBS FOR INDOOR BLOOM

The familiar spring bulbs are the usual candidates for coaxing into winter bloom. Extend the blooming period by planting bulbs of early, midseason, and late varieties. Different kinds of bulbs, and even different cultivars of the same species, have different blooming times, so it's best not to mix bulbs. Plant just one type in a container. Try these : crocuses (*Crocus* spp.), daffodils (*Narcissus* spp.), Dutch irises (*Iris xiphium* hybrids), grape hyacinths (*Muscari* spp.), hyacinth (*Hyacinthus orientalis*), Siberian squill (*Scilla siberica*), star-of-Bethlehem (*Ornithogalum arabicum*), tulips (*Tulipa* spp.), and windflower (*Anemone blanda*).

256

Plant the Pots

Early October is a good time to pot up bulbs for winter bloom. To prevent last-minute panic, order your bulbs early. Some mail-order catalogs offer prechilled bulbs that will bloom after a shorter storage time. If you're selecting bulbs in a store, choose the largest ones. Pick those that are sound, with no nicks, blemishes, or evidence of disease.

In addition to bulbs, you'll need pots and potting soil. Special bulb pans—short, wide flowerpots—are nice because they offer a larger planting surface than the usual tall, narrow pots. But you can use regular pots, too, either clay or plastic. Whatever kind of pots you use, be sure they have drainage holes. Bulbs will rot if waterlogged. Wash pots that have been used before to remove traces of mold and dirt.

A pot with a diameter of 4 to 5 inches at the top will hold one large daffodil, tulip, or hyacinth bulb, or several crocuses. A 6- to 10-inch pot will support six of the larger bulbs or a dozen crocuses. Pots usually look best planted as full as you can get them.

The soil you use to fill the pots needn't be rich. Flower bulbs have within them all the nutrients necessary to bring their buds to bloom. Use commercial potting soil to fill the pots, or make your own by mixing equal parts of soil, sand, and peat moss or leaf mold. (Substitute vermiculite or perlite for the sand if you wish.) Some people lighten the commercial soil mix by adding some sand or perlite to it. Later, when the bulbs are planted in the garden, good soil is helpful to nourish the leaves that will make

Hourglass-shaped hyacinth vases are fun for young and old. The glass neatly supports the bulb, even with a fat spike of flowers. Tip the vase once a week to drain old water; gently refill with fresh water.

more plant food to support *next* year's growth and bloom.

Ready to pot up some bulbs? Here's how.

1. Pat a 2-inch layer of soil mix into the bottom of the pot to form a good base for the roots.
2. Set bulbs pointed end up and almost—but not quite—touching.
3. Add soil mix, making sure it sifts down well into the cracks between bulbs. If you're planting daffodils, cover the bulbous part of the bulb with soil but leave the protruding central stem stub uncovered. For tulips, hyacinths, crocuses, and most other bulbs, spread ½ to 1 inch of soil mix over the bulbs. Leave at least a ½-inch watering space at the top of the pot, between soil level and pot edge.
4. After planting the bulbs, water the pots. An easy way is to set them in a basin of water. Remove the pots when the surface of the soil feels moist.

Find a Cool, Dark Hideaway

Now you need to find a likely nook to tuck those potted bulbs away—some place dark and cool that will foster good root growth. The ideal spot has a temperature of 38° to 48°F. You won't have the same control over the temperature under home conditions that florists have in their cold storage setups, but one or more of the following hiding places should work well.

- A root cellar—either in your basement or dug into a hill—is cold, damp and dark—just what you need.
- Try a cold frame with perlite insulation. Perlite is a lightweight insulating material that won't absorb water. Stash the pots away in a covered cold frame, but first spread one inch of perlite on the ground so pots won't freeze to the soil. Keep the pots 6 inches away from the sides of the frame and at least 4 inches away from the glass cover. Pack perlite all around the pots, and heap it over them to a depth of 1 to 2 inches. When your pots have come in from the cold, you can rebag the perlite for next year or use it for making potting soil mixtures.
- Bury pots in leaves in an unheated garage. Move them to a cold house basement or other cool-but-not-freezing spot if outdoor temperature turns frigid.
- Put the covered pots on the north side of an unheated enclosed

FORCING BULBS IN WATER

A few kinds of bulbs—hyacinth, narcissus, and crocus—may be brought to flower in water, but for those few, the process is quicker than planting in soil. Paperwhite narcissus will flower in only five to six weeks, hyacinths in six to eight weeks, and crocuses in about ten weeks.

Start the bulbs on their way in a shallow waterproof container, twice as deep as the size of the bulbs. Fill the container half full with pebbles, and set the bulbs on this base about ½ inch apart. Slowly pour in water till it touches the base of the bulbs. Then fill in between the bulbs with more gravel, to help keep them in position. Some people put a small amount of activated charcoal in the water to keep it fresh.

A hyacinth vase may be used for forcing sweet-scented hyacinths into bloom indoors. This vase is hourglass-shaped, with a constriction in the middle to hold the bulb above the water. Fill the bottom part of the vase so that the water level just touches the bottom of the bulb. Change the water each week. No pebbles are needed for this arrangement.

Put the planted dishes or vases in a dark, cool place (38° to 48°F) to encourage roots to develop, which takes two to four weeks. Add water from time to time so that the roots are continuously in water, but don't flood the bulbs above their bases. Watch for emerging leaves, and when they're about 3 inches high, put the containers in a warmer place (65°F or so) in bright, indirect light. When flower buds appear, give the plants plenty of direct light to bring them into bloom. Then return them to bright, indirect light so the flowers last longer. Bulbs that have been brought into bloom in water are usually discarded after flowering, but there's no harm in sticking them into an odd corner of the garden.

porch, perhaps in an insulated picnic cooler. Be sure to cover them to keep them in the dark.

- More work, but a traditional cooling arrangement: Dig a trench 1 to 1½ feet deep. Line with a board or straw to keep the pots from getting stuck to the ground, and cover with a foot or more of insulating mulch—straw, leaves, peat moss—and a tarp.

Wherever you store the potted bulbs, check them regularly to see if the soil has dried out and needs watering. Pots kept on a porch or garage, away from the damp ground, may need watering more often. Avoid overwatering. Soggy soil lacks vital air and leads to rotting of bulbs and roots.

Into the Light

After the pots have been in storage for about 12 weeks, pull out a few and check for root development. If you see roots in and around the pot's drainage hole and about 2 inches of leaf bud poking above the soil, the bulbs are ready to bring indoors. It's time for the next step up in your flower encouragement program—more warmth and light. For a longer show of bloom indoors, bring in a pot or two each week so that new buds will be unfolding as others are fading.

For better, longer-lasting flowers, introduce the potted bulbs to indoor conditions *gradually*. Water the pots when you bring them indoors. At first, keep them in a cool room, and give them plenty of bright indirect light. (Crocuses need a very gradual transition from dark to light.)

After two to three weeks of transition, the buds will begin to show color. That's the time to move them to a warmer spot, around 70°F, with stronger, more direct light. Be sure to keep the soil moist during this stage; if soil is too dry, buds may form but fail to open. If the stems need some support, poke some green plant stakes or short dowels into the soil in the pot and tie a string around them to encircle the plants, or for a more attractive solution, put the pot in a larger container—perhaps a handsome crock or copper pot—and fill in the spaces with moss. Once plants are in bloom, keep them out of direct sun and away from radiators, stoves, and other heat sources so the blossoms will last longer. When a plant finishes blooming, continue to water the soil in the pot until the leaves die back naturally. If possible, give the resting bulb a few doses of liquid fertilizer, too. Then you can plant the bulbs in the garden. They'll recover in a year or two and go on to bloom some more outside, but should not be forced again. Once in a bulb's lifetime is enough.

PART FOUR

*hed no tear! O shed
    no tear!
The flower will bloom
    another year.
Weep no more! Weep
    no more!
Young buds sleep in the
    root's white core.*

—John Keats (1795–1821)

WINTER

Make Your Yard Bird-Friendly

263

Without the birds and the bees, our gardens wouldn't amount to much. Pollinating bees help keep the cucumbers, squash, apples, and pears coming. And birds do far more than most of us realize to keep insect pests under control.

While birds seldom completely eradicate a pest, they are capable of coming close: Studies show that birds can consume as much as

90 percent of a cabbage moth population. The use of pesticides, with all its attendant risks, can control only about 95 percent. Recent news that some insect larvae have begun to display immunity to the bacterium *Bacillus thuringiensis,* or Bt, a popular larval control, makes us appreciate birds all the more. Insects can't develop immunity to birds!

Some studies indicate that birds as a group eat more insects than any other kind of food. A single wren can eat several hundred insects a day. In spring, chickadees, warblers, and vireos pick bugs off leaves and twigs, keeping your trees and shrubs healthy. Robins, larks, quail, sparrows, and starlings patrol the ground for insects, eggs, and larvae. Even the often-maligned crow eats bugs when he's not pulling up your corn.

264

You can bring birds to your yard by filling any one—or all three—of their basic needs: food, water, and shelter. One way to attract more birds to your property is to establish plantings that will give them shelter and food. Birds of various kinds are attracted not only by insects but also by seeds, fruits, nuts, and flowers. The raucous blue jay eats mainly weed seeds and bugs, and song sparrows and juncos also subsist on weed seeds. Overwintering birds depend on tree, weed, and flower seeds, and on berried trees and shrubs.

Inviting birds to your yard benefits both you and them. Insect-eaters like this chickadee provide plenty of entertainment as they forage in bark crevices or hang upside down from twigs.

No matter what season they visit your yard, birds help keep pests in check. Summer resident birds, those that linger to build nests and raise their young, take care of a lot of insect pests during the growing season. Winter residents, those familiar feeder birds that flock to your tray for a handout of sunflower seeds, earn their keep by scouring bark crevices of winter trees for hidden insect eggs and hibernating pests.

HOME SWEET HOME

Nesting boxes will help to attract and keep interesting birds in your area. Birds have very specific housing requirements; the preferred size of the box and the diameter and height of the entrance hole are different for different species of birds. Even the height at which the box is mounted and the character of the surrounding terrain are important considerations.

You can purchase birdhouses made with certain species in mind, or make your own. Check your library for plans. If you want to paint your nest box, do so at least one month before nesting season so it can air out. Some birds have very modest requirements. Robins are informal nesters that will set up housekeeping in a simple U-shaped shelter of a roof, back, and floor, with front and sides left open. Swallows need even less structure: Each year, barn swallows settle on our swallow nest shelves, short boards that Mike put up in our barn. They refurbish the mud nests they (or their cousins) made on these shelves in previous years.

If you own any wooded land, leave standing any dead trees with holes and hollows for birds (and other wildlife) to nest. This is the easiest way of all to provide bird housing, and one that many birds prefer.

265

Planting for the birds means triple benefits: insect control, weed control, and bird-watching pleasure. Many of the trees, shrubs, and vines you plant to encourage birds will also beautify your grounds. Your landscaping improvements may possibly offer even a fifth dividend: increased property value. If you've ever seen a crab-apple tree festooned with a group of visiting cedar waxwings, you know that the pleasure of watching the birds is as good a reason as any to attract them.

Designing for the Birds

You may already have a good base of bird-attracting plants on which to build. Trees and shrubs, especially those that bear tempting, tasty berries, are the basis of the bird-friendly yard. Evergreens for shelter are important to birds, too.

If you're just beginning to develop your property, think of the natural progression from open meadow to forest. In the wild, many bird species live in the transition zone, the brushy area where field gives way to forest. For the widest range of bird species, plant tall trees at the edge of your land, taper to shorter trees, then shrubs, then open lawn or meadow. But if your yard space or budget is limited, you can still attract more birds by adding a small planting just for them.

Vines and Shrubs for Feasting

If you have a post, fence, trellis, or dead tree to offer support, consider planting a fruiting vine to attract foraging winter birds. Many attractive shrubs produce berries that last well into winter. A single berry-laden bush can attract birds by the dozen. Here is a sampling of plants birds favor.

Bayberry (*Myrica pensylvanica*). Bayberry is right at the top of the birds' list: 73 species enjoy its waxy gray-green fruits. It's a commonly sold shrub that can be used in borders or naturalistic settings.

Bittersweets (*Celastrus* spp.). Although some consider these vines to be rampant pests, bittersweets produce a bounty of orange berries. The twisted stems jeweled with their bright fruits are a special delight of autumn for me, and I confess that I'm trying to start some here on the farm because I love it so. Bittersweet rambles and can choke out desirable live trees, so choose the site carefully.

Staghorn sumac (*Rhus typhina*). A plant of the hedgerows, staghorn sumac is equally at home in a naturalistic garden planting. Sumac is a good bird staple—the clusters of fuzzy brownish red fruits are eaten by 93 species of birds!

Virginia creeper (*Parthenocissus quinquefolia*). Well-loved by more than three dozen kinds of birds, Virginia creeper has leaves that turn gorgeous shades of red and orange in fall. The vines produce an abundance of deep blue-black berries that last well.

Other bird favorites include: Russian olive (*Elaeagnus angustifolia*), which has fragrant spring flowers and reddish fall fruits eaten by 25 species of birds; Japanese barberry (*Berberis thunbergii*), whose leaves and berries turn an attractive red in the fall; and American cranberrybush viburnum (*Viburnum trilobum*), which produces red winter berries eaten by 34 bird species. White-berried snowberries (*Symphoricarpos* spp.) and firethorns (*Pyracantha* spp.), with their clusters of bright orange-red fruit, are also good choices.

Multiflora rose (*Rosa multiflora*) is sometimes recommended for plantings, but it reseeds itself so readily that it can become a serious pest. Rugosa roses (*Rosa rugosa* hybrids and cultivars) don't produce the multitude of rose hips the multiflora does, but their thick, bushy growth makes good shelter. Add other dense shrubs, such as privet or rhododendrons, to give birds cover and perching posts on their way to and from trees and feeders.

Invest in a Tree for the Birds

Birds appreciate almost any tree that produces nuts, berries, or seeds. Alder and birch cones feed redpolls, siskins, goldfinches, and other favorites. Acorns serve as bird food, too, for larger species like blue jays, grackles, thrashers, quail, and woodpeckers. Seeds of tulip poplar and ash make excellent bird fodder. The blue berries of the hackberry are relished by 36 kinds of birds. Cedar and pine trees, while not such good wild cafeterias, offer dense protective cover and serve as winter windbreaks. Here are some of my favorite trees for the birds. Consult with your local nursery owner for recommended species or cultivars for your area.

Crab apples (*Malus* spp.). Crab apples blossom prettily in spring, attracting many small insects—and insect-eating birds. Their white, pink, or red flowers are followed by yellow, orange, or red berries in fall. The abundant fruit is enjoyed by up to 26 species of birds all fall and winter. They are small trees, 15 to 25 feet tall. Look for disease-resistant cultivars.

Flowering dogwood (*Cornus florida*). The dogwood is a handsome tree with showy white spring flowers. Its clusters of red winter berries feed as many as 86 species of birds. Dogwoods are small trees, 20 to 30 feet tall. Dogwoods don't mind light shade as long as they get some dappled sun. Water them well in a drought. If dogwood blight is a problem in your area, plant your dogwoods in a mixed shrub border rather than as a single specimen, or try the blight-resistant kousa dogwood (*Cornus kousa*) instead.

Hawthorns (*Crataegus* spp.). Hawthorns have fragrant white or pink flowers and nutritious red berries that help support up to 33 species of birds. They are small to medium trees, 15 to 30 feet tall. One heavy-fruiting species good for attracting birds is Washington thorn (*Crataegus phaenopyrum*), a deep-rooted tree that tolerates some shade and does well in cities.

Hollies (*Ilex* spp.). Holly bushes and trees furnish dense nesting and hiding cover. Researchers have counted 45 species of birds enjoying the red berries. Be sure to plant both a male holly for pollination and a female holly for berries. There are both evergreen and deciduous species. Depending on the species, hollies can be shrubs or trees, ranging from 8 to 50 feet. Protect hollies from winter winds by planting in a mixed border or on the leeward side of a windbreak of evergreens.

Mountain ashes (*Sorbus* spp.). Mountain ashes are airy, small trees with clusters of white flowers in spring. They feed 15 species of birds with their many small, brightly colored berries. The fall fruit of the American mountain ash (*Sorbus americana*), native to eastern North America, is eagerly sought by ruffed grouse. Mountain ashes are medium to tall trees, depending on the species, and range from 15 to 60 feet.

Dinner for 50

Simple feeders will attract a variety of bird species to your home place—and encourage them to stay. Here are some tips to get your bird banquet underway.

- Pick a location away from walls or steps, from which a cat could jump to attack feeding birds. To further discourage cats, use a smooth metal pole to support the feeder, or attach a metal cone guard to the pole just below the feeder.
- Evergreens near the feeder provide wind protection and cover. If possible, put a feeder away from the house for shy species.
- An open platform is a simple feeder many birds prefer. Make yours about 2 feet square, with an edge of quarter-round molding to help prevent seed scattering; mount on a 5-foot pole. In winter, a cov-

ered feeder may be easier, so you won't have to scrape snow off each time you feed.

- Feed sunflower seeds and bird-feeding mixes. Cracked corn and commercial chicken feed are economical alternatives. Birds also enjoy household leftovers such as bread crumbs, stale crackers, crumbled bacon, raisins, pieces of fruit, and cooked rice.
- For a high-calorie fat source to keep birds warm, mount chunks of suet in hardware-cloth cages or purchased suet feeders, or hang suet in plastic mesh bags, like those used for onions. To serve peanut butter, mix it with as much cornmeal as you can work into it. This gives it a gritty instead of sticky texture, so it doesn't gum up the bird's mouth and throat. Chink a large pinecone with this mixture and hang it in a tree, or spread directly on tree bark.
- Once you've started stocking the feeder, replenish the food regularly to keep the birds coming.
- Birds need water, just as we do. They like a shallow container holding only an inch or two of water, and a perching spot so they can drink without getting wet. Try using a large flowerpot saucer with a rough, flat rock in the center to provide good footing for the birds. We keep a spare in the house so we can replace the water daily in freezing weather. You can also buy electric cables to heat your birdbath.

Many people think that birds that are encouraged to stay around might starve if those feeders go empty. Recent studies indicate, though, that even birds that habitually dine at a feeder still get 75 to 80 percent of their food from trees, bushes, and weeds in the surrounding area. Even when they have come to depend on feeders, birds seem to retain the ability to forage on their own when the free lunch is removed. Still, in severe weather, the extra calories you provide might give some birds the edge they need for survival.

CHAPTER FORTY-ONE

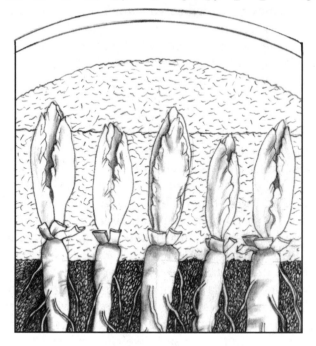

Grow Belgian Endive for Winter Salads

270

The crisp, almost buttery-tender heads of witloof chicory plants sell in city greengrocers for several dollars a pound. When they *are* available commercially, these delicacies are trucked from California, or sometimes even imported from Belgium or France, where procedure and equipment have been developed for raising the chicory heads, or chicons, in large quantities.

Gardeners who have grown their own chicory can only smile at this cumbersome arrangement. Few vegetables are easier to raise than chicory roots. The sprouting process is simple, requiring only an hour or less of preparation, a few leaky buckets, and a box of sand. It is another example of the beautiful simplicity of backyard gardening: Any gardener can grow chicory that far surpasses the shipped-in product in flavor and texture, all for a dollar packet of seeds and a little—very little—time.

The Belgan endive we await so eagerly in midwinter is the blanched leafy head of common chicory (*Cichorium intybus*). Its flame-shaped, blanched shoots are called chicons, and the popular name "witloof" means "white leaf."

Closely related to endive and escarole, chicory is native to Europe and northern Africa. Cultivars offered in seed catalogs have been developed for forcing, with larger roots that are better equipped to store the energy needed to produce a crisp, leafy sprout in winter.

Plant a Row of Witloof

The salad delicacy that can make a January menu special begins in the most prosaic way, with the sowing of a short row of witloof chicory seeds in May or June. Dig the roots before the ground freezes hard, and replant indoors in containers for forcing. A 10-foot row will produce plenty of roots for your first sprouting venture.

PRACTICE WITH DANDELIONS

If you don't have roots of witloof chicory to dig up this season, substitute dandelion roots. They also force well, in just the same way, and will give you some practice for next year. Surprise your favorite gourmet with this distinctive salad treat just when winter seems to be winning.

Ordinary garden soil is fine for chicory. Work it deeply, removing rocks, so the roots develop evenly. The seeds sprout in a week or two, depending on soil temperature. Thin young plants to 5 inches apart when they have grown large enough to grasp. Then just keep them weeded and let them be.

The plant doesn't seem to be attractive to insects. You won't be tempted to eat the leaves, either—they're rather bitter in summer and there are many better garden greens around. Once established, a row of witloof chicory demands no summer care other than weeding and occasional watering in a real drought.

Digging the Roots

By mid- or late fall, when the flood tide of corn and tomatoes is behind you, those chicory roots are ready for your attention. They will sprout more readily if they've been subjected to several freezes before you dig them up, but be sure to rescue them before the ground freezes solid. If you dig the roots and pot them before frost, leave the containers out in the cold to get a good chill in order to encourage sprouting.

When you're all set to prepare your chicory, follow these steps.

1. Use a garden fork or spade to dig the roots. Dig deeply; some roots may be more than a foot long.
2. As you dig the roots, set aside the largest ones to be sprouted first. A good-sized root measures an inch or more at the top and tapers to a length of 10 to 12 inches. Save the remaining roots for forcing later.
3. With a sharp knife, cut the leafy crown from the plant, leaving a 1-inch stub.
4. Trim the roots to a uniform length of about 9 inches.
5. Keep the roots in a cool, dark place. You can pot them up all at once, bringing containers into the warmth as you need them, or you can store the roots as you would other root crops like carrots, and pot up a bucketful at a time.

Potting

It's important to exclude light from the developing sprout, to keep it mild flavored and tender. This requires deep containers. Most households can muster enough punctured kettles, buckets, and wastebaskets to hold the roots. If your planter is still intact, knock a few holes in its base for drainage.

Traditional directions call for plunging the roots vertically into a 10-inch substratum of soil and topping that off with another 6 to 8 inches of sand or sawdust. The soil is mostly for support and the conveyance of moisture to the root, not for nutrients. The power that will produce a crisp, delicate salad head is all in the root.

ZOOM WITH WATER

Several recently introduced chicory cultivars, including one called 'Zoom', may be forced without soil. Just pack the roots in standing position in a plastic tub. Add water to a depth of 2 inches or so. Then pop a carton over the "planted" roots to keep light out. Allow a 10-inch space between the tops of the roots and the carton, to give the head room to grow. Keep the roots at 55° to 68°F till chicons appear.

I've also tried placing the roots on their sides in a shallow container—an old drawer or basin, for example—with equally good results, as long as I topped the roots with a 6- to 8-inch layer of sawdust. I've also simply covered the planted bucket with a paper grocery bag to keep out light, and that has worked well, too, as long as a few inches of sawdust covered the roots.

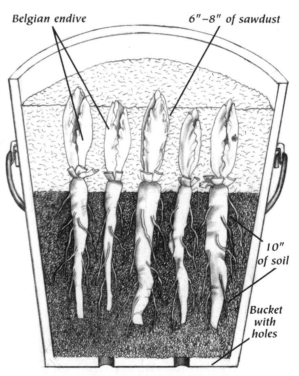

Belgian endive · *6"–8" of sawdust*

10" of soil

Bucket with holes

Gourmet witloof chicory flourishes in a leaky bucket. Dig roots from the garden before the ground freezes solid and cram them into a bucket of soil. Emerging shoots are kept pale and tender thanks to a thick layer of sawdust that blocks the light.

Forcing

Here's how to prepare roots for forcing.

1. Plant them in containers filled with

273

about 10 inches of soil—any kind of soil. You can even use peat moss. Jam the roots tightly together, packing some soil between them so they aren't exposed to the air.

2. Cover with at least 6 inches of sawdust or sand, which blanches the green shoot as it reaches for daylight. I prefer sawdust because it's easier to wash off.

3. Keep the planted containers in a cool, dark place at 32° to 40°F. Bring them in for sprouting gradually, as you need them.

4. When you're ready to start the roots on their way, move them to a warmer place. A temperature of at least 50°F is necessary to induce sprouting. Mine have done well at about 60°F. Keep them no warmer than the mid- to upper 60's for best sprout quality.

5. Water the planted roots when you bring them in, and weekly thereafter. It takes two to three weeks for them to sprout.

6. When the leaf tip shows through the thick top layer of sawdust, the head is ready to cut. Six-inch-long heads are a good size for cutting, but you can cut even 3-inch heads if you can't wait. Push away the sawdust and slice the head off, close to the root. Be careful to keep the crown of the root uncut.

7. Replace the sawdust and harvest a second, smaller witloof chicory head from the same root two to three weeks later.

CHAPTER FORTY-TWO

Grow a Traditional Medicine Garden

275

In this season of colds and flu, when people all around you are sneezing, do you ever wonder what our ancestors did when they suffered the winter miseries? In America 200 years ago, people turned to their gardens for relief from ailments. The early American garden was an indispensable resource from which the colonial housewife plucked not only fresh 'sallets' and 'garden sass' (an old New England term for vegetables), but also the herbs she depended upon to keep her family well and cure their ills. Indeed, so vital was the eighteenth-century kitchen garden that even in a household with many children or abundant hired help, the woman of the house reserved to herself the responsibility of growing and preparing simples, as the early herbal remedies were called.

The eighteenth-century family kitchen gardens were largely green gardens. By the early nineteenth century the wholesale raising of ornamental flowers in the style of the colorful, jumbled English cottage garden became commonplace, gradually replacing the herbs on which earlier generations had depended.

More than 100 different plants were widely grown in these early gardens, and most of them served a purpose. Even the flowering plants—gilly flowers, marigolds, calendulas, flax, hollyhocks, bouncing bet—were grown for healing, eating, or household use. A great many gardens also harbored one or two varieties of poisonous plants, which were sometimes used in small doses to dull pain or induce sleep.

Herbalist How-Tos

The books of the seventeenth-century herbalists John Gerard, John Parkinson, and Nicholas Culpeper were often kept on the mantel, next to the Bible, in colonial homes. These herbalists, noted for their copious use of secondhand information as well as for their helpful descriptions of plants and their common uses, influenced the shaping of early gardens.

Eating periwinkle, for example, was said to "cause love between man and wife." I can't vouch for the safety or effectiveness of that suggestion, but other herbalist prescriptions such as eating wild cress or watercress for scurvy, and consuming sorrel when citrus fruits were scarce, were right as rain. These green leafy foods, and many others similarly recommended in old-time herbals, contain significant amounts of vitamin C, the official "antiscorbutic."

According to the "doctrine of signatures," still taken seriously during the eighteenth century, plant shapes and colors were considered clues to their efficacy in treating certain diseases. The plant hepatica, with its liver-shaped leaf, was thought to be an effective treatment for hepatic ailments. We may smile at this unsophisticated reasoning, but it was not an illogical outgrowth of the Puritan's conviction that

EVERY INCH COUNTED

Most people think of intricate knot gardens with elaborate geometric beds when they hear the term "colonial garden." It's true that many early gardens were constructed in a formal, mannered order, especially on large estates and elegant town properties, where there were plenty of servants to take care of the weeding and clipping. Knot gardens require meticulous planning and intensive continuous care to keep them shapely and prevent weed takeover. The average early American garden was less formal and more useful.

In settlements where Indian raids were a regular threat, families built their houses close together in a little town, with the large open fields for raising crops situated just at the edge of town. Beside each house there was room for a small garden, which was often enclosed, along with the house, in a tall stockade fence. Later, in more gracious and less precarious times, and especially in the South, low, dense hedges of boxwood were used to outline and to partly protect the kitchen garden.

In such a circumscribed plot, every inch counted. Even the informal herb gardens had a sense of order, an 'each plant in its place' layout that permitted the raising of a maximum number of plants in a minimal space. Paths often crossed the garden, but in the smallest gardens the beds between paths were usually planted in a solid block of vegetables or herbs, rather than in space-wasting rows. The effect was one of casual but disciplined abundance.

the earth was created for man's use. What could be more natural than to suppose that the Creator had somehow marked the plants to help man discover their proper uses?

Despite some of the bizarre cures that make me, for one, very glad to be living here and now, I find it remarkable that so many plants now recognized for their high vitamin and mineral content were recommended and used correctly by traditional herbalists, with only hearsay, tradition, and observation to guide them.

A Corner of Special Plants

Whether you call it a medicine garden, an herb garden, or a kitchen garden, you will find great satisfaction in setting up a corner devoted to these plants. Imagine a small garden alive with small, neat mounds of thyme; shrubby, needle-leaved rosemary; vigorous, vining hops. Experiment with some of the mild, nontoxic healing agents, like catnip, chamomile, fennel, horehound, and sage. Group them in a small plot, add an edging of parsley or chives, and you've revived an old and ever-useful tradition.

Such a small garden—a source of savory seasonings, insect-repellent aromatics, and even helpful healing tonics—will give you pleasure out of all proportion to its size. One of my gardening friends has a 3-by-5-foot semicircle planted with herbs and pansies near the back (main) door of her eighteenth-century stone house. There's sage, dill, thyme, geraniums, parsley, chives—just a few of each. That little plot seems to attract even more admiring attention than the brightly colored flowers in borders surrounding the house.

Here is a sampling of plants found in early gardens, and still worth growing today in your own garden corner for use or ornament. I've left out the dangerously poisonous ones and those chosen for the significance of their shapes. Think of these suggestions as a beginning, and fill your garden with the plants you find most useful or interesting.

Annual Plants for the Medicine Garden

Basil (*Ocimum basilicum*)

Many present-day gardeners grow basil especially to season their tomatoes. Long before tomatoes were even accepted as edible, basil was a favorite Old World and colonial herb. My favorite kinds are lemon basil (*O. basilicum* 'Citriodorum'), bush basil (*O. basilicum* 'Minimum'), and 'Genova' basil (*O. basilicum* 'Genova').

Growth habit:	Bushy annual; 12 to 18 inches tall.
Where to grow:	Full sun; well-drained, rich soil.
How to start:	Sow directly in the garden when weather and soil have warmed. Or start seeds indoors two to three weeks before the last spring frost date.
Spacing:	Space plants 1 foot apart.
Growing tips:	Pinch the growing tips to encourage bushy growth.

| *Uses:* | Some herbalists believe basil tea (1 teaspoon dried leaves per cup) may help remedy headaches and nervous tension. |

Calendula (*Calendula officinalis*)

Calendula, also called pot marigold, bears bright orange or yellow flowers that may be used in soups and broths, as well as for their reputed healing qualities. This plant makes a cheerful spot of color in your medicine garden.

Growth habit:	Annual; 15 to 18 inches tall.
Where to grow:	Full sun; ordinary to poor garden soil.
How to start:	Plant seeds directly in the garden, or indoors in late winter for earliest bloom.
Spacing:	Space plants 10 inches apart.
Growing tips:	Calendulas prefer cool weather. They tolerate cold temperatures and even light frost. I always make a second planting in July for fall flowers.
Uses:	Dried petals were powdered and mixed with lard, turpentine, and resin to make a healing salve in the seventeenth and eighteenth centuries. Even today, calendulas are recommended by some herbalists for healing skin problems such as warts and rashes.

Parsley (*Petroselinum crispum*)

A perfect edging plant, parsley forms a low, neat row of intensely green, fine cut leaves. Parsley is occasionally visited by a yellow-, black-, and green-striped caterpillar—the larva of the black swallowtail butterfly—but seems otherwise immune to pests and disease. The problem with parsley is getting the slow-germinating seed to sprout. Although most catalogs say that it takes three weeks, my experience has been that it's closer to four in early spring when soil is cold.

Growth habit:	Neat mounds; 12 to 18 inches tall.
Where to grow:	Full sun to partial shade; ordinary garden soil. Hardy to Zone 9, but may survive winters in colder regions.
How to start:	Sow seeds directly in the garden. Or start indoors eight to ten weeks before the last spring frost.
Spacing:	Space plants 6 inches apart.
Growing tips:	Soak seeds in water overnight to leach out the germination-inhibiting chemicals they contain.

	To speed up outdoor plantings, pour a fine stream of very hot water over the just-planted seeds.
Uses:	Old uses of parsley included treating kidney and liver ailments. In addition to its value as a garnish and as a source of vitamins A and C, we use it today as an antidote to garlic breath: Just chew on a sprig of parsley after eating garlic. Parsley chlorophyll tames the garlic fumes.

Summer Savory (*Satureja hortensis*)

Savory has a long-standing international reputation for aiding in the digestion of what Gerard called the "windie pulses," or what we call dried peas and beans. In Germany, in fact, it is called *Bohnenkraut,* the bean herb. Some gardeners think the herb also protects bean plants from bean beetles and other pests, but I haven't found this to be true in my garden.

Growth habit:	Neat and bushy; 12 to 18 inches tall.
Where to grow:	Full sun; well-drained, ordinary garden soil.
How to start:	Plant seeds directly in the garden. The seeds are very tiny but grow well in open rows if you comb the soil to a fine tilth.
Spacing:	Thin plants to 1 foot apart.
Growing tips:	Begin snipping leaves when plants reach 6 inches tall. Nip off branch tips to delay flowering.
Uses:	The first cutting usually has the best flavor. In addition to tucking a sprig of savory into baked beans, try the seventeenth-century practice of mixing dried savory with fine bread crumbs when breading veal or other meat. And if you're stung by a bee or other insect, rub a fresh savory leaf on the punctured spot for quick relief.

280 Sweet Fennel (*Foeniculum vulgare* var. *dulce*)

Sweet or Florence fennel is an aromatic, anise-flavored plant closely resembling dill. Its lower stem thickens like a plump stalk of celery. All parts of the plant—seed, root, stalk, and leaf—are edible. Try it in salads and as a cooked vegetable. The seeds contain an oil that may irritate sensitive skin.

Growth habit:	Feathery; 4 feet tall.
Where to grow:	Full sun; well-drained, ordinary garden soil.

How to start:	Plant seeds directly in the garden.
Spacing:	Thin plants to 18 to 24 inches apart.
Growing tips:	Fennel is often planted in a bed of its own because it seems to inhibit growth of several garden vegetables, including beans and tomatoes.
Uses:	Fennel was once used to encourage milk flow in the nursing woman and to treat kidney ailments, among other things. Present-day uses include brewing leaves and stems for a hot facial and using fennel solution as an eyewash.

Perennials for the Medicine Garden

Catnip (*Nepeta cataria*)

Catnip is a rather strong-tasting, rank-growing mint—not the best choice for tea if you have more mellow mints in your garden. It is a familiar barnyard and roadside weed across the country.

Growth habit:	Bushy, vigorous; 1 to 3 feet tall.
Where to grow:	Full sun; well-drained, ordinary to poor soil. Hardy to Zone 3.
How to start:	Seed is very fine; start in pots or flats. Cuttings root easily in spring. Or transplant from a donor's yard; keep moist until established.
Spacing:	Space plants 12 inches apart.
Growing tips:	Pinch the growing tips to keep catnip in bounds.
Uses:	Catnip is a well-known traditional tea plant, especially esteemed for its soothing effect on the digestive system. It is also a good insect chaser. Strew a few sprigs on your kitchen shelves and counters to banish ants. The effect lasts three to four days and then the cuttings must be renewed.

Creeping Thyme (*Thymus praecox* subsp. *arcticus,* also offered as *T. serpyllum*)

The tiny-leaved thyme plant is more powerful than it looks. Its use in remedies is legendary. And the flavor is good. We like pinches of thyme in casseroles, soups, stews, and salads. I sometimes pot up a plant or two from the border to provide indoor cuttings during the winter. If you have a stony place where foot traffic is not heavy, scat-

281

ter seeds of creeping thyme between the stones to make an aromatic carpet. Creeping thyme, also called mother-of-thyme, likes sun and good drainage, but it's an adaptable plant, not hard to please.

Growth habit:	Forms spreading mats; 2 to 4 inches tall.
Where to grow:	Full sun to partial shade; ordinary garden soil. Hardy to Zone 5.
How to start:	Sow seeds directly in the garden or start indoors four to six weeks before last spring frost.
Spacing:	Space plants 6 inches apart.
Growing tips:	Creeping thyme grows slowly, and stays small, creeping farther than its height. Older plants get woody and produce a scanty supply of leaves; periodically start new plants from seeds or cuttings.
Uses:	Thyme is famous for its use in cough remedies; in addition, it was once administered to heal worms, sciatica, hiccups, whooping cough, and toothache. Try thyme tea (1 ounce of dried leaves to 1 pint of water) to help throat irritation or stomach upset.

Elecampane (*Inula helenium*)

This robust, hairy-leaved perennial, bears large, bright yellow, daisylike flowers. You may have noticed it growing wild in moist, shady spots; elecampane escaped from colonial gardens years ago.

Growth habit:	Tall and sturdy; 4 to 6 feet tall.
Where to grow:	Part to full shade; moisture-retentive soil. Hardy to Zone 3.
How to start:	Plant seeds directly in the garden. Or plant root divisions in fall.
Spacing:	Space plants 2 feet apart.
Growing tips:	Sometimes called wild sunflower, elecampane is at home in a shady wildflower garden, too.
Uses:	Elecampane roots were recommended for a wide variety of ills, from what Galen called 'passions of the hucklebones' (we call it sciatica) to cough, itching, worms, shortness of breath, and digestive problems. It's grown by herbal healers today for its effect on respiratory problems; a reputedly soothing tea may be made from a bit of root steeped in boiling water.

Feverfew (*Chrysanthemum parthenium*)

This old healing staple earns a place in today's garden by virtue of its neat habit of growth and attractive white and yellow button flowers. Whenever I've grown a garden, I've cherished feverfew for bouquets. The plant is easy to grow.

Growth habit:	Bushy; 1 to 3 feet tall.
Where to grow:	Full sun to partial shade; ordinary to poor soil. Hardy to Zone 5.
How to start:	Seed is fine; start in pots or flats. Divisions with a bit of root from the mother plant take hold quickly.
Spacing:	Space plants 1 foot apart.
Growing tips:	Pinch the growing tips to keep feverfew low and bushy. Self-sows freely.
Uses:	Feverfew's leaves are bitter, so you'll probably not be tempted to use it. But it's been used to treat inflammation, depression, and toothache.

Horehound (*Marrubium vulgare*)

Anyone who has ever sampled the musky, aromatic, sweet/bitter flavor of horehound cough drops can appreciate why this penetrating herb was a popular remedy for all kinds of throat ailments. An ancient plant, horehound is one of the five bitter herbs, traditionally eaten at the Passover Feast.

Growth habit:	Bushy; 2 to 3 feet tall.
Where to grow:	Full sun; well-drained, sandy soil. Hardy to Zone 4.
How to start:	Plant seeds directly in the garden. Or start from cuttings or young plants.
Spacing:	Space plants 12 to 18 inches apart.
Growing tips:	Horehound's square stems give it away as a member of the big mint family. Though it doesn't spread by underground stems, it self-sows generously.
Uses:	Early herbalists recommended horehound for liver and spleen problems, for consumption, and to aid in childbirth. While I'm not so sure of those claims, horehound does deserve its reputation for soothing throats irritated by coughs and cold. The leaves can be brewed as a tea. You can make a syrup cooked down from

283

sweetened tea or lozenges by boiling the syrup to the hard-crack candy stage.

Houseleek (*Sempervivum tectorum*)

Also called hens-and-chickens, houseleek is a familiar dooryard plant. Frequently found around the foundations and back steps of old houses, houseleeks make good edging and rock garden plants. Some of the seventeenth century (and earlier) herbalists maintained that a planting of houseleeks could fend off lightning. Although no one expects that of it any more, it is an attractive, long-lasting, trouble-free plant to have around.

Growth habit:	Low, spreading rosettes; 4 to 6 inches tall.
Where to grow:	Full sun; well-drained, even dry soil. Hardy to Zone 5.
How to start:	Buy young potted plants or "chicks" offshoots.
Spacing:	Space plants 1 foot apart.
Growing tips:	Houseleeks are good container plants, and tolerate well those occasional lapses when we forget to water them.
Uses:	Houseleek leaves were mainly external applications for the healing of burns, ulcers, skin inflammations, corn removal, and gout. They're still used, especially in Europe, to heal skin problems and relieve insect stings.

Marjoram (*Origanum majorana*, sweet marjoram; *Origanum vulgare*, wild or pot marjoram)

Marjoram adds texture and shape to the dooryard garden. The attractive plant has many small branches bearing small gray-green oval leaves and round, knotlike flower buds. Sweet marjoram has a more delicate flavor than wild marjoram. A half-hardy perennial, sweet marjoram seldom lives over the winter for me but will survive in the South if given some protection.

Growth habit:	Wiry, bushy; *O. majorana*, 8 to 12 inches; *O. vulgare*, 12 to 24 inches.
Where to grow:	Full sun; well-drained, ordinary garden soil. *O. majorana*, hardy to Zone 9; *O. vulgare*, to Zone 5.
How to start:	Start the slow-germinating seeds indoors four to six weeks before last spring frost. Plant out after air and soil have warmed.

Spacing:	Space plants 6 to 12 inches apart.
Growing tips:	Weed the small seedlings faithfully. Pinch lightly to keep them bushy and in shape.
Uses:	One of the most ancient of herbs, marjoram was a widely accepted remedy for asthma, rheumatism, and what the herbalist Gerard so expressively called "wamblings of the stomacke." In Elizabethan times it was a favorite strewing herb. Bertha Reppert, who grows and sells herbs in her Mechanicsburg, Pennsylvania, shop, suggests making a small pillow of dried marjoram for asthma sufferers. Sweet marjoram is used to flavor soups, stews, omelets, sausage, and salads.

Sage (*Salvia officinalis*)

Always a much-loved kitchen herb, especially good with pork, poultry, bread stuffings, and cheese dishes, sage was also much relied on for healing. Garden sage is quite hardy, but where winters are severe, set the plants on the warm south side of a building. Don't cut from them after September. Older plants develop large patches of bare woody growth and produce fewer leaves, so plan on renewing the clump every three years or so.

Growth habit:	Bushy; 2 to 3 feet tall.
Where to grow:	Full sun; ordinary garden soil. Hardy to Zones 4 to 8, depending on cultivar.
How to start:	Sow seeds directly in the garden or start indoors three to four weeks before last spring frost. Propagate established plants by layering or root cuttings.
Spacing:	Space plants 18 to 24 inches apart.
Growing tips:	Cut back growing tips to encourage bushiness.
Uses:	Some of the many troubles that sage was said to alleviate include sunburn, plague, palsy, cough, pain-in-the-side, headache, and overeating. Our amusement over such encyclopedic claims should not obscure the very real virtues of the plant when taken as a tea to relieve headaches and coughs.

CHAPTER FORTY-THREE

Layer Shrubs to Produce New Plants

S ome Saturday morning, when you're doing outside chores, take a few extra minutes to do some layering. In its simplest form, the procedure goes like this: Scuff the soil a bit to loosen it, and bend a supple young branch to the bare ground. Cover the branch at the point of contact with a handful of loose soil. Put a rock or a brick on the part of the branch that touches the soil to keep it in place until roots form. Easy, huh?

EASY LAYERING

You'll find layering is as easy as pie. Try it with berry bushes such as currants and gooseberries, bramble fruits such as raspberries and blackberries, and grapevines (*Vitis* spp.). Layering is an easy way to propagate groundcovers such as periwinkle (*Vinca minor*) and pachysandra (*Pachysandra terminalis*) as well as a wide variety of ornamentals. Try using it on barberries (*Berberis* spp.), clematis (*Clematis* spp.), daphne (*Daphne* spp.), flowering quinces (*Chaenomeles* spp.), forsythias (*Forsythia* spp.), lilacs (*Syringa* spp.), magnolias (*Magnolia* spp.), mock oranges (*Philadelphus* spp.), rhododendrons and azaleas (*Rhododendron* spp.), shrub roses (*Rosa* spp.), viburnums (*Viburnum* spp.), willows (*Salix* spp.), and wisterias (*Wisteria* spp.).

Many plants even layer naturally, when a low branch happens to touch the ground and sprout roots. It was, in fact, the spontaneous rooting of low branches in my gooseberry bush that prompted me to start intentionally rooting more branches. I've fostered dozens of new gooseberry bushes from a single bush of my favorite cultivar in this way, just casually plunking a rock on a branch when I thought about it. Inducing root formation on a plant's branch by keeping it in close contact with the soil is one of the easiest ways to propagate bushy plants.

When to Layer?

Fall, winter, and early spring are the best times to start layering because branches are dormant then and other garden work isn't so pressing. I've done layering in summer, too, and some bushes rooted by fall. It's best to put the branch in contact with the soil when the soil is soft and loose, not frozen hard.

Unlike a cutting, a layered branch continues to be nourished by its parent plant while it's forming roots. Timing isn't so critical: You can wait a month or more before severing the young plant from the larger bush. Its roots won't rot while actively growing in the ground as they might if kept in water or wet vermiculite.

Step-by-Step to a New Plant

The bare-bones layering technique I described is adequate for many plants. If you're willing to add a couple more steps, which will take only a few minutes, you'll get even better and often quicker results. It's all right to layer a number of branches from a single bush. I've had as many as eight gooseberry branches pegged down for layering, and they all "took." You can even anchor a single branch to the ground at more than one spot, a technique known as serpentine layering. For plants you intend to give or sell, layer a branch into a buried flowerpot using the following technique.

1. Remove any leaves that will be buried by the soil covering.
2. Peel the bark from an inch or two of the underside of the stem, where it will touch the ground, or nick a V-cut into the branch. Wounding the branch causes a concentration of plant hormones to accumulate at the cut, and this helps to start root formation. Take only a thin strip.

A GRAIN OF WHEAT FOR EXTRA ENCOURAGEMENT

An old cottager's custom was to insert a grain of wheat or an oat into a slit in the branch. The grain serves two purposes: It keeps the cut open, and, as it sprouts in contact with damp earth, it also releases plant hormones that stimulate rooting. Most of the plants on our easy-to-root list (see Easy Layering on page 287) shouldn't need any special treatment, but if you're having difficulty persuading a plant to root, it's worth a try. Short on oats this winter? You can also dust the wound with a commercial rooting compound.

3. Hold the branch to the ground with a sturdy piece of wire, bent into a U-shape.
4. Pile a few inches of soil over the contact point and pat it down.
5. Put a rock on top of the soil mound to anchor the branch and to conserve moisture.
6. It may take as long as four months to develop a strong root system.

Shrubs like barberry, forsythia, and weigela are simplest of all to propagate. Just bend a branch, cover with soil, and plunk down a rock. When you see new green leaves, lift the rock and investigate for roots. Then cut away from the mother and transplant.

Check in eight weeks or so to see whether the layered branch has started to root. Remove the rock and check for visible roots. Tug at the branch. If it seems well anchored, feel for roots in the soft surrounding soil.

7. If the branch has rooted and is producing green leaves, it's ready to grow on its own. It's best to transplant the young bush when it is dormant, in late fall or early spring. I've gotten away with potting up little gooseberry plants at other times, though, by coddling them—providing shade, watering well, and covering them with plastic bags for several days.

8. Cut the "foster" branch close to the new plant, dig it up retaining as much soil as possible around the roots, and replant promptly in its permanent spot.

Layering is one more way to get more pleasure and productivity from whatever ground and plants you have to call your own. A single bush can come up with the makings of a whole hedge in just one year, with a little help from you.

CHAPTER FORTY-FOUR

Make a Cone and Pod Wreath

I have yet to decide whether I go on walks to gather material for wreaths, or if I make wreaths to use the dried plant findings that I can't help collecting. Anyway, it is good to have an excuse to go hiking and a reason for collecting. The myriad ways in which seeds are protectively cased, the variety and beauty of the forms, keeps the autumn and winter landscape full of interest and wonder even after the flowers and leaves have faded.

Years ago, a friend showed me how to make simple wreaths out of the pods, cones, and nuts found in woods and wayside. I call them field and forest mosaic wreaths. These festive decorations gather mementos of different wild places into a permanent form that is attractive on a wall, door, or even a table.

Open Your Eyes

The first step—collecting the materials—is pure pleasure. Beginning in the backyard, let's see what we can find.

The hemlock windbreak is full of small, plump cones, and the rose-of-Sharon bush, gone to seed, leaves straw-colored, starry pods. Over in the perennial bed, iris seed heads, shaped like brown trumpets, are in their own way as handsome as the flowers were. Silver dollar plant stems are ready to be picked, dried, and peeled down to their satiny white, paper-thin medallions. Clusters of brown rhododendron pods may be added to our collection. Sprays of columbine pods are delicate but useful. Even the husk of the large marigold has a place in the wreath.

The hard frost that loosens the filberts for harvest leaves their fringed husks, rusty brown and usually in clusters of three. Almond, walnut, butternut—as we roam the hedgerow and nut grove, we compete with the squirrels and add samples of each of these wild or cultivated nuts to our baskets.

Brisk fall and winter days summon us beyond our own yards to the meadows and woods. In the woods—whether it's your own woodlot, a city park, or a nearby forest—you will find many interesting dried things to put in your wreath, such as: acorns of all varieties, beech nuts, big cones and little cones, nuts, locust pods, and tulip tree "umbrellas."

Hickory and black walnut trees are often found in hedgerows and at the edges of woods, as are redbud trees, which have interesting flat pods. Check under specimen or curbside plantings in residential areas in town. Chestnut burrs and nuts, gum tree burrs, "button balls" from the sycamore, and pods on shrubbery are often common in older parts of town. Remember to ask before you collect.

Roadsides and meadows offer still other plant pod treasures. It's impossible to make an exhaustive list of the variety of decorative dried forms to be found in open and so-called waste places for there

Collecting seedpods, cones, acorns, and other woodland treasures is a good excuse for a walk on a brisk, inviting day. Create a wonderfully textured wreath by gluing your finds to a cardboard frame. White pinecone "petals" make a neat edging.

292

is a wide local variation in available species. Without walking far from my home, I can gather a bagful of teasel, milkweed pods, ground-cherry husks, alder cones, thistle, evening primrose seedpods, and a good many others. We often wonder whether it is our peculiarly pack-rat nature that makes us do this—or is it a primal memory of a dimly sensed life that depended on fall collecting for survival?

On vacations and trips, look for pods that will be choice additions to your collection. We treasure the pinon pinecones we gathered in Colorado and the odd prickly-crown pods of water chestnut (*Trapa natans*) from the Hudson River Valley. My husband and son collected water chestnut pods for me while fishing near our campsite in New

ARTFUL CONSTRUCTION

The wreath will be more interesting if you plan for some contrasts in texture and color: a shiny horse chestnut flanked by a prickly gum tree burr and a woody peach stone, for example. Or a blond English walnut shell, greenish velvet wisteria pod, and dark brown hickory nut case grouped together.

To add another dimension of interest to the wreath, include several stages of a nut—for example, a hickory nut case, the four sections showing cleavage but still surrounding the nut; the whole, hulled hickory nut; and a broken hickory nut showing the inside chambers. Stripping a pinecone of its larger "petals" leaves a "flower" with a long "pistil"—a good filler for medium-sized spaces. Pinecones look good when placed stem up, too. An acorn cap turned stem side up works well next to several complete acorns. I also like to include nuts and husks that show the markings of animal life—tooth-marked nuts, squirrel-ravaged pinecones, gnawed-open husks.

York State. I considered it a truly great present. (We appreciated the help of our biologist friend, Jeff, in researching the plant's identity.)

Shaping the Wreath

Wreaths may be made of any attractive mixture of dried pods and cones. You can build the wreath gradually, adding more material as you find it. If you have all the material you need, though, you can complete a wreath in an evening.

The final content of the wreath is up to you. Be sure your pods, cones, acorns, or other wild findings are ripe and dry; green, incompletely dry plant material might become moldy and ruin your project.

A Cardboard Doughnut and Your Creativity

The base of the field and forest mosaic wreath is a doughnut of sturdy corrugated cardboard. Use white glue to attach the dried materials to the base and to each other. Use the following steps to create your wilderness wreath.

1. Trace around a dinner plate or use a compass to draw a cardboard circle about 10 inches in diameter. Cut the cardboard along the lines with a craft knife, serrated steak knife, or saw.
2. Cut an inner hole 4½ to 5 inches in diameter, leaving a "doughnut" about 5 inches wide to be covered with dried findings.
3. For the outer edges of the wreath, strip the "petals" from several pinecones. This is a good fireside job. These pine shingles or petals make a neat, attractive border for the wreath.
4. Squeeze a trickle of white glue around the outer edge of the base. Place the pinecone petals, points in, so that they cover the edge. Press each small shingle so that it is in contact with the glue. Then cover the inner edge of the wreath in the same way, using white glue and pinecone shingles.
5. When the border has dried, start to build up the wreath. Select the largest pieces from your collection—the pinecones, milkweed pods, teasel heads, black walnut shells, and such—and glue them, arranged closely together, around the wreath.
6. Arrange medium-sized material—acorns, thistles, rose-of-Sharon stars, larch cones, tulip tree umbrellas, ground-cherry husks—in the open spaces. Put a dab of glue on each piece before adding it to the mosaic, and press it in place.
7. Finally, add tiny pieces to fill in the chinks so no cardboard can be seen. Use hemlock cones, rhododendron stars, and other small pods.
8. After the glue has thoroughly dried, spray the completed wreath with clear varnish. Glue a hanger to the back.

A Wreath for Remembrance

The richness of the natural brown tones makes the wreath a perfect "harvest home" symbol and a mellow holiday decoration appropriate for both the fall and winter, and durable enough to hang year-round. You might find that your wreath becomes, as mine has, a composite memento of trips taken, hikes enjoyed, and backyard and wayside strolls. I *have* managed to give some wreaths away, though. In fact, some years ago, I made them to sell.

Now I'm looking forward to making more with my grandchildren. The wreaths last a long time, as long as they're kept dry. My parents still display one that I made for them 20 years ago!

CHAPTER FORTY-FIVE

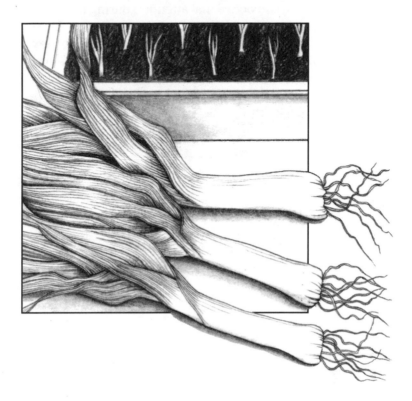

Start Some Hardy Leeks

295

Many a savory winter soup begins with a shivering dash to the garden to pick a wrist-thick leek from its sheltering bed. Milder in flavor than onions, and also slower-growing, leeks (*Allium ampeloprasum*, Porrum group) compensate by surviving winter in the garden, even in New England. Though they're sometimes considered special gourmet fare, leeks are easy to grow, and they're super-hardy.

The ever-ready fortitude of leeks in winter is our reward for giving it garden space and occasional attention during its long, slow, 120- to 130-day growing season. Because young leek seedlings are thready and easily overwhelmed by weeds, I've found that they do best for me when I start them indoors from seed. Sow seed indoors in January and February for these slow growers.

Planting seeds indoors is good therapy for those deep winter days when we crave the sight of some green, growing thing—but know perfectly well that it's too early to start tomatoes or even cabbage. Fast-growing cultivars like 'Titan' and 'King Richard' mature in mid- to late summer. For winter harvest, select the hardier traditional leeks such as 'Unique', 'Blue Solaise', 'Nebraska', or 'Alaska'.

Sow leeks indoors in winter so the thready seedlings are large enough to fend for themselves when transplanted into the garden come spring. By early fall, your leeks will be stout-stemmed and ready for the soup pot.

Leek seed can also be planted directly in the ground three or four weeks before the last frost date. To save garden space, sow the slow-growing leeks in a nursery bed, and transplant seedlings later to their permanent garden site. Southern gardeners can plant leek seed in late summer for winter and spring crops.

296

Life Story of a Leek

Leeks are best raised to maturity in trenches. As they grow, add more soil to the trench. The slowly rising soil level encourages the development of a longer bulb stem—the tender white part that is so good to eat. If you plant leeks on the soil surface rather than in trenches, the tougher green leaves tend to flag off from the central bulb closer to the ground, limiting the amount of edible stalk.

By the time winter arrives, these exceptionally cold-hardy plants are still growing, staunchly weathering snow and ice until we harvest them for dinner. Here's how to get started on a crop.

1. Plant seeds in flats indoors in mid- to late winter.
2. Thin seedlings to stand 1 inch apart in the flats.
3. When the seedlings are at least 6 inches high, harden them off outdoors in a sheltered place.
4. Use a shovel to dig a wide-bottomed trench about 6 inches deep and 6 inches wide.
5. Plant the seedlings in the bottom of the trench about 6 inches apart. Leave the trench open for the first few weeks while the plants get established. The trench gives you working space to cover the bulb gradually as it grows.
6. When the leaves are 6 to 8 inches high, rake or hoe fine soil into the trench, about an inch at a time, every three weeks. Keep the soil level at or just below the point where the green leaves diverge from the stem in order to help the plant build a longer stretch of bulb stem. Keep the plants well watered throughout this process.
7. By early fall, the trench will be filled in completely. The once-tender plants will have turned into stout muscled stalks, all the more tender because you blanched them as they grew.

Growing Superb Leeks

For a superb stand of leeks, give the plants deeply dug, well-drained, near-neutral or slightly acid soil, rich in humus. To beef up the soil's humus content, substitute an inch of fine compost for soil on one or two of the regular trench fillings. To help supply the leek's heavy demand for nitrogen, fertilize with manure, compost tea, or diluted fish emulsion once or twice during the growing season.

Perpetual Leeks

Once you've grown some leeks, you have an even easier option than growing from seed. Simply replant the small bulbs, or corms, that cluster around the base of the overwintered mother bulbs in early spring. These grow into plants sooner than seeds do, giving you a head start on the long leek season.

The leek grown from a corm will give you a bunch of perfectly good corms after *it* matures and overwinters in your garden. So, if you don't eat them all before spring, you can have "perpetual" leeks with very little effort.

You can also replant the root tips to start new plants. Just cut off the bottom inch or two of the leek, trim the straggly roots to 1 to 2 inches long, and replant the nubbin of root tip. Root tips can be replanted only once: If you plant a root tip from a leek that was tip-grown last year, it will go to seed. This ploy works best in spring and fall when soil temperature is moderate. Nubs tend to rot in very cold weather and dry up in very warm soil.

Cold-Weather Care

Continue to hill up soil around the bases of the plants every few weeks, stopping just before the point where the green leaf pleats begin to fan out, so that the soil won't wash down between the leaflets of the bulb. Hilling encourages the formation of additional inches of tender bulb.

Before the ground freezes hard, pile on 10 to 12 inches of mulch to keep the soil workable for another few weeks and, later, to protect the leeks from extremely cold weather. If the ground freezes hard early in your area, replace some of the mounded-up soil with mulch to permit easier access to the bulbs. Straw, leaves, and aged sawdust make good weed-free mulches. If deep freezing would lock your leeks in place until a thaw, dig some leeks before the ground hardens and store them in sand in a cold cellar.

If you've mulched the ground early to retard deep freezing, you can probably harvest leeks for a steaming cup of vichysoisse in January. Use a fork to harvest. Dig from the side of the row to avoid cutting into the bulbs.

Rinse the leeks thoroughly before cooking to wash out soil trapped between the loose upper layers. Some people plunge the leeks upside down into a bucket of water to swish out dirt particles. And keep an eye on the calendar. Before long, perhaps one day after you've enjoyed a warming bowl of cock-a-leekie soup, it will be time to start another crop of leeks.

CHAPTER FORTY-SIX

Build Your Own Cold Frame

"Gardening," writes Ann Leighton in *Early American Gardens,* "offers a chance for man to regulate at least one aspect of his life, to control his environment. . . ." We begin by taming a piece of ground, growing vegetables in rows, flowers in beds, herbs in pots. We like to think we have control over this small territory.

But we're still at the mercy of the weather. An early fall frost can wipe out a row of perfect table-ready lettuces. In spring, late frosts and slow-melting snow can keep us out of the garden. At this time of year, we restlessly poke at our seedlings and are sorely tempted to dig in the still-sodden earth, though we know we shouldn't, just to get some green thing growing.

Gardeners are forever trying to stretch the growing season, even in benign climates. We want an extra-early start, another month of harvest. So we do what gardeners have done for ages: We set aside a tiny plot in which we can more completely control the climate. In this microclimate, parsley and pansies live over the winter, cabbage starts early, lettuce thrives in summer shade, spinach keeps producing till Christmas. We accomplish all this—and more—with a simple glass-covered box: a cold frame.

Just a Box with a Lid

In its simplest form, a cold frame is a bottomless box covered with a lid that admits light. Without consuming a single kilowatt of power, the cold frame magnifies the sun's warmth and shelters tender plants

That old piece of window sash stacked behind the garage is the humble beginning of a very useful cold frame. An angled lid catches the sun, and a bank of leaves provides insulation from cold. Try an early crop of lettuce or radishes.

from wind and other weather extremes. When well managed, it can extend your growing season by a month in the spring and as much as two or three months in the fall.

The best site for your cold frame is a south-facing, sunny spot, with good drainage and some protection from the wind. It's helpful to have a source of water nearby, but that's not essential. Pick a location that gets lots of sun, especially during the winter and early spring. An overhead tree can provide protection from the scorching summer sun—as long as it loses its leaves for the cold months, when you'll want all the sun you can get. A cold frame in part shade year-round is fine for propagating shrubs and perennials, but not for general use.

Build your frame with the north side—the high end—against a wall, hedge, fence, or even a compost pile to shield it from the wind. You can even back the cold frame up to the window of a heated cellar so you can open the window and warm the frame on bitter cold nights.

KEEP IT COZY

On very cold nights, your frame needs extra protection to keep the plants from freezing. Since heat escapes readily through the glass, it's most effective to pile insulating materials on top of the frame. Use old blankets, straw or hay, feed bags stuffed with pine needles or crumpled newspapers, lengths of roofing paper, scrap lumber, or whatever else is handy. Banking leaves, straw, or hay around the perimeter of the frame helps, too. A layer of snow makes good insulation, but brush off thick, heavy snow to spare the sash.

There's no such thing as a standard-size cold frame, but 3 by 6 feet seems to be a generally agreed-upon size. A frame smaller than 2 by 4 feet is too small to be useful; a frame wider than 3 feet makes plants hard to reach. The size of the frame is often determined by the dimensions of the discarded windows used for the top. For a bigger frame, just use two or more windows for the lid. Make the frame slightly smaller than the size of the lid, at least an inch less wide and about 2 inches less long, so water drains off the edge instead of into the frame.

Creative Construction

The construction of a cold frame, for most of us, is determined by the materials we have at hand. The box is most commonly made of wood, a fairly good insulator; the lid is often a recycled storm window. We made ours of discarded, wood-framed storm sash and 2-inch locust boards milled from our own trees. Your attic or garage, classified ads, or local garage sales might yield a window for your cold frame lid. If not, use fiberglass or rigid plastic panels. Even 6-mil plastic sheeting tacked to a frame makes an acceptable lid. No wood on hand for the box? Stone, brick, or concrete structures are even more durable and retain more heat than wood. (Metal is not a good choice unless you insulate around the perimeter.)

Some gardeners use ½-inch or ¾-inch exterior plywood. Cedar, cypress, and redwood are good choices for the box; they're decay-resistant woods that often outlast the sash. To prolong the life of a wood frame, brush on several coats of linseed oil or a nontoxic preservative such as Cuprinol. Avoid using creosote, pentachlorophenol, or mercury compounds to treat wood in which you intend to grow plants.

Construction details vary, depending on the materials you use and whether the frame is a permanent or a portable structure. Frame sides may be screwed, bolted, hooked, or nailed together. Make the rear wall of the frame 4 to 6 inches higher than the front so that the lid is sloped. Most frames range from 6 to 12 inches high for the front board, and 12 to 18 inches high for the rear. A sloping lid makes the most effective use of the sun, and its angle allows ready drainage of rainwater and melting snow.

Ideally, the sun's rays should strike the glass at a 90-degree angle. Since the sun is low in the sky in winter and high in summer, it's impossible to maintain a 90-degree orientation year-round with a fixed lid position. So we compromise and build a frame angled to catch the March and April sun, when we need it most. (Or perhaps the November and December sun, if you prefer.) Or we add a wedge to each side of the frame in early autumn to boost the angle of the glass to 55 degrees, thus catching more of the sun's rays head-on.

Extra Support

Reinforce the corners of a wood frame, unless it's designed to be taken apart for moving or storage. We nailed 2-by-2-inch stakes upright in each corner of our frame. Interior supports interfere with placement of seed flats, though; those who wish to make efficient use of every inch of the frame prefer to nail 1-by-3-inch boards to the exterior corners for bracing.

Some lids may need additional support. A horizontal wood strip, nailed flat against the inside front and back walls, adds extra support for the window sash. For a long frame, or for a frame using long windows, or where snow cover is heavy, nail one or two 1-inch strips of wood across the frame to support the sash. Notch the crosspieces into the front and rear boards. (It's easier to work in the cold frame when there are no obstructions. If your cold frame uses a reasonably sized, well-angled single sash, there's usually no need to add crosspieces.)

Hinge the window lid to the back of the frame. If there is a building in back of the cold frame, use hooks, thumbscrews, or other improvised means to catch the sash so it doesn't blow down with a glass-breaking bang in heavy wind. (If you suspect that I learned this the hard way, you're right!)

Get Ready to Grow

Simply place your wood frame on level ground. You can even attach handles to the ends of the cold frame to make it portable and use it to cover special row crops in the garden. If you build a brick, stone, concrete block, or poured-concrete frame, lay the bottom layer a few inches below the frost line to avoid disruption of the structure when the ground freezes and thaws. For extra insurance, drive supporting stakes into the ground around the cold frame to keep it well anchored.

Grow your cold-frame plants in flats, in individual pots, or directly in the ground. Feeding, watering, and other care can be easily tailored to each plant's needs when you use containers or flats. But if you're growing a single crop of lettuce or spinach, planting directly in the soil makes sense.

303

To be sure of excellent drainage, dig out 3 or 4 inches of existing soil inside the frame and replace it with a layer of coarse gravel. Top with at least 6 inches of loamy soil, raked or screened to a fine tilth. The soil needn't be extra rich: Both spring seedlings and protected, wintering plants are sturdier when not overfed. Sappy, succulent plants are more sensitive to frost. A mixture of 2 parts good garden loam, 1 part sharp sand, and 1 part compost, leaf mold, or aged manure will serve you well.

Caring for Your Garden under Glass

Gardeners who have the best luck with cold frames are those who take time to observe and tinker with the setup. Temperature and moisture are the two most important management factors.

Temperatures on a clear, sunny day, even in early spring, can zoom higher than 90°F in the cold frame. To cool the frame, open the sash. Use scrap wood to make a prop with several stops to hold the window open at different levels. I've found James Crockett's advice accurate and helpful: When the outdoor temperature reaches 40°F, open the cover 6 inches. When it reaches 50°F, open the cover completely. Close the cover in midafternoon to trap the midday heat.

Many gardeners keep a maximum-minimum outdoor thermometer in the cold frame. In general, keep the temperature no warmer than 80°F; below 75°F is even better. Tender plants thrive at 60° to 75°F, half-hardy plants do well at 50° to 60°F, and hardy plants at 45° to 60°F. You can buy automatic venting devices from some seed catalogs and greenhouse supplies. These gadgets use temperature-sensitive metals that bend at certain temperatures to open the frame automatically.

Without a regular supply of rain, plants in the cold frame may need to be watered, especially those in flats that dry quickly. Check them every other day. Water in the morning. The dampness from evening watering lingers, encouraging fungal growth. Should you have trouble with damping-off disease of seedlings planted in the cold frame, spread a 1- to 2-inch layer of vermiculite on top of the soil and plant the seeds in that. Keep seedbeds evenly moist but never soggy.

PUT YOUR FRAME TO WORK YEAR-ROUND

Many gardeners use their cold frames all year round. In early spring, your cold frame will warm up sooner than the garden, and seeds of cold-weather vegetables, herbs such as chives and parsley, and hardy annual flowers like snapdragons and calendula may be sown directly in the soil or in flats set in the frame. When summer heats up, cover your cold frame with lath or screening or whitewash it to shade houseplants or summer lettuce. In fall, take off the shading devices and fill the frame with flats of fall-planted wildflower seeds and pots of bulbs for winter forcing.

Here are some other seasonal suggestions to guide you in your cold-frame gardening.

Spring. Raise early crops of lettuce, spinach, and radishes. Sow hardy seedlings weeks ahead of outdoor planting time. Root cuttings of shrubs and perennials. Start cucumber and melon plants in pots. Harden off seedlings started indoors.

Summer. Root cuttings of perennials. Grow summer lettuce under light shade. Sow biennials such as foxglove and Canterbury bells that appreciate winter protection. Dry fruits and vegetables, with ventilation. Sow pansies in August for early spring bloom.

Autumn. Sow seeds in flats for spring seedlings. Grow late crops of leafy plants. Transplant young parsley plants from garden to frame for early spring use. Protect garden crops from frost with portable frames.

Winter. Grow winter salad greens in well-insulated frame. Hold half-hardy perennials over winter. Store potted bulbs for forcing.

Plan On
Oriental Vegetables

At least 300,000 species of plants have been identified, and there are still thousands of other species of plants growing on earth that have not yet been described and named. Sometimes I ponder this awesome fact when I'm trying to decide whether to serve carrots or beans for dinner. Not all of these undiscovered treasures are food plants, of course. Still, there are many more species of food plants in the world than most people realize.

Vegetables are supremely important in the Orient especially, where not enough arable land is available to raise grain for feeding livestock. Their flavor and texture *make* the meal. Not so incidentally, the marvelous cuisine that has developed around fresh vegetables in these ancient cultures is now recognized as an eminently sane way to eat, and healthier than "overnutrition" based on heavy use of red meat, saturated fat, and sugar.

Oriental Specialties for American Gardens

Since vegetables are so necessary and so widely appreciated in China and Japan, many different kinds are grown. Some of them are beginning to be introduced here in America. From my experiments with them, the vegetables described here seem to be good choices. For something interesting and delicious to serve along with your familiar garden standbys, or for a truly authentic Chinese or Japanese meal, grow and cook some of these special oriental vegetables.

Cee Gwa

Some seed catalogs refer to cee gwa (*Luffa acutangula*) as Chinese okra. There is a resemblance between the slim, ridged, 6-inch-long fruits of this member of the cucurbit family and the pods of an okra plant, but they aren't related botanically. Actually an edible gourd, cee gwa, also known as sing-kwa, thrives in warm weather and rich soil.

This is a good plant to train to a trellis or fence by tying up the vines as they grow. Sow seeds directly in the garden, about 2 inches apart, and thin to retain the strongest plants. Northern gardeners can get a head start on a crop by sowing seeds in peat pots in the house in late winter. Plant outside after danger of frost is past. Space plants about 6 inches apart in the row. Fruits appear about three months after planting.

Pick the fruits when they're young and tender. The older gourds turn tough and fibrous. Use young cee gwa like zucchini or cucumbers: After trimming off their ridges, serve raw in salads; steam or stir-fry for soups or side dishes.

Chinese Cabbage

It is natural, I suppose, to explain an unfamiliar vegetable in terms of a more familiar one. Still, the term "cabbage" never seems to properly describe this vegetable, which is quite a different food from the widely grown, solid round heads we use to make cole slaw. Like our garden cabbage, wong bok (*Brassica rapa,* Pekinensis group) and bok choy (*Brassica rapa,* Chinensis group) are good steamed and buttered, or cooked in soup. It is in salads that they excel, though, particularly in late fall when lettuce has given out. The leaves are more tender than those of common garden cabbage, and the base and heart have the crispness of celery without the strings—all with a mild flavor.

Wong bok, also known as pe-tsai or Chinese celery cabbage, is the heading form of Chinese cabbage; bok choy, also known as pak-choi or Chinese mustard, is the leafy type. Most cultivars go to seed quickly if they mature in hot weather. Unless you plant one of the new heat-resistant strains, you'll have a larger, tastier harvest if you plant the seed in summer for a fall crop. June and July plantings do well for me. We eat the thinnings in August and September and cut the mature plant in October or even November, if I've given them some protection from frost.

Good fertile soil and a steady supply of moisture help to produce tender, fastgrowing leaves. Unlike regular cabbage, wong bok and bok

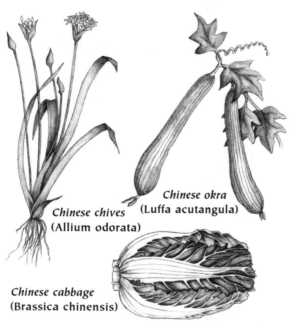

Chinese okra
(Luffa acutangula)

Chinese chives
(Allium odorata)

Chinese cabbage
(Brassica chinensis)

308

The names are exotic, the plants unusual, and the vegetables are some you've never seen before. But American gardeners and cooks are beginning to discover oriental specialties like cee gwa, or Chinese okra; gow choy, or Chinese chives; Chinese cabbage; and mao gwa, which looks like a fuzzy zucchini.

choy often go to seed when transplanted. Sow the seeds in individual pots or directly in the garden so the roots won't be disturbed. Thin seedlings to stand 18 to 24 inches apart in the row.

Daikon

Daikon (*Raphanus sativus* 'Longipinnatus') is as popular in Japan as the potato is in America. These large, pungent oriental radishes, which can reach 2 feet long, are more substantial and versatile than our small, crisp, early spring radishes. They are served raw, either sliced or grated, steamed as a vegetable, cooked in soup, and pickled.

Plant the seed in early spring directly in the garden. Thin the seedlings of large daikon cultivars so that they are spaced 10 inches apart in the row. Early summer plantings yield a fall crop that may be stored in a cold place for a month or two. You can't do that with a delicate spring radish.

A SPICY INTRODUCTION

For an introduction to peppery daikon, try a relish made from the Chinese radish. Mix equal parts of the grated raw root with cooked, coarsely grated beets. Season the mixture with salt and lemon juice. Here are some good cultivars of daikon to try.

'Miyashige'. Fine-quality, thick, blunt root. A good fall crop which is good for storage. Plant in midsummer.
'Sakurajima'. Famous for its ability to achieve prodigious size. Sow in spring.
'Tokinashe'. The pointed roots are pungent. Sow in spring or summer.

Gai Choy

A planting of gai choy (*Brassica juncea*) makes good use of garden space. We like these leafy Chinese mustard greens because they have a rich but mild flavor; they're not at all pungent or bitter like some greens. Be sure to pick them young, though, for they shoot to flower as soon as the weather turns hot. We use the whole plant top, snipping leaves and stems into a pan of butter for a brief sauté.

Plant gai choy in early spring directly in the garden. Thin the seedlings to 3- to 4-inch spacing (save the thinnings for the evening's soup). The greens are ready to pluck about five weeks after planting. Flea beetles, tiny black jumping insects that chew small round holes in the leaves, can be hard on seedlings of gai choy and other members of the cabbage family. Powdered diatomaceous earth, available as Perma Guard, helps to control flea beetles without poisoning the vegetable or the soil.

Gai Lohn

Gai lohn (*Brassica oleracea,* Alboglabra group) is sometimes known as Chinese kale or Chinese broccoli. The florets are smaller and less solid than those of the familiar western broccoli, but both leaves and stem are good to eat. To enjoy the flower buds at their best, pick them before they bloom. Gai lohn is often stir-fried or steamed, and served while still tender-crisp. Cook this vegetable briefly, stopping short of that unappetizing gray-green shade too often seen in overcooked broccoli.

Gai lohn thrives in rich soil and cool weather. Its best growth periods are in spring and fall, so it is a good vegetable to plant in early spring and again in midsummer for fall use. Sow seeds directly in the garden, thinning the plants to about 6 inches.

Gow Choy

Gow choy (*Allium tuberosum*) is easy to grow, decorative, and versatile. Known as Chinese chives, this perennial member of the onion family forms handsome clumps of slender, flat leaves. The flavor has more than a hint of garlic and blends pleasingly with many salads and mixed meat and vegetable dishes. Add the finely snipped leaves shortly before serving time; long cooking makes them limp and stringy.

310

Sow seeds of gow choy right in the garden row, or start seedlings indoors in late winter and transplant seedlings in April. Light frost won't hurt the young plants. Space the plants 8 to 10 inches apart or plant them in an herb bed in groups. Start cutting the tops when they're 5 or 6 inches high, and continue to cut throughout the season as new growth appears. By season's end, the plants will be well established and strong enough to endure winter freezes if covered with a protective mulch.

Heung Kuhn

Known as Chinese celery, heung kuhn (*Apium graveolens*) is a slow-growing plant, somewhat less robust than western celery. I add a leaf or two as well as a few chopped stems to soups, stews, and casseroles. Sometimes I dry the leaves, too, and use them in the same way over winter.

Sow seeds of heung kuhn indoors in March. Plant seedlings out in late April or early May, spacing the plants 8 to 10 inches apart. Rich soil and a steady supply of moisture will assure a succulent stem and a bushy crop of leaves. When planted in April, heung kuhn forms an 8-inch-wide clump of thin, leafy celery stalks by August. The plants, usually untroubled by insects, are quite cold-hardy, but should be protected from hard frosts.

Hinn Choy

Hinn choy (*Amaranthus gangeticus*) is a good warm-weather spinach. This plant varies more widely in color than many garden vegetables. Most are green, but you may find some with mahogany red leaves or streaks. The flavor of hinn choy, also called Chinese spinach, is mild and good, blending well with other sharper-flavored greens in a mixture.

Hinn choy likes warm weather. Plant seeds directly in the garden after the weather has settled and the soil has warmed. Thin to 4 inches apart. Plants that are started in April or May will be just right for eating by midsummer, when the early cool-weather greens have petered out.

Mao Gwa

The 4- to 5-inch-long fruits of mao gwa (*Benincasa hispida*) assume a comfortable, rounded pear shape when fully developed. The green rind is somewhat tougher than that of a zucchini, and the fuzz must be peeled off before cooking. Sometimes known as wax gourd or fuzzy gourd, the plant is a tender, rambling vine that grows somewhat like a cucumber vine. It will perform best when given some support—tied to a trellis, fence, or wooden rack. The sliced cooked fruits look and taste like a slightly meatier zucchini. They are good in vegetable soup or braised with onions.

Mao gwa likes comfort and luxury—warm weather, rich soil, and a steady supply of moisture (1 inch per week). Plant seeds after danger of frost, when soil is warm. To give these long-season vegetables an early start, presprout the seeds by wrapping in damp paper towels for a day or two. Tuck the sprouted seed gently under 1 inch of compost in the row. Thin to about 6 inches.

Shungiku

Some of the oriental vegetables mentioned in this chapter have western counterparts, but shungiku (*Chrysanthemum coronarium*) is in a class by itself. Sometimes called chop suey greens, shungiku is actually an edible type of chrysanthemum. The leaves of this hardy annual have the familiar chrysanthemum-like lobes, and the yellow, single-petaled, daisylike flower forms a bright note amid the gray-green cauliflower and brussels sprouts of late summer.

Despite some seed catalog warnings about its pungency, we found shungiku to be a pleasantly aromatic addition to a salad or a pan of stir-fried vegetables. But it's not the sort of vegetable you'd prepare by the bucketful or eat every day. The pungency isn't at all on the sharp or bitter side, though. It's more on the order of garden mint— a plant that makes a splendid, subtle flavor contribution when used in small amounts.

Plant seeds in early spring directly in the garden, or in an herb garden. When the leaves have grown to a height of 6 inches, you can start to harvest. Pull the whole plant to thin the row (3- to 4-inch spacing is about right), or cut the leaves and let more grow. Flavor is best before the plant blooms, but I've snipped a few leaves from a blooming plant into our lunchtime salad and no one complained.

CHAPTER FORTY-EIGHT

Experiment with Companion Planting

313

A lot of nonsense has been written about companion planting. So much untested advice has been repeated that the core of truth is often obscured by an overlay of wishful thinking. Some plants do seem to affect others growing nearby, either positively or negatively, but how do you weed out fact from fiction?

Let's begin with a definition. Companion planting is the intentional interplanting of two or more species of plants for such beneficial results as improved growth and protection from insects. Chamomile, for example, has the reputation of improving the growth and flavor of other herbs growing nearby. Aromatic herbs are often planted to repel crop-damaging insects. Other plants, especially legumes, benefit their neighbors by enriching the soil. Some plants attract beneficial insects and pollinators. Others are used as decoys or traps to lure insect pests away from valuable crops. For example, nasturtiums are often planted to attract aphids, and alfalfa rows are included in fields of cotton to trap damaging lygus bugs.

Recorded observations of the effects plants have on each other go back to early Roman times. The naturalist Pliny recommended sowing chick peas with cabbage to repel caterpillars. Farmers in ancient Rome planted grain between their fruit trees and grapevines, and Chinese gardeners centuries ago planted beans with most of their grain crops.

This long tradition of intentional interplanting confirms that companion planting often does produce good results. After all, those farmers of old might not have had formal training in botany, but they were observant. They managed to domesticate and breed plants and even work out sound crop-rotation and fertilizing practices.

314

According to folklore, borage improves the flavor of strawberries. Though this effect has never been proved, other plant combinations have shown their value in controlled testing. Try some companion trials in your own garden.

Research in the Home Garden

Much work remains to be done on which repellent plants work, and why. What little research has been done on companion planting is not always conclusive, but it has demonstrated clearly that monocropping—planting large stands of a single species—encourages pests and diseases.

If you want to try companion planting in your garden, start with some of these plant combinations, which have been proven to be effective.

- Beans planted with corn were infested with fewer leafhoppers in one study.
- Black nightshade, a common hedgerow weed, attracted potato beetles away from potato plants.
- Collards planted with beans had four times less aphids than those planted alone—the result of a higher population of beneficial parasitic wasps.
- Companion plantings of dill and basil protected collards from flea beetles and helped to decrease cabbage worm damage.

UNHAPPY COMPANIONS

Allelopathy, or the suppression of growth, is the negative side of companion planting. Perhaps the best-known allelopathic plant is the black walnut tree, which produces juglone, a strong toxin that retards the growth and even the seed germination of many other plants.

Studies have confirmed that cabbage is retarded by rue or grapes growing nearby, oats by thistles, and wheat by decomposing sweet clover. Most species of eucalyptus release growth-suppressing substances, as do sunflowers. Goldenrod seems to be allelopathic to some trees, including black locust and sugar maple. And certain weeds, especially yellow nutsedge, giant foxtail, and quack grass, are known to produce substances that are highly toxic to many plants. The production of such toxins is essentially the plant's attempt to define its territory, to eliminate competition.

- Cucumbers planted with corn or broccoli suffered less disease because they were infested with fewer cucumber beetles.
- French marigolds have been shown to control root-knot nematodes, especially when they are planted close together and allowed to grow all season long. Interestingly, odorless marigolds are more susceptible to insect attack, especially by spider mites, than the pungent conventional cultivars.
- Tomatoes interplanted with collards reduced flea-beetle infestations.
- Tomatoes planted next to cabbage have been shown to repel whiteflies and diamond-back moths.

Word-of-Mouth Planting Lore

Companion-planting lore as repeated from one gardener to another is voluminous, often contradictory, but often right on target. Though these long-standing traditions aren't supported by current research in the scientific community, the home garden is the ideal place to conduct your own experimental studies. Here are some of the more popular folklore companion-plant combinations for you to try. Folklore has it that:

- Basil dislikes rue.
- Borage improves the flavor of strawberries and tomatoes and stimulates their growth.
- Calendula stimulates growth of tomatoes.
- Carrots repel onion flies.
- Chamomile improves the growth and flavor of onions, cucumbers, and aromatic herbs.
- Hyssop and legumes encourage grapes.
- Horseradish at the corners of a potato patch repels potato beetles.
- Lovage improves health and flavor of nearby plants.
- Marjoram, basil, oregano, and lovage help the growth of peppers.
- Peppers should be kept away from fennel and kohlrabi.
- Radishes discourage squash borers.
- Sage stimulates growth of carrots, cabbage, strawberries, and tomatoes, but don't plant sage near cucumbers or rue.
- Tarragon enhances growth and flavor of nearby plants.
- Tomatoes do well with cabbage, asparagus, onions, carrots, sage, basil, or parsley, but not with fennel or potatoes.

Getting Educated

If you decide to conduct some companion-planting experiments, take the time to set up the plots carefully and be conscientious about observing and recording the results. Weather and insect populations vary so much from year to year that any successful experiment should be repeated, preferably several times, in order to be considered conclusive.

Don't expect companion planting to solve all your pest problems, but use it as one part of an integrated garden-management program that includes crop rotation, use of pest- and disease-resistant cultivars, and natural soil enrichment.

CHAPTER FORTY-NINE

Raise Houseplants from Seed

In the cold months, we turn our attention indoors again after a season of outdoor gardening. We see more places in our homes where a new houseplant would be just right, or we want to putter with seeds and potting soil. Perhaps we've just added a sunroom to the house that we want to fill with colorful flowers and interesting foliage, or we've read another article about the value of houseplants in reducing pollution of indoor air.

This absorbing process offers a lot of satisfaction for a small investment of time. It's the perfect weekend project. Planting the seeds takes only a few minutes and in a few weeks you have tiny seedlings to transplant—another relaxing Saturday task. There's no weeding or harvesting to do, and because you're dealing with a few pots at a time rather than a whole rowful of plants, the project stays within manageable proportions. Yes, it *is* true that you can get 100 gloxinia plants from a single packet of seed. But then you can enjoy the luxury of having a lavish selection of plants from which to choose—and plenty to give away.

Seed-Starting Basics

Let's start with some general directions for seed starting. You can start houseplants from seed at any time of year. Some houseplants grow slowly from seed, but watching them grow is part of the fun. You don't need any special equipment or any special skills for houseplant seed starting.

1. Fill a planting flat or individual seed-starting pots with damp vermiculite, shredded sphagnum moss, or sterile potting soil. Soak the planting medium before sowing the seeds so they won't be dislodged by a stream of water applied after planting.
2. Keep the planted seeds warm and moist—but not soggy—until you see sprouts. Bottom watering is best. Use lukewarm water to avoid shocking young plants.
3. Put the flat or pots under fluorescent lights or in direct window light as soon as sprouts appear.
4. Fertilize young seedlings with a liquid fertilizer solution, such as fish emulsion, at one-fourth to one-half strength every one to two weeks.
5. Thin the seedlings to 2 inches apart. Transplant seedlings from flats to 2-inch pots when they're 2 inches high.

Choose Your Favorite

If you're new to seed starting, start with one of the easier species like coleus. But don't hesitate to try a special favorite, tricky or not. Your desire to succeed will give you a growing edge.

Easy-Growing Choices

These easy-to-germinate plants are good choices for beginning seed starters.

Achimenes

Known in various circles as orchid pansy, mother's tears, or cupid's bower, achimenes (*Achimenes longiflora*) is a perfect hanging basket plant for a partly shady place. Its waxy, tubular blossoms come in a range of soft, pleasing colors and almost smother the plant with bloom.

Achimenes are easy and rewarding to grow from seed. The seeds are minute, and must be left uncovered. A temperature of 70° to 80°F is best for germination, which can take two to three weeks.

Softly colored achimenes, *top right,* and striking coleus, *bottom right,* in magic-carpet colors are among the easiest houseplants to grow from seed. Geraniums, *top left,* can be a bit more tricky, requiring patience and careful care.

Growing plants and mature specimens prefer the same temperature range for day, with nighttime temperatures of 60° to 65°F. An east window with some morning sun suits them well.

Achimenes grow actively, flower profusely, and then enter a period of dormancy. During their period of growth, give the plants plenty of water, but don't let them get soggy in standing water. When mature, they form small, scaly rhizomes. Collect the rhizomes and store in a cool place for four to five months, just as you would store gladiolus. After their rest, replant the rhizomes, three to five of them to a 10-inch pot, and water well for another season of bloom.

320

Cacti

Many species of cactus will grow slowly but easily from seed. A packet of mixed cactus seeds could be the start of a whole new windowsill garden. Sow them directly into small pots any time of year. Many cacti will bloom indoors in late winter.

Cactus seeds need moisture for germination just as other seeds do, and the seedlings must have a steady supply of moisture, too. Alternating between cool temperatures of about 65°F and warmer temperatures around 80°F seems to encourage germination, which can still take three to seven weeks. When transplanting the seedlings, keep soil moderately damp but don't overwater. Roots bruised from handling rot quickly. Pot seedlings in your regular potting-soil mixture, with a cup of sand and a handful of perlite added for good drainage.

Mature cactus plants are able to store water, so they can survive underwatering better than many other plants. They *do* require water, though—weekly, biweekly, or monthly, depending on the size and site of the plant. Keep your cactus plantation on a sunny windowsill.

Calceolarias

Brightly colored, speckled pouches of yellow, orange, red, and bronze make calceolarias (*Calceolaria* spp.), sometimes known as slipper flower or pocketbook plant, make a showy ornament for the table or windowsill. Try 'Anytime', a dwarf, early-blooming cultivar. Seeds planted in December will bloom in March.

Calceolaria seed is very fine; leave it uncovered. A germination temperature of around 70°F will give the best results, but seed will sprout (although more slowly) as low as 55°F. Calceolarias like excellent drainage and soil on the sandy side. Don't overwater the seedlings, but do keep plants well watered when in bud and in bloom. Give them indirect light and a cool spot while they're blooming; high temperatures cut short the blooming period.

321

Coleus

Coleus (*Coleus* × *hybridus*), the foliage plant with magic carpet colors, is another houseplant that's easy to raise from seed. A packet of mixed colors and varieties is great fun to grow. Colors include burgundy, copper, fuschia, dusty pink, apple green, and an elegant green and ivory mixture.

Just press the seeds gently into the soil surface. Germination takes a week to ten days at 65° to 75°F. The little plants soon show their true colors, which are especially vibrant when the plants are grown under fluorescent lights. Give the plants bright light—but not necessarily full sun—all day. Dwarf coleus plants are a good choice for indoors. Pinch off the growing tips periodically to encourage the plant to grow bushy rather than leggy.

Wax Begonias

Wax begonias (*Begonia* Semperflorens-Cultorum hybrids), also called fibrous begonias, grow readily from superfine seed. The neat, mound-shaped plants are perfect for window boxes and container gardens, and are a mainstay of flower beds across the country. As houseplants, they're a longtime favorite for kitchen windows.

Settle the dustlike seeds on a bed of damp vermiculite or fibrous potting soil. Leave the seeds uncovered; light promotes germination. Stretch a layer of plastic wrap over the flat to admit light and retain moisture. In a warm place (70° to 75°F), with plenty of light, the tiny seedlings begin to appear in two to four weeks. With less light and warmth, it may take six weeks or more. Keep the young plants under lights or on your brightest windowsill. Fertilize the seedlings weekly, starting when they are quite small. Wax begonias grow well in a loose, well-drained soil that is moist but not soaked. They like morning sun.

A Little Tricky, but Worth It

Once you've got some experience under your belt, try your hand at growing some of these plants. They're trickier, but well worth the effort.

Geraniums

Zonal geraniums (*Pelargonium* × *hortorum*) take patience. They germinate in two to four weeks at 65° to 75°F, and flower three to four months later. Many hybrids are fast, vigorous growers and a good choice for the indoor gardener. Seeds sown in December or January will be in bloom by midspring.

322

To hasten germination, nick or file the seeds so they absorb water more readily. Try to keep the soil temperature of the seedbed between 70° and 75°F; fluctuation can delay germination even more than usual. Geranium plants need good drainage; add perlite to your potting soil mix when transplanting the seedlings. A steady supply of moisture is essential during flowering. Geraniums need plenty of light. Put them on your sunniest windowsill.

Gloxinia

Gloxinia (*Sinningia speciosa*) is a showy plant with large, richly colored flowers and handsome, velvety leaves. It is a challenge—not as adaptable as, say, coleus. But when given the conditions it requires, it can be a truly impressive houseplant.

Start by sowing the fine seeds on a bed of damp, milled sphagnum moss or potting soil. Leave the seeds uncovered, and protect the flat with glass or plastic wrap to prevent drying. Germination takes two to three weeks. Plants raised from seed can flower in five to six months, but some take as long as eight months. Gloxinia 'Early Giant', a more tolerant cultivar with extra-large flowers, blooms in four months from sowing.

Keep the soil moist but not soggy. Many growers keep their gloxinias on trays of moist pebbles to maintain 50 to 60 percent humidity—hard to achieve in heated houses. A temperature of around 70°F, dropping to 65°F at night, is just right. Gloxinias need lots of light. A bright east window is a good spot for gloxinias in spring and summer, changing to a southern exposure for winter. They also do very well under fluorescent lights.

Ornamental Peppers

These perky, bushy, foot-high plants will warm and brighten any winter room with their abundant, small, red, round or pointed fruits. You can eat ornamental peppers, which belong to the genus *Capsicum* (they're the same species as the familiar garden pepper, *C. annuum*), but be warned—they're very hot! *Don't* eat fruits of the often similar-looking Christmas or false Jerusalem cherry (*Solanum capsicastrum*), a member of the nightshade family that bears a round red or orange fruit.

Most cultivars of ornamental peppers fruit in four to six months from seed. Cover the seeds and don't overwater; pepper seeds can germinate in fairly dry soil. They do like to be warm, though—75° to 80°F is a good range. Give the plants bright light with as much direct light as possible, at least 3 to 4 hours a day. Set the pots on trays of moistened gravel; humidity helps to prevent blossom drop. Once they start to bear fruit, keep the plants on the cool side for a longer display.

Be a Backyard Researcher

324

Catalog claims can be confusing, and even the advice of trusted experts must often be fine-tuned to suit particular conditions. There's only one way to determine whether a certain vegetable, planting technique, or soil amendment is one you want to use in your garden, and that's to try it yourself. You'll learn more from home-garden trials if you conduct them systematically.

When checking out a new vegetable cultivar, consider flavor, yield, earliness, resistance to diseases and insects, cold-weather tolerance, and length of storage life. A vegetable that doesn't rate high on all these counts may still be worth growing; once you know what to expect, you can make complementary plantings to fill the gaps. 'Buttercup' squash, for example, has the best flavor of any squash I've grown, but for me it yields less than 'Butternut'. So I always plant some of both: 'Butternut' for everyday, 'Buttercup' for special meals.

Applying the Scientific Method

Perhaps you want to assess the effectiveness of a new mulch, or attempt an extra-early planting. Maybe you mean to test growing conditions in different parts of your garden, or find a safe and effective insect deterrent. Could be you want to keep some vegetables alive later in the fall, or you're curious about the effects of different soil amendments and fertilizers. Then your garden, or part of it, becomes an informal test plot. In order to draw any meaningful conclusions from your trials, you'll need to borrow a few principles from the scientific method.

Regular Records Are a Plus

Good records can multiply the usefulness of your garden experiments. If you regularly jot down your observations, you'll build up a valuable guide-from-gardens-past that will add to your enjoyment of each new gardening season.

Such a record can be very simple—in fact, it is more likely to be used if not housed in an imposing bound book. Mine is a feed-store calendar with a square for each day of the month, on which I record dates of sowing seed or transplanting, weather conditions, frost dates, first pickings, insect control measures used, fertilizers added, amounts canned and frozen, final pickings for the season. Once you're at it, you dash off a note when the swallows return, the bluebirds are nesting, and the first peepers sing in the woods. Experimenting in the garden hones the skill of appreciation. Sometimes you even learn something.

A Control Is the Standard

A control is simply an untreated sample, a baseline with which you can then compare your experimental specimens. You'll need to include a control if you're comparing two cultivars, testing an insect repellent, or evaluating a certain mulch.

A wall calendar makes a handy place to jot gardening notes. Keep records of planting and picking dates, frosts and droughts, first and late harvests. Paging through the entries is a help when ordering new seeds or supplies—and reliving the gardening year is a nice relief from winter doldrums.

If you're trying to decide on the merits of a new vegetable, grow your most similar familiar cultivar next to it. When testing vegetables, treat the control plot exactly like the trial plot. When comparing treatments, apply the treatments to the same kind of plants growing in the same kind of soil as the untreated plants. Only then can you make valid comparisons.

Weather is one of the variables that affects plants the most, so for a true comparison, test the plants under consideration in the same season. Don't compare this year's new cultivar with memories of an old standby grown last summer. Recently the new 'Ormavon' brussels sprouts tempted me with their advertised ability to form a small cabbage head atop the plant in addition to the sprouts clustered along the stem. Perhaps they do well in milder British winters, but here— even in an exceptionally mild December—they produced small sprouts and only a loose rosette of leaves. Growing 'Jade Cross'

326

brussels sprouts next to the new cultivar gave me a standard for comparison.

Likewise, when testing for flavor, serve your standard cultivar at the same meal with the new one, and prepare it in the same way. It might be fun to have a "contest" and take a family vote. Such a game is not only amusing, but also a good reminder to truly savor the fine fresh flavors of the food you grow. When you're judging, you really "listen" to the taste.

INFORM YOURSELF

We have a saying around our place that—for us—constitutes a homely truth because we learned it the hard way: "When all else fails, read the directions."

To succeed with some of the new cultivars, it helps to be informed. The new 'Jersey Golden Acorn' squash, for example, seems to be more sensitive to cold weather than some other winter squashes, and should be planted about one week after 'Butternut'. Supersweet corn cultivars also tend to be more easily discouraged by cold soil. 'New Zealand' spinach is a warm-weather plant, but the seed germinates best in cold soil. (Says so on the packet, or should.) 'Sweet-100' tomatoes really should be staked or caged, or you'll lose a lot of fruit. I've tried it both ways, and the directions are right. If the seed packet has inadequate instructions, and some do, consult the seed catalog or a gardening book.

Repeat the Experiment

In the scientific community, successful experiments must be repeated before firm conclusions can be drawn. You don't need to have your Great Zucchini Trial replicated by the whole neighborhood before you decide which kind to grow next year. But it certainly does make sense to repeat insect-control experiments that worked in order to decide whether, for example, the wasps you bought to eat the bean beetle larvae control the pests well enough to be worth their cost. Did the aluminum-foil mulch really make a difference in your eggplant yield—or was it the warm, wet summer?

CHAPTER FIFTY-ONE

Make Your Own Planting Flats

Planting flats are like compost—you seldom have more than you need! Though many gardeners nowadays start their seeds in individual pots, old-fashioned wood flats still come in handy: They're sturdy and durable and cost little to make, except for the investment of a Saturday morning or two. Flats are not only for starting seeds—they also make convenient, portable holders for individual pots. And you can custom-fit them to make the best use of your windowsill or lighted plant stand.

It's a rare gardener who couldn't use more growing space for starting seeds indoors. A good seed-starting container provides ample space for plant roots and is well drained so standing water doesn't drown plant roots. Though you can plant seeds in all sorts of containers, the best choices are free and easily replaceable (milk cartons, yogurt cups, foam coffee cups), or strong and long-lasting. Milk cartons are a good size for seed starting and certainly affordable, but they give the patio a helter-skelter look when they're lined up outside in spring to harden off the seedlings. The shallow, topless wood boxes called flats are easier on the eyes, they last much longer, and they'll hold more plants. Flats are virtually free when made with scrap wood, unless you count the cost of the nails. The wood flat is a classic that is, I think, unlikely ever to be superseded entirely by clever plastic gadgets that work well but cost more.

HANDLES ARE A HELP

You'll find simple handles helpful when you must lug around a lot of large flats. Before constructing the flat, nail a cleat to two opposite sides of the flat for a handhold. The size and shape of the cleat isn't critical. A scrap of wood an inch or so wide and three inches long is satisfactory. Nail the cleat from the outside. If the nail protrudes inside, hammer it down flat.

Cleats do take up an extra few inches of space. If your flats must fit together tightly in a limited space, make the two short sides higher and drill holes for finger holds. Note, though, that these flats won't stack as neatly for storage as flats with sides that are uniform in height.

Size and Materials

The size of your shelf or planting bench and the materials you have available determine the dimensions of your flat. In general, a flat should measure no more than about 14 by 18 inches, or it will be too heavy to handle easily when filled with wet soil. Rectangular flats are traditional, but there's no law against making a square flat if that's what you want. Measure the space you have available before you

Classic wood flats are strong and long-lasting and just as useful as ever. Make a good supply of these versatile containers from scrap wood and a few nails. Fill with soil and plant seeds or cuttings. Or group individual pots in an easy-to-carry flat that's custom-fitted to your windowsill or shelf space.

begin construction. For instance, six 12-by-16-inch flats will fit neatly on the shelf of a 26-by-48-inch fluorescent-lighted plant stand.

One-inch-thick boards make a sturdy flat. Half-inch boards, which you can salvage from discarded crates or pallets, make a lighter flat but are more difficult to nail without splitting the wood. The sides of the flat must be deep enough to hold 2 to 3 inches of soil. The bottom of the flat is made of slats, which can vary in width, with a bit of space between for drainage. Use what you have.

Constructing the Flat

Building flats is a good job for a rainy weekend, especially when you're gearing up for a busy planting season ahead. The first flat you put together may be an awkward operation, but the next ones you make will go together more easily. Here's how to get started.

1. Keeping in mind the space you have available, measure and cut the boards for the sides of the flat.
2. Add handles or drill handholds, if you want them, in the two short sides of the flat.
3. Calculate how many bottom slats you will need, allowing for 1/16

to ⅛ inch of space between the boards for drainage. Cut the bottom slats to length so they are flush with the sides of the box when nailed on.

4. Use a clamp to stabilize the boards while you are nailing them, or if need be, prop the boards or ask a helper to hold them for you. Remember to line them up squarely before nailing.
5. Using four-penny box nails, nail one of the long sides to each of the two shorter sides. Drive three nails at each corner.
6. Nail the other long side to the unattached ends of the two short sides, to form a four-sided frame.
7. Put the open frame on a flat surface. It is still loose-jointed at this point. Check the corners with a square to make sure the frame is straight.
8. Nail on the first bottom slat. This will stabilize the frame and keep the corners from shifting.
9. Nail on the rest of the bottom slats, leaving about ⅛ inch between the slats to allow for drainage.

CHAPTER FIFTY-TWO

Nudge Some Shrubs into Bloom

Just when winter begins to seem like a permanent condition, you have a chance to bring a preview of spring indoors, to foster some budding tree or shrub branches on their way to flowering. Mid- to late winter is the perfect time to cut some flowering branches for indoor bloom. You're ready for a breath of spring, the buds have matured enough to be capable of producing flowers, and often the plants need to be pruned anyway.

Coaxing the Best Bouquet

Bring in a few cuttings every week or so to have a steady succession of indoor blossoms till the spring gardening season begins. In late winter and early spring, as the natural blooming season grows closer, you'll find that cut branches take less time to bloom indoors than they did in January. Follow these tips for greatest success.

- Cut branches on a day when temperatures are relatively moderate—not bitter cold.
- Look for branches that have abundant flower buds. (Hint: Leaf buds are slimmer, more pointed; flower buds are rounder, fatter.)
- Use sharp, clean tools to cut the branches. Pruning shears make a quick, neat cut. Don't break branches off; that leaves a ragged cut that doesn't heal well.

Crush the cut ends of the branches to expose more plant tissue, so that water can be absorbed more readily. I put the cut ends of the branches on the chopping block in my husband's workshop and tap them with a hammer, splintering the bottom inch or two. Then plunge the branches into a bucket of lukewarm water.

The following morning, put the branches in fresh, cool water. Keep them in a cool place away from bright light until the buds are closer to flowering. Mist them daily with a spray of water from a plastic bottle with a trigger nozzle.

For best bloom quality, keep branches where temperatures range between 60° and 70°F. Warmer air encourages quicker bloom but the flowers will be smaller and paler, and they won't last as long as those that come to bloom in cooler conditions.

When the buds begin to swell, remove the branches from their storage bucket, arrange them in an attractive container, and give them more light. Keep them away from heat, though. Branches bloom for a longer time if moved to a cool room at night (and even during the day if you're off at work).

Mock oranges, magnolias, and flowering crab apples are delicate and lovely, but the blossoms last only a few days. You can count on a solid week of bloom from wisterias, peaches, apples, forsythias, dogwoods, witch hazels, and serviceberries. Branches of flowering cherries, mountain laurels, horse chestnuts, deutzias, and pears will bloom for up to two weeks. Alder, birch, oak, and pussywillow catkins often last even longer.

BEST BLOOMERS

Spring-blooming shrubs and trees are your best candidates for late-winter bouquets. Try some of these suggestions, or experiment with whatever you have available. You needn't limit your bouquets to flowers; many trees have interesting catkins, and even tiny, unfurling leaves make a nice arrangement.

Shrubs

Bridal-wreath (*Spiraea* × *vanhouttei*)
Chinese witch hazel (*Hamamelis mollis*)
Deutzias (*Deutzia* spp.)
Flowering almonds (*Prunus* spp.)
Flowering quinces (*Chaenomeles* spp.)
Forsythias (*Forsythia* spp.)
Lilacs (*Syringa* spp.)
Mock oranges (*Philadelphus* spp.)
Pussy willows (*Salix caprea*, *S. discolor*)
Rhododendrons and azaleas (*Rhododendron* spp.)
Wisterias (*Wisteria* spp.)

Trees

Apples and crab apples (*Malus* spp.)
Common horse chestnut (*Aesculus hippocastanum*)
Flowering cherries (*Prunus* spp.)
Flowering dogwood (*Cornus florida*)
Magnolias (*Magnolia* spp.)
Peach (*Prunus persica*)
Pears (*Pyrus* spp.)
Serviceberries (*Amelanchier* spp.)

USDA PLANT HARDINESS ZONE MAP

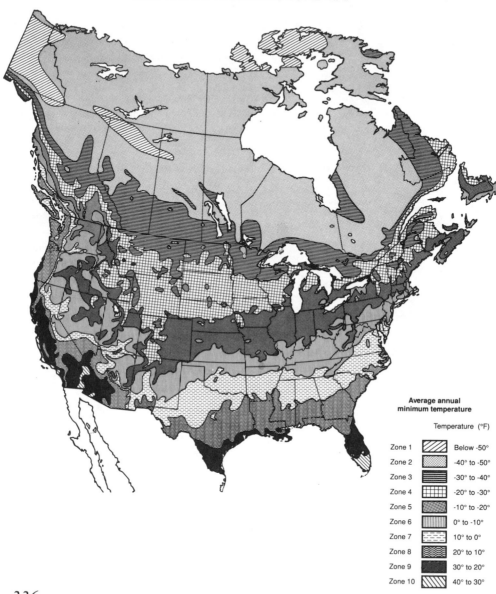

Average annual minimum temperature

Temperature (°F)

Zone 1		Below -50°
Zone 2		-40° to -50°
Zone 3		-30° to -40°
Zone 4		-20° to -30°
Zone 5		-10° to -20°
Zone 6		0° to -10°
Zone 7		10° to 0°
Zone 8		20° to 10°
Zone 9		30° to 20°
Zone 10		40° to 30°

R E S O U R C E S

Here, arranged chapter by chapter, you'll find sources for information, seeds, plants, and supplies—even butterfly larvae. Several of the books are out of print, but you might want to try finding them at libraries or used-book dealers. A self-addressed, stamped, business-size envelope (SASE) will be appreciated by plant societies and other nonprofit groups and by small businesses from which you request information. Unless otherwise noted, catalogs are free. Prices were current at the time this book was published.

General Resource Books

Barton, Barbara J. *Gardening by Mail 3.* 3d ed. Boston: Houghton Mifflin Co., 1990.

Whealy, Kent, ed. *Fruit, Nut, and Berry Inventory.* Decorah, Iowa: Seed Saver Publications, 1989.

———. *Garden Seed Inventory.* 2d ed. Decorah, Iowa: Seed Saver Publications, 1988.

Chapter 1

Seeds

The Cook's Garden
P.O. Box 535
Londonderry, VT 05148
($1) Mizuna, peppergrass

Garden City Seeds
1324 Red Crow Rd.
Victor, MT 59875
($1) Peppergrass

Pinetree Garden Seeds
Rt. 100
New Gloucester, ME 04260
Spinach, tyfon

Chapter 2

Seeds

Bowman's Hill Wildflower Preserve
Washington Crossing Historic Park
Washington Crossing, PA 18977
(Contribution)

Native Gardens
Rt. 1, Box 494
Greenback, TN 37742
($1)

Native Seed Co.
14590 Triadelphia Mill Rd.
Dayton, MD 21036

Association

The New England Wildflower Society, Inc.
Garden in the Woods
Hemenway Rd.
Framingham, MA 01701

Books

Art, Henry W. *The Wildflower Gardener's Guide.* Pownal, Vt.: Storey Communications, Garden Way Publishing, 1987.

———. *Wildflower Perennials for Your Garden.* New York: Hawthorn Books, 1976.

Phillips, Harry R. *Growing and Propagating Wildflowers.* Chapel Hill, N.C.: University of North Carolina Press, 1985.

Sperka, Marie. *Growing Wildflowers.* Magnolia, Mass.: Peter Smith Publishers, 1984.

Chapter 3

Plants and Seeds

Lost Prairie Herb Farm
805 Kienas Rd.
Kalispell, MT 59901
($1)

Richter's
P.O. Box 26
Hwy. 47
Goodwood, Ontario L0C 1A0
($2.50)

The Rosemary House
120 S. Market St.
Mechanicsburg, PA 17055
($2)

Books

Carr, Anna, et al. *Rodale's Illustrated Encyclopedia of Herbs.* Emmaus, Pa.: Rodale Press, 1987.

Lathrop, Norma. *Herbs: How to Select, Grow, and Enjoy.* Los Angeles: Price Stern Sloan, HP Books, 1981.

Ortho Books Editorial Staff. *The World of Herbs and Spices.* San Ramon, Calif.: Ortho Books, 1979.

Chapter 4
Supplies
The Dramm Co.
P.O. Box 1960
Manitowoc, WI 54221

Rootstocks
Northwoods Nursery
28696 S. Cramer Rd.
Molalla, OR 97038

Pacific Tree Farms
4301 Lynwood Dr.
Chula Vista, CA 91910
($2)

Rocky Meadow Orchard
& Nursery
Rt. 2, Box 2104
New Salisbury, IN
47161
(3 first-class stamps)

Books
Garner, R. J. *The Grafter's Handbook.* New York: Oxford University Press, 1979.

Kaufman, Peter, et al. *Practical Botany.* text ed. Englewood Cliffs, N.J.: Prentice-Hall, Reston, 1983.

Chapter 5
Plants
Comanche Acres Iris
Gardens
Rt. 1, P.O. Box 258
Gower, MO 64454
($3 for 2-year
subscription)

Grandview Iris Gardens
HC 86, Box 91
Bayard, NE 69334
(1 first-class stamp)

Lilypons Water Gardens
6800 Lilypons Rd.
P.O. Box 10
Buckeystown, MD
21717
($5) Irises for water

Books
Cassidy, G. E., and S. Linnegar. *Growing Irises.* Portland, Ore.: Timber Press, 1982.

Kohlein, Fritz. *Iris.* Gardener's Library. Translated from German by Molly Peters. Portland, Oreg.: Timber Press, 1988.

Warburton, Bee, ed. *The World of Irises.* Tulsa, Okla.: American Iris Society, 1978.

Chapter 6
Plants
Fred's Plant Farm
P.O. Box 707
Dresden Rd.
Dresden, TN 38225

Books
Martin, Franklin, W., et al. *The Sweet Potato Cookbook.* Ft Myers, Fl.: ECHO, 1989.

Chapter 7
Seeds
General seed catalogs may also offer seeds of extra-early tomato cultivars.

Siberia Seeds
P.O. Box 3000
Olds, Alberta T0M 1P0
(SASE)

Tomato Growers
Supply Co.
P.O. Box 2237
Ft. Myers, FL 33902

Supplies
Solar Garden Co.
Box 909
Cherry Hill Cottage
Stockbridge, MA 01262
Umbrella greenhouse

Chapter 8
Seeds
R. H. Shumway
P.O. Box 1
Graniteville, SC 29829

Southern Exposure Seed
Exchange
P.O. Box 158
North Garden, VA
22959
($3)

Chapter 9
Plants
Edible Landscaping
P.O. Box 77
Afton, VA 22920
($2)

338

J. E. Miller Nurseries, Inc.
5060 West Lake Rd.
Canandaigua, NY 14424

St. Lawrence Nurseries
R.D. 5, Box 324
Potsdam-Madrid Rd.
Potsdam, NY 13676

Chapter 10
Supplies
Gardener's Supply Co.
128 Intervale Rd.
Burlington, VT 05401
Swan-neck hoe

Chapter 11
Books
Neal, Avon. *Ephemeral Folk Figures: Scarecrows, Harvest Figures and Snowmen.* New York: C. N. Potter, 1969.

Chapter 12
Seeds
Seeds Blum
Idaho City Stage
Boise, ID 83706
($3)

Books
A Guide to Cooking with Edible Flowers. 1987. Available from Paradise Farms, P.O. Box 346, Summerland, CA 93067.

Lenz, Louisa. *Dried, Cut, and Edible Flowers for Pleasure, Food and Income.* 1990. Available from Ecology Action of the Mid-peninsula, 5798 Ridgewood Rd., Willits, CA 95490.

Tillona, Francesca, and Cynthia Strowbridge. *A Feast of Flowers.* New York: Gramercy Publishing, 1969.

Chapter 13
Plants
Lamb Nurseries
E. 101 Sharp Ave.
Spokane, WA 99202

White Flower Farm
Litchfield, CT 06759

Woodlanders, Inc.
1128 Colleton Ave.
Aiken, SC 29801
($1)

Chapter 14
Supplies
Gardener's Supply Co.
128 Intervale Rd.
Burlington, VT 05401

Smith & Hawken
25 Corte Madera
Mill Valley, CA 94941

Chapter 15
Seeds
Native Seeds/SEARCH
2509 N. Campbell Ave. #325
Tucson, AZ 85719
($1)

The Pepper Gal
10536 119th Ave. N
Largo, FL 33543
(SASE)

Plants of the Southwest
930 Baca St.
Sante Fe, NM 87501
($1.50)

Chapter 16
Plants and Seeds
The Country Garden
P.O. Box 3539
Oakland, CA 94609
($1)

Select Seeds
180 Stickney Hill Rd.
Union, CT 06076
($2)

Books
Fell, Derek. *Annuals: How to Select, Grow, and Enjoy.* Los Angeles: Price Stern Sloan, HP Books, 1983.

McGourty, Frederick, and Pamela Harper. *Perennials: How to Select, Grow, and Enjoy.* Los Angeles: Price Stern Sloan, HP Books, 1985.

Vaughan, Mary J. *Complete Book of Cut Flower Care.* Portland, Oreg.: Timber Press, 1988.

Chapter 17
Plants
Edible Landscaping
P.O. Box 77
Afton, VA 22920
($2)

Raintree Nursery
391 Butts Rd.
Morton, WA 98356

Southmeadow Fruit Gardens
15310 Red Arrow Hwy.
Lakeside, MI 49116

339

Chapter 18

Supplies

Butterfly eggs, larvae, cocoons, and equipment for raising butterflies are available from these sources.

Carolina Biological Supply Co.
2700 York Rd.
Burlington, NC 27215

Connecticut Valley Biological Supply Co.
82 Valley Rd.
P.O. Box 326
Southampton, MA 01073

Associations

Lepidopterists' Society
Ron Leuschner, President
1900 John St.
Manhattan Beach, CA 90266

Xerces Society
10 S.W. Ash St.
Portland, OR 97204

Books

Schneck, Marcus. *Butterflies: How to Identify and Attract Them to Your Garden.* Emmaus, Pa.: Rodale Press, 1990.

Tekulsky, Mathew. *The Butterfly Garden.* Boston: Harvard Common Press, 1985.

Chapter 19

Supplies

Mellinger's Inc.
2310 W. South Range Rd.
North Lima, OH 44452

Plant Collectibles
103 Kenview Ave.
Buffalo, NY 14217
(2 first-class stamps)

Smith & Hawken
25 Corte Madera
Mill Valley, CA 94941

Lillian Vernon
510 S. Fulton Ave.
Mt. Vernon, NY 10550
Plant stands with casters, for heavy planters

Books

Newcomb, Duane. *The Apartment Farmer.* Los Angeles: Jeremy P. Tarcher, 1976.

Ortho Books Editorial Staff. *Gardening in Containers.* Edited by Ken R. Burke, San Ramon, Calif.: Ortho Books, 1983.

Stevens, David, and Kenneth A. Beckett. *The Contained Garden.* New York: Penguin USA, Studio Books, 1983.

Chapter 20

Plants

Daylily Discounters
Rt. 2, Box 24
Alachua, FL 32615
($3)

Klehm Nursery
Box 197, Rt. 5
South Barrington, IL 60010
($4)

Gilbert H. Wild & Son, Inc.
1112 Joplin St.
Sarcoxie, MO 64862
($3)

Association

American Hemerocallis Society
Elly Launius, Executive Secretary
1454 Rebel Dr.
Jackson, MS 39211

Books

Munson, R. W., Jr. *Hemerocallis: The Daylily.* Portland, Oreg.: Timber Press, 1989.

Stout, Arlow B. *Daylilies.* Millwood, N.Y.: Sagapress, 1986.

Chapter 21

Books

Chesanow, Jeanne. *Honeysuckle Sipping: The Plant Lore of Childhood.* Camden, Maine: Down East Books, 1987.

Gjersvik, Mary Anne. *Green Fun.* Riverside, Calif.: Chatham Press, 1974.

Chapter 22

Plants

Fox Hill Farm
440 W. Michigan Ave.
P.O. Box 9
Parma, MI 49269
($1)

Well-Sweep Herb Farm
317 Mt. Bethel Rd.
Port Murray, NJ 07865
($2)

Books

Vivian, John. *Building Stone Walls.* rev. ed. Pownal, Vt.: Storey Communications, Garden Way Publishing, 1979.

Chapter 23
Supplies
Smith & Hawken
25 Corte Madera
Mill Valley, CA 94941

Lillian Vernon
510 S. Fulton Ave.
Mt. Vernon, NY 10550

Books
Black, Penny. *The Book of Pressed Flowers.* New York: Simon & Schuster, 1988.

Chapter 24
Seeds
Most cultivars mentioned are available from general seed catalogs.

The Cook's Garden
P.O. Box 535
Londonderry, VT 05148
($1)

Le Jardin du Gourmet
P.O. Box 75
St. Johnsbury Center, VT 05863
($.50) The turnip cultivar 'Des Vertus Mateau'

Chapter 25
Supplies
Cambridge Wire Cloth Co.
P.O. Box 399
Cambridge, MD 21613
Stainless steel screens and mesh by the roll

Gardener's Supply Co.
128 Intervale Rd.
Burlington, VT 05401
Food driers

Solar Survival
P.O. Box 250
Cherry Hill Rd.
Harrisville, NH 03450
Plans for solar drier, $13

Books
Farm Journal Food Editors. *How to Dry Fruits and Vegetables at Home.* Philadelphia: Countryside Press, 1975.

Klippstein, Ruth, and Katherine Humphrey. *Home Drying of Foods.* Bulletin #399IB120. rev. ed. New York: Cornell Cooperative Extension, 1984.

Chapter 26
Plants and Seeds
Dabney Herbs
P.O. Box 22061
Louisville, KY 40252
($2)

Gurney Seed & Nursery Co.
110 Capital St.
Yankton, SD 57079
Elderberry bushes

Lost Prairie Herb Farm
805 Kienas Rd.
Kalispell, MT 59901
($1)

Supplies
Nichols Garden Nursery
1190 N. Pacific Hwy.
Albany, OR 97321
Self-seal bags for making your own teabags

Chapter 27
Seeds
Abundant Life Seed Foundation
P.O. Box 772
Port Townsend, WA 98368
($1)

Thompson & Morgan, Inc.
P.O. Box 1308
Jackson, NJ 08527

Plants
Little Valley Farm
R.R. 3, Box 544
Spring Green, WI 53588
($1)

Niche Gardens
1111 Dawson Rd.
Chapel Hill, NC 27516
($3)

We-Du Nurseries
Rt. 5, Box 724
Marion, NC 28752
($2)

Chapter 28
Supplies
Abundant Life Seed Foundation
P.O. Box 772
Port Townsend, WA 98368
($1) Cloth seed bags, seed envelopes, seed thresher, screens for seed cleaning, and more

Southern Exposure Seed Exchange
P.O. Box 158
North Garden, VA 22959
($3) Poly bags and heat sealers, seed envelopes, silica gel, labeling supplies, corn sheller, and more

Association

Seed Savers Exchange
R.R. 3, Box 239
Decorah, IA 52101

Books

Ashworth, Suzanne. *Seed to Seed*. Decorah, Iowa: Seed Savers Exchange, 1990.

Jabs, Carolyn. *The Heirloom Gardener*. San Francisco: Sierra Club Books, 1984.

Chapter 29
Seeds

The Flowery Branch Seed Co.
P.O. Box 1330
Flowery Branch, GA 30542
($2)

Goodwin Creek Gardens
P.O. Box 83
Williams, OR 97544
($1)

Seeds Blum
Idaho City Stage
Boise, ID 83706
($3)

Shepherd's Garden Seeds
30 Irene St.
Torrington, CT 06759
($1)

Books

Jacobs, Betty. *Flowers That Last Forever*. Edited by Sarah M. Clarkson. Pownal, Vt.: Storey Communications, Garden Way Publishing, 1988.

Thorpe, Patricia. *Everlastings*. New York: Facts on File, 1985.

Chapter 30
Supplies

Charley's Greenhouse Supply
1569 Memorial Hwy.
Mt. Vernon, WA 98273
($2)

A. M. Leonard, Inc.
6665 Spiker Rd.
P.O. Box 816
Piqua, OH 45356

Chapter 31
Seeds

Abundant Life Seed Foundation
P.O. Box 772
Port Townsend, WA 98368
($1)

Henry Field Seed & Nursery Co.
415 N. Burnett St.
Shenandoah, IA 51602

Seeds Blum
Idaho City Stage
Boise, ID 83706
($3)

Chapter 32
Seeds

For best selection of gourd seeds, see ads in *The Gourd*, the quarterly newsletter of the American Gourd Society. A number of varieties are also available through the Seed Savers Exchange.

Henry Field Seed & Nursery Co.
415 N. Burnett St.
Shenandoah, IA 51602
Birdhouse, dipper, and bushel gourds

R. H. Shumway
P.O. Box 1
Graniteville, SC 29829
Birdhouse, bottle, calabash, caveman's club, bushel, and mixtures of small and large-type gourds

Associations

American Gourd Society
P.O. Box 274
Mt. Gilead, OH 43338

Seed Savers Exchange
R.R. 3, Box 239
Decorah, IA 52101

Books

Gourds, Their Culture and Craft. Boston: Gourd Society of America, 1966.

Heiser, Charles B., Jr. *The Gourd Book*. Norman, Okla: University of Oklahoma Press, 1979.

Mordecai, Carolyn. *Gourd Craft*. New York: Crown Publishers, 1978.

Wilson, Eddie W. *The Gourd in Folk Literature*. Boston: Gourd Society of America, 1947.

Chapter 33
Plants

Bear Creek Nursery
P.O. Box 411
Northport, WA 99157
(2 first-class stamps)

Chestnut Hill Nursery, Inc.
Rt. 1, Box 341
Alachua, FL 32615

Nolin River Nut Tree
Nursery
797 Port Wooden Rd.
Upton, KY 42784

Waynesboro Nurseries,
Inc.
P.O. Box 987
Rt. 664
Waynesboro, VA 22980

Supplies
Potter Walnut Cracker
Co.
P.O. Box 930
Sapulpa, OK 74067
(SASE) Nutcrackers for
hickory nuts and
black walnuts

Hunt's Black Walnut
Cracker
Box 3
Hartford, IA 50118

Association
Northern Nut Growers
Association
9870 S. Palmer Rd.
New Carlisle, OH 45344

Books
Jaynes, Richard A., ed.
*Nut Tree Culture in
North America.* Ham-
den, Conn.: Northern
Nut Growers Assoc.,
1979.

Ortho Books Editorial
Staff. *All About Grow-
ing Fruits, Berries and
Nuts.* rev. ed. Edited
by Barbara Ferguson.
San Ramon, Calif.:
Ortho Books, 1987.

Chapter 34
Association
Seed Savers Exchange
R.R. 3, Box 239
Decorah, IA 52101

Chapter 35
Seeds
Abundant Life Seed
Foundation
P.O. Box 772
Port Townsend, WA
98368
($1) Milk pumpkin,
Mescher lettuce, Black
Turtle beans, Long
Season beet, flint and
flour corn, including
blue corn and Black
Mexican

Comstock, Ferre & Co.
263 Main St.
P.O. Box 125
Wethersfield, CT 06109
White Egg turnip

The Cook's Garden
P.O. Box 535
Londonderry, VT 05148
($1) Gilfeather turnip

Seeds Blum
Idaho City Stage
Boise, ID 83706
($3) Wren's Egg bean,
Black Turtle bean,
Tennessee Sweet
Potato squash,
Arikara squash, Long
Season beet

Association
Seed Savers Exchange
R.R.3, Box 239
Decorah, IA 52101

Chapter 36
Supplies
The Corn Crib
P.O. Box 164
R.R. 2
Madison, MO 65263
(SASE)

Chapter 37
Supplies
Mellinger's Inc.
2310 W. South Range Rd.
North Lima, OH 44452

Chapter 38
Seeds
The Cook's Garden
P.O. Box 535
Londonderry, VT 05148
($1)

Johnny's Selected Seeds
Foss Hill Rd.
Albion, ME 04910

Pinetree Garden Seeds
Rt. 100
New Gloucester, ME
04260

Supplies
Gardener's Supply Co.
128 Intervale Rd.
Burlington, VT 05401
Spun-bonded row
covers

Johnny's Selected Seeds
Foss Hill Rd.
Albion, ME 04910
Spun-bonded row covers

Solar Garden Co.
Box 909
Cherry Hill Cottage
Stockbridge, MA 01262
Umbrella greenhouse

343

Chapter 39
Bulbs
Dutch Gardens
P.O. Box 200
Adelphia, NJ 07710

Peter de Jager Bulb Co.
P.O. Box 2010
South Hamilton, MA
01982

Van Engelen, Inc.
313 Maple St.
Litchfield, CT 06759

Chapter 40
Plants
Southmeadow Fruit
Gardens
15310 Red Arrow Hwy.
Lakeside, MI 49116

Associations
National Wildlife
Federation
1400 16th St. NW
Washington, DC 20036

North American
Bluebird Society
P.O. Box 6295
Silver Spring, MD
20916

Books
Bird Watcher's Digest
(periodical). P.O. Box
110, Marietta, OH
45750.

DeGraaf, Richard M.,
and Gretchin M.
Whitman. *Trees,
Shrubs, and Vines
for Attracting Birds:
A Manual for the
Northeast.* Amherst,
Mass.: University of
Massachusetts Press,
1981.

Sunset Editors. *Attract-
ing Birds to Your
Garden.* Menlo Park,
Calif.: Lane Books,
1974.

Chapter 41
Seeds
The Cook's Garden
P.O. Box 535
Londonderry, VT 05148
($1)

William Dam Seeds
P.O. Box 8400
Dundas, Ontario
L9H 6M1
($2)

Chapter 42
Plants and Seeds
Sandy Mush Herb
Nursery
Rt. 2
Surrett Cove Rd.
Leicester, NC 28748
($4)

Well-Sweep Herb Farm
317 Mt. Bethel Rd.
Port Murray, NJ 07865
($2)

Association
Society for Economic
Botany
Economic Botany
Business Office
P.O. Box 1897
Lawrence, KS 66044
Membership includes
subscription to the
quarterly journal
Economic Botany.

Books
Carr, Anna, et al.
*Rodale's Illustrated
Encyclopedia of
Herbs.* Emmaus, Pa.:
Rodale Press, 1987.

Duke, James A., and
Steven Foster. *A Field
Guide to Medicinal
Plants: Eastern and
Central North
America.* Peterson
Field Guide Series.
Boston: Houghton
Mifflin, 1990.

Leighton, Ann. *Early
American Gardens.*
Amherst, Mass.:
University of Massa-
chusetts Press, 1986.

Tyler, Varro E. *The New
Honest Herbal.* Phila-
delphia: George F.
Stickley Co., 1987.

Weiss, Gaea and Shan-
dor. *Growing and
Using the Healing
Herbs.* Emmaus, Pa.:
Rodale Press, 1985.

Chapter 43
Books
Hill, Lewis. *Secrets of
Plant Propagation.*
Pownal, Vt.: Storey
Communications,
Garden Way
Publishing, 1985.

Chapter 44
Supplies
Seedpods, pinecones,
and other materials
are readily found.

Chapter 45
Seeds
William Dam Seeds
P.O. Box 8400
Dundas, Ontario
L9H 6M1
($2)

Johnny's Selected Seeds
Foss Hill Rd.
Albion, ME 04910

Nichols Garden Nursery
1190 N. Pacific Hwy.
Albany, OR 97321

Chapter 46
Supplies
Charley's Greenhouse
  Supply
1569 Memorial Hwy.
Mt. Vernon, WA 98273
($2) Automatic cold
  frame opener

Johnny's Selected Seeds
Foss Hill Rd.
Albion, ME 04910
Automatic cold frame
  opener

Chapter 47
Seeds
Sunrise Oriental Seed
  Co.
P.O. Box 10058
Elmwood, CT 06110
($1)

Kitazawa Seed Co.
1748 Laine St.
Santa Clara, CA 95051

Books
Harrington, Geri. *Grow
  Your Own Chinese
  Vegetables.* Pownal,
  Vt.: Storey Communi-
  cations, Garden Way
  Publishing, 1978.

Kraft, Ken and Pat.
  Exotic Vegetables.
  New York: Walker &
  Co., 1977.

Chapter 48
Books
Carr, Anna. *Good
  Neighbors: Companion
  Planting for Garden-
  ers.* Emmaus, Pa.:
  Rodale Press, 1985.

Rice, Elroy L. *Pest
  Control with Nature's
  Chemicals.* Norman,
  Okla.: University of
  Oklahoma Press,
  1983.

Chapter 49
Seeds
Park Seed Co.
Cokesbury Rd.
P.O. Box 31
Greenwood, SC 29647

Stokes Seeds, Inc.
P.O. Box 548
Buffalo, NY 14240

Thompson & Morgan,
  Inc.
P.O. Box 1308
Jackson, NJ 08527

Association
Indoor Gardening
  Society of America
Mrs. R. D. Morrison
5305 S.W. Hamilton St.
Portland, OR 97221

Books
Gilbert, Richard. *Two
  Hundred Houseplants
  Anyone Can Grow.*
  Los Angeles: Price
  Stern Sloan, HP
  Books, 1988.

Reader's Digest Editors.
  *Success with House-
  plants.* New York:
  Reader's Digest Asso-
  ciation, 1979.

Chapter 50
Books
Levitan, Lois. *Improve
  Your Gardening with
  Backyard Research.*
  Emmaus, Pa.: Rodale
  Press, 1980.

Chapter 51
Supplies
Materials are readily
  available at any
  building supply store.

Chapter 52
Plants
Holbrook Farm &
  Nursery
115 Lance Rd.
P.O. Box 368
Fletcher, NC 28732
($2)

Tripple Brook Farm
37 Middle Rd.
Southampton, MA
  01073

Valley Nursery
P.O. Box 4845
2801 N. Montana Ave.
Helena, MT 59604
(2 first-class stamps)

I N D E X

Note: Page references in *italic* indicate tables. **Boldface** references indicate illustrations.